FARMS AND ESTATES –

A CONVEYANCING HANDBOOK

FARMS AND ESTATES –
A CONVEYANCING HANDBOOK

Christopher Jessel
Farrer & Co

JORDANS
1999

Published by
Jordan Publishing Limited
21 St Thomas Street, Bristol BS1 6JS

British Library Cataloguing-in-Publication Data
A catalogue record for this book is available from the British Library

ISBN 0 85308 552 8

Typeset by Mendip Communications Ltd, Frome, Somerset
Printed by MPG Books Ltd, Bodmin, Cornwall

v

Preface

This book is for those involved with buying and selling land in the countryside. It is written by a practising lawyer and I hope it will be of use not only for lawyers but also for surveyors, investment advisers, for landowners, trustees and directors and for all who have to advise or take decisions on acquiring or disposing of rural land.

The law relating to agricultural land, and particularly its transfer from one person to another, has for most of our history comprised most of the work of most lawyers. Down the millennia, when virtually the only form of wealth was in agriculture, and power and influence came from the control of rural land, this is what lawyers did.

That is no longer the case. Very few lawyers are now concerned with transferring farms and rural estates. Only a limited amount of largely theoretical information is imparted in the law schools and newly qualified practitioners can find it difficult to pick it up easily from their more experienced colleagues.

Equally, surveyors and those advising on investment in agricultural land may find the legal complications daunting and hard to understand.

This book is intended to go some way to fill that gap. The only way to learn how to handle the many problems of buying and selling land in the countryside is to do it. I hope, however, that this will provide an introduction as well as a reassurance that what may appear to be an intractable and formidable mass of rules can be an attractive and fascinating discipline. I hope also that it will explain the reason for some of the complications.

I am grateful to Jordans, and particularly Martin West, for suggesting that I set down (in as logical an order as I can) knowledge that has been gained over the years. I am grateful to those of my colleagues at Farrer & Co who have looked through the text and let me have their comments but, of course, all faults are mine. Above all, I am grateful to clients for giving me the opportunity to work in what sometimes seems literally to be a field of law with its own pattern of growth and its own depth. I must also acknowledge the loan of many pairs of gumboots, without which this book could not have been written.

CHRISTOPHER JESSEL
Farrer & Co
March 1999

Contents

Table of Cases

References are to paragraph numbers in Part 1, and to other Parts of the book.

Table of Statutes

References are to paragraph numbers in Part 1, and to other Parts of the book.

Table of Statutory Instruments

References are to paragraph numbers in Part 1, and to other Parts of the book.

Table of EC Legislation

References are to paragraph numbers in Part 1, and to other Parts of the book.

Table of Abbreviations

AH	Agricultural holding
AHA 1986	Agricultural Holdings Act 1986
AONB	Area of Outstanding Natural Beauty
AT	Agricultural tenancy
BOAT	Byway open to all Traffic
CGT	Capital gains tax
CAP	Common Agricultural Policy
EA	Environmental Agency
FBT	Farm business tenancy
IACS	Integrated accounting and control system
MAFF	Ministry of Agriculture, Fisheries and Food
MoD	Ministry of Defence
PAYE	Pay-as-you-earn
RSPB	Royal Society for the Protection of Birds
RUPP	Road used as a public path
SSSI	Site of special scientific interest
VAT	Value added tax
WTO	World Trade Organisation

Part 1

NARRATIVE

Chapter 1

INTRODUCTION

1.1   THE LONG-DISTANCE VIEW

This book outlines the issues that need to be considered when advising a buyer or seller of rural land. The land may be a few fields, a working farm, or a landed estate. It may be purely agricultural or involve other activities such as forestry, mining, leisure or sport.

The book is intended only as a broad outline. There are a great many detailed texts on specialist aspects of the subject, such as the environment, planning, land taxation, mortgages, covenants, easements, the common agricultural policy (CAP), which examine every relevant statutory provision and the case-law that govern each specialist area. In farming terms, they are rather like a close examination of the left foreleg of a cow or the number of ears on a sprig of barley. This book is more like a long-distance view from a hill or an aeroplane.

1.2   THE LONG-TERM VIEW

For those who are not familiar with the details of agricultural conveyancing, the topic can appear at first sight to be confusing and intractable. The book begins, therefore, with an outline of the details of a transaction, and is aimed specifically at the topic of buying and selling rural land. Many other issues arise simply during the course of ownership and these will, of course, have an impact on decisions taken and advice given when the land is bought and sold, but there are many matters that arise at the time the land changes hands which can, for practical purposes, be ignored during the years of continued ownership. For most people, that is a very long-term matter, although a few commercial or residential farms can change hands frequently. The traditional pattern in England and Wales, as in the rest of Europe, is of the family farm handed down through the generations, and the family estate handed down through the centuries. When such land changes hands, it constitutes a major upheaval in the life not only of individual owners and occupiers but of other people who live around or on the land itself.

Many estates have been, and continue to be owned by institutions, the Crown, the Church, charities and pension funds, which generally view the ownership of land as an investment decision; but even there, it is a long-term matter. It does not make economic sense continuously to buy and sell large areas of rural land.

It follows, therefore, that, when such land comes to be sold, there may be little information conveniently available in a form needed by a buyer. If a typical house in the suburbs or a flat in the city centre, or even a cottage in a village change hands every five years, there will be available a great deal of information about boundaries, water supplies, dry rot guarantees and other matters which can be assembled quickly and cheaply in a package and kept in a house 'logbook'. The information may already be kept with the deeds package. That is not the case with rural land. The information may, of course, exist in files held by professionals who have advised the owner over the years. The seller is under a legal duty to answer enquiries correctly and, for that purpose, to consult his advisers, but often it needs a good deal of effort to collate the information. As this book demonstrates, the wide range of issues that need to be considered means that careful preparation over as long a period as possible is needed to make the transaction go smoothly.

Rural conveyancing also requires many skills which are not necessary in other transactions. Although, increasingly, properties in towns and cities have registered titles, that is still relatively unusual in rural areas where unregistered land is still the norm. Rural transactions involve issues arising under European law to an extent that is rarely seen in normal commercial sales of, for example, shops and offices. Lawyers handling such matters also need to be familiar with topics which are not always relevant in urban areas, such as septic tanks, wildlife conservation and ancient monuments.

This book is aimed primarily at lawyers seeking to become familiar with this topic but I hope it will also be of use to others involved in a professional team including surveyors, farm managers and environmental experts, so that they may understand some of the issues that lawyers will need to tackle and the questions that will be raised. I hope also that this book will be of some use to those who are buying or selling their own land or taking investment decisions on behalf of institutions and who need to understand the broader issues involved.

Chapter 2

THE TRANSACTION

2.1 INTRODUCTION

This book is about the sale and purchase of farms and estates. Advisers need to be aware of the objectives of their clients in order to complete transactions as efficiently as possible. If possible, advisers of one party should also be aware of the objectives of the other party since, frequently, it is possible to structure a transaction in a way that suits the interests of both parties. The form of the transaction will be affected by and will affect other aspects of a client's concerns such as taxation, powers of management and family arrangements. It can prove important that the sale or purchase is made by or to a company, trustees or partners and that it is carried out by a transfer of land, a lease or the transfer of shares in a company.

2.2 THE FARM

'A farm', in modern usage, is an area of land occupied for agriculture, and usually comprises the whole of a particular agricultural business. The popular image of a farm is an area of land lying within a ring-fence with a farmhouse in the centre. At least one boundary lies along a public highway and it is possible for the farmer to pass between any part of the farm without crossing another highway or a river or similar obstacle. Close to the farmhouse are farm buildings, usually arranged around a farmyard. Further away is a row of cottages to house farm workers. The farm may comprise arable areas growing crops, and pasture areas carrying cattle, sheep and pigs. Fields are divided by hedges or fences and there may be areas of woodland.

Although this represents an accurate picture of many farms, it is far from typical. Most farmers occupy areas held under different tenures. The farmer may himself own and occupy some freehold land. Some land may belong to the farmer's family, for example a relative or a family trust, some land may be rented, either as a protected agricultural holding or as a farm business tenancy, while other land may be held under grazing licences or through various forms of farming partnership, contract farming and other arrangements. The farm land may be scattered over an area of several miles, in a number of separate parcels. The farmer may live away from the farm land in a village, as may most of his employees who may own their own homes. The farm buildings may be scattered and may be modern structures. The farm may produce only one type of crop or livestock, be used for industrial purposes and/or other diverse activities such as leisure or tourism.

When the farm changes hands, the land may be divided in different ways. The farmer may sell only some of his fields, or he may sell his own land but retain occupation of other family land or tenanted land.

2.3   THE ESTATE

The traditional 'landed estate' comprised a number of farms and other rural areas such as woods, moorland, villages and often parts of towns. Where the estate belonged to a private landowner (often known as the squire), there would be a great house where the squire lived with his family and a large number of domestic servants. Where the estate belonged to an institution such as the Crown, the Church or a College, then normally there would be no specific centre. Until about 1850, land was the basis of wealth and therefore power, and all powerful individuals and institutions depended on estates not only for income but also to provide a basis for control of the countryside and a prestigious seat.

Today, there are fewer traditional landed estates, and those that remain are reduced in size. A modern estate may still include the home of the squire although he may have moved out of the old mansion into a converted farmhouse and no longer have resident domestic employees. The institutional estate is now managed generally for an economic return and may form part of the portfolio of an endowed charity or an insurance company, when it will be regarded as an investment to be bought, managed and sold in accordance with the needs of the portfolio.

Many estates are still retained for sporting purposes in order to run an effective shoot or, increasingly, to protect a hunt. Conservation estates are also becoming important as new charities are set up for environmental purposes either to preserve the traditional countryside or to conserve wildlife. Other amenity bodies hold areas of land for public access.

2.4   FARM OR ESTATE

The same area of land may be seen as comprising both a farm and an estate. Many traditional family landowners have been able to take over the former farms, each typically of 100 acres, and combine them together in a home farm, usually in excess of 1,000 acres. Individual farm houses and most of the farm workers' cottages are sold or let at a rent. The farm itself will be managed commercially, but it may also be valued for sporting purposes, for an amenity such as providing a good view from the owner's residence, or simply providing the pleasures of ownership, and, in that case, may be regarded more properly as an estate. The brochure of the selling agent may, therefore, represent the land either as a functioning agricultural unit or as an enjoyable part of the countryside.

Although farms, as such, are primarily focused on agricultural production, the effect of environmental controls and subsidies and the increasing reliance on diversification to support farming income have meant that the old distinction between a farm and an estate has become blurred. Nevertheless, in general terms, a farm will be the aggregate of land occupied by the farmer for production, while the emphasis of the estate will be on land of varying character and types of occupation, let at rents in order to produce an income and capital growth.

2.5   SALE AND PURCHASE

The typical transaction considered in this book is the outright passing of freehold ownership in return for a single payment. In the case of farms, this will normally be accompanied by a change of occupation, although many farm employees may remain. In the case of estates, it will involve the transfer of the right to receive income, although, frequently, estates include a substantial home farm and may include nothing else. The transfer may be carried out through a lease where the farmer holds a lease or where there is a sale and lease-back, but such arrangements are not typical. A large number of farm business tenancies are granted, but they are usually of a short-term nature and the emphasis is on rent rather than a single capital payment.

Many of the considerations which are relevant to sale and purchase will also apply to other transactions such as mortgages, gifts, transfers into and out of trust, re-financing arrangements and transmission of assets between companies contained in the same group. Such transactions are not the subject of this book, although as they are very often prepared in a legal form which appears to be and has many of the characteristics of a sale, it will be important for third parties to know the true nature of the transaction. For example, where there is true sale at arm's length, the parties will normally have carried out the necessary searches and have checked the existence of various rights. In the case of other transactions such as transfers within a family or within a group of companies, it may appear to be a sale, but the same detailed examination of the necessary rights may not have been carried out. Consequently, if a third party purchases a farm or estate subsequently from the recipient under such a transaction, it may be that the necessary rights do not exist or the appropriate searches have not been made.

Normally, the seller will not retain any interest in the land after the transaction. Where the sale is a part of the farm or an estate then rights may need to be reserved for the benefit of the retained land. In a few cases the seller will wish to retain a right of overage (see **26.4**), for example if there is a prospect of development. It is also common for sellers to retain rights such as minerals in case they acquire value in the future. Such examples are considered as appropriate but, as a general rule, the seller will be transferring the property and everything that goes with it and will not be creating new rights. The buyer will therefore need to check what rights exist and will usually not have the opportunity of obtaining details from some independent source. It is this that underlies the need for detailed searches and enquiries.

Chapter 3

THE SALE

3.1 METHODS OF SALE

A number of practices have developed in relation to the sale of agricultural land because of the nature of what is being sold and its special requirements, particularly the seasonal timing of the sale of arable land and the need to coincide with harvest.

As with any other property, a sale of land can be concluded in one of two ways. The first is a negotiated bargain between parties – a sale by private treaty; the second is an offer to a number of people or to the public at large with the bidders making offers on the basis of the terms put forward by the seller – a sale by auction or tender. The decision as to which method to use will be determined by the preferences of the seller, the current state of the market, the nature of the property being sold and, in particular, whether it should be divided into lots, whether or not adjoining land will be retained and, if so, whether rights need to be kept for the benefit of that land, and the market both in the locality and in the country generally.

Normally, a sale will be preceded by active marketing. A pure commercial farm may simply be advertised in the farming press and details circulated to those likely to be interested or their known advisers. Land with residential or sporting interests will often be advertised more widely. Most farms will be sold on the basis of an illustrated brochure, which is expensive to produce, and an estate will usually be sold with a full brochure containing numerous photographs and maps, perhaps on several scales. Where the farm or estate is likely to be of particular interest to certain groups of people, such as those looking for a sporting estate or seeking to benefit from tax reliefs, details may be circulated to firms known to be acting for such groups.

A private treaty sale will usually be preceded by an informal tender or a request for best offers. An informal tender is a version of the more formal tender (see below) which does not lead to a concluded contract immediately but leaves the field clear subsequently for the successful bidder (who at that stage is not legally bound) to proceed to formal exchange with the seller.

Best offers involve the selling agents contacting a number of people who have expressed interest and inviting them to put forward their best and final offers. The seller will then exchange contracts with the successful applicant.

A sale of a farm by auction will generally be used where there is strong competition and where the seller needs to exchange contracts by a specific date. The excitement of the auction room may produce higher bids than might have been expected by negotiation, but it is expensive and if the property does not meet the reserve price this expenditure may be wasted.

A tender involves sending a form of contract to a number of prospective buyers and inviting them to submit their bids in writing and without knowledge of those put forward by other people. As such, there is none of the immediate competition produced by an auction room, but a tender can sometimes produce an unexpectedly high bid particularly from a special purchaser such as an adjoining landowner. In the case of a formal tender, all the parties making offers will be legally committed and the seller will usually choose the highest tender. However, the seller normally reserves the right to refuse any tender where there may be reasons for suspecting the credit worthiness of the highest bidder, for example if it is a limited company without assets. An informal tender is similar but it does not lead immediately to a concluded contract, allowing the successful bidder to negotiate that subsequently.

3.2   LOTTING AND SUB-SALE

The seller must consider at the outset whether the property is to be sold as a whole or divided into lots. In the case of auctions, a farm or estate is generally offered as a whole first, and only if it does not meet the reserve will parts of it then be offered as separate lots. In the case of a farm within a ring-fence, lotting will be unusual, but if the farm is in detached pieces, or there is known to be strong interest in part of the land from neighbouring farmers, or the house is out of scale or is capable of being sold on its own, then lotting may be appropriate.

In the case of estates, lotting will be the rule. The estate will comprise several farms and, particularly if some of them are let, the tenant may be interested in bidding for his farm alone. The land may also consist of houses, cottages, woods, mines, rivers, playing fields and other areas which may be of interest to different buyers. Before the Second World War, it was common for estates to be sold initially as a single lot with a long completion period of perhaps six months. The seller was often an estate owner who simply wished to dispose of the property knowing that the immediate buyer would probably not wish to take the whole estate but would look for a number of sub-purchasers who would take conveyances of their parts direct from the original seller. Such sales are now unusual because the seller will usually wish to have at least a share of the extra profit from the break-up; however, where the sub-sales are likely to involve a great deal of work and added value, single lot sales can still be appropriate. A common method of sub-sale applies to farms where two or three adjoining farmers are interested in acquiring the farm land but do not want the farmhouse. They may therefore form a consortium, agreeing to divide up the land between them and to sell the farmhouse on. Sub-sales are therefore common and accepted in relation to farm and estate sales.

3.3   LET AND NEWLY VACANT FARMS

The trigger for an estate landlord to sell a farm may be that a tenant is retiring and has served notice to quit. In such cases the landlord may prefer not to find a new tenant or to take on the land himself but to sell it, with completion timed to coincide with the date the tenant gives vacant possession. It is possible to negotiate a surrender by the sitting tenant either in return for a fixed payment or for one calculated by reference to the sale price. The sale price may be divided simply by giving the tenant a percentage of the net proceeds after expenses of sale. More usually, the first slice of the proceeds will be allocated to the landowner and the remainder will be divided between owner and tenant. Where this happens, the tenant will often have rights under the Agricultural Holdings Act 1986 to compensation for improvements or tenant right matters, and it will have to be agreed how those will be dealt with as between the landlord, the tenant and the ultimate buyer. A number of other matters will need to be resolved, including the IACS (that is, Integrated Accounting and Control System) payments, farm workers' cottages, transfer of undertakings of employees, environmental agreements and other issues. The buyer will expect protection against outstanding claims from the selling landlord since many of these matters will be under the tenant's control.

Special problems arise if the tenant is not giving up his tenancy voluntarily and it has been terminated by notice to quit by the landlord, for example, for non-payment of rent, or by forfeiture, or where a farm business tenancy is coming to an end and the tenant has no incentive to co-operate. All of these matters, which are dealt with in more detail later, will affect the timing and the nature of the sale, and the terms and factors that need to be taken into account in determining the method of sale.

3.4   TIMING

Timing is critical for agriculture, and traditionally most sales take place at Michaelmas (29 September or, in some parts of the country, 6 or 10 October) with a smaller number at Lady Day (25 March or occasionally 6 or 10 April). This is related to the requirements of harvest for arable farms. In fact, Michaelmas is now a little late. Harvest will normally take place at any time from July onwards and the land will usually be clear by early September at the latest, although, occasionally, depending on the weather and the type of crop, this may run on into October and specialist crops such as carrots may be lifted later still. Once the harvest has been taken, the land will need to be cultivated for the next year's harvest and any autumn sowing that will need to be started. For that reason, it is usually necessary to negotiate either early entry for the buyer or holdover for the seller. Other factors can affect the timing, including the dates of IACS payments and the qualifying dates for grants and allowances in relation to the ownership of sheep and cattle. Other factors that may be relevant are the need to conclude a deal either before or after the end of the tax year on 5 April, the pressure from a lending bank, the need to carry out a transaction within the accounting year of a company, as well as purely personal matters affecting individuals such as a date of emigration or the need to coincide with the purchase of another property. Because of the complexity of agricultural sales and the number of issues that need to be resolved, timing must be considered well in advance. The sale process is often protracted because of the need to prepare particulars and carry out numerous surveys and searches, and it is essential at the outset of the sale process to consider whether any special date is critical for exchange of contracts or completion.

3.5   ALTERNATIVE METHODS OF SALE

The standard method of sale is by way of transfer of the freehold, and that method will be assumed throughout in this book. However, a number of other methods can be used. One variant is the sale and lease-back where a working farmer owns his farm and wishes to remain in possession but needs to raise capital. He may therefore sell the freehold subject to a lease-back to himself. Before the coming into force of the Agricultural Tenancies Act 1995, this was sometimes done by taking back an annual agricultural tenancy which gave the farmer lifetime security and (if it was granted before 1984, security for two successors). If the sale and lease-back is under a farm business tenancy, it can be for a defined period such as 20 years so that the buyer knows that there will be an income stream for that length of time, following which he will obtain possession. In such cases, negotiations of the terms of the lease will usually be the most critical aspect of the deal.

Where the farmer occupies under the terms of a saleable lease, in what ever way this may have arisen, the transaction can be carried through by assigning the lease. The consent of the landlord will usually be required under the terms of the lease, and the provisions of s 19 of the Landlord and Tenant Act 1927, which provide that consent cannot be unreasonably withheld, do not apply to farm business tenancies (FBTs). It follows that unless the words of s 19 are specifically included in the assignment clause of the lease the landlord will have the right to refuse consent to a sale and impose terms such as the payment of a sum of money. Long leases of agricultural land were common in the early part of this century but these are now rare, although they are coming back following the introduction of FBTs.

It may also be possible for a landlord to sell a farm for a period of time by granting an FBT at a premium, for example for 30 years. The rent review will need to be considered carefully in the light of the mandatory provisions of the Agricultural Tenancies Act 1995, but provided a satisfactory formula can be developed, possibly by taking an initial ground rent and indexing it or having a peppercorn or fixed rent, this would seem to be an acceptable method of sale for a limited period.

Many farming enterprises are set up with the farm and the live and dead stock together making up all the assets of a specific farming company (see **22.5**). It may therefore be worth considering a sale of the company. Buyers are usually wary about this unless they can be certain that there are no hidden liabilities in the company. However, if there are definite advantages, such as the availability of substantial tax reliefs which have built up in the company, this may be acceptable to a buyer.

3.6   SALE OF THE FARM BUSINESS

If a farm business is not part of the company being sold a decision will have to be taken as to the method of selling the various assets of the business. Apart from the land, such assets will include live and dead stock as well as machinery. Intangible assets, such as milk quota, may be disposed of separately or included with the land. There may be an argument for selling certain assets such as hefted sheep, or animals having the benefit of premium rights, along with the land.

It is common practice to hold a machinery sale or a sale of live and dead stock between contract and completion of the sale of a farm, and this right will usually be reserved specifically in the contract of sale although, strictly speaking, it is not necessary since the seller is free to do what he wishes on the land. In a very few cases, the seller may want to hold a sale of stock after title to the land has passed to the buyer and, in such a case, special provisions will be needed.

Where cultivations and other tenant right matters exist that have separate values which cannot be known at the time of contract, and which can be ascertained only at the date of sale, these may need to be included separately under the contract. Where the landlord is selling a farm on the termination of a tenancy and the tenant has tenant right claims, this provision will be normal.

Care needs to be taken where the seller is retiring and seeks to obtain the benefit of retirement relief from capital gains tax (see Chapter 28) since this is conditional on the disposal of effectively all the assets of the business. Capital gains tax relief on retirement is now being phased out but, if the seller is able to claim it, he will need to sell all the assets at the same time (although not necessarily to the same person) and such sale must be coordinated. This may present problems if, for example, the milk quota has been leased out and an opportunity to sell the land arises subsequently and has to be taken. However, provided the seller's advisers are aware of the position, they can usually take steps to overcome such problems, for example by selling the milk quota subject to the leasing contract.

Chapter 4

THE PRINCIPALS

4.1   INTRODUCTION

The various parties to the transaction will have differing needs, legal powers and functions. In the case of sellers, such matters may influence the form and timing of the transaction. Buyers will usually have to fit in with the requirements of the seller, but a private treaty sale will often go more smoothly if the seller is aware of any special requirements of the buyer. This is not usually practical in the case of auctions and formal tenders, unless the class of people invited to bid is restricted.

In this book, the parties are normally assumed to be private individuals or companies, but special rules relate to other types of buyers and sellers such as trusts, pension funds, charities, local authorities and consortiums.

4.2   THE WORKING FARMER

A working farmer who wishes to sell his farm may have various motives which will affect the sale. If he is moving to another farm in another part of the country, he will need to coincide the sale and purchase in very much the same way as an individual moving house. He will usually be more concerned to ensure that his purchase is secured before the sale, because the risk of being without a farm is greater than the problems (including financial) of having to own and run two farms. If the farmer is retiring, he will need to be able to wind down his business and dispose of the assets, and tax considerations, particularly retirement relief, could be important. The farmer may be under pressure for cash, for example from a bank, which will wish to have a say in the terms of the disposal. Many farms are sold today in order to fund divorce settlements. The farmer who owns the land may have moved out of the farmhouse leaving the wife in occupation; in such a case, a buyer will need to ensure that possession of both the land and the house is available on completion. In this respect, a farm sale is unlike a residential sale because it is common for the husband to continue to work the farmland, even though he is not living in the farmhouse.

A farmer may simply want to sell a few fields which are surplus, or raise a limited amount of cash.

Similarly, a working farmer as buyer may acquire a whole new business, or may simply acquire additional fields in order to expand the business or to spread fixed costs.

The working farmer as purchaser may also be taking advantage of rollover relief – where another farm has been sold, often at a considerable profit for development, tax will be attracted unless the proceeds are reinvested in a new business within a limited time.

4.3   THE AMENITY FARM

It is common for individuals who have made or inherited money and wish to live in a pleasant environment to purchase a farm mainly as a residence but perhaps partly in order to carry on a rural occupation. Such farms are not necessarily operated as businesses. If the area of land is small, the farm land may be used as pony paddocks and, if larger, the land may be used for sporting or other amenity purposes, or to protect a view. In these cases, owners may retain occupation of the house and immediate grounds while giving grazing tenancies to local farmers of the grassland beyond. The amenity farmer will often be less concerned with commercial issues such as IACS or the quality of the land but more interested in issues such as sites of special scientific importance and ancient monuments. However, if the land is crossed with footpaths, the value of a farm to an amenity farmer who seeks privacy may be less than to a working farmer who may not be so concerned.

4.4   THE INVESTOR

Farms, and particularly estates, may be acquired as an investment to secure an income with long-term capital growth. Farm land cannot normally compare with the stock market for short-term investment purposes, and usually needs to be held for a period calculated at least in decades in order to secure a proper return. In the 1970s, many pension funds invested heavily in farm land in the hope that it would be a more sound home for their money than the stock market, but experience has shown that the needs of such funds are not really suited to farm land. As an investment, it needs a great deal of management and regular expenditure even where the land is fully let. Where land is purchased subject to an Agricultural Holdings Act tenancy, then, in the long term, there may well be prospects of a capital gain when vacant possession is eventually achieved. In addition, if the farm land can be sold subsequently for building purposes, this can realise very large gains, but if the chance of planning permission is only a few years away the price will normally fully reflect this 'hope value' so, again, this is a long-term investment.

Historically, most rural land in England was owned by aristocratic families or institutions such as the Crown and the Church, largely to produce income. These owners still retain a great deal of land for this purpose although their holdings have dramatically reduced in size during this century. However, whilst foreign investors and property companies are still prepared to invest in large farms and estates to create income, many owners of land have tried to rationalise their estates by selling off poorer quality farm land or land which is in uneconomic units and to acquire better quality land so that, even among long-term investors, there is a steady shift from one farm to another. A buyer of land for a long-term investment will wish to ensure that the investment is as sound as possible, that buildings are in good order (because normally the landlord is responsible for repair), and will need to have regard to all the same factors that would be relevant to a working farmer. If the land is purchased when already let, the investor will need to investigate the strength of the tenant's covenant (that is, his ability to pay rent and farm the land separately) and the likelihood of the land being re-let if the tenant leaves.

4.5   TRUSTEES AND EXECUTORS

Many estates are held by family trusts and the trustees will often be professionals or institutions who will not themselves have any direct personal benefit under the trust. They will therefore need to take account of objective considerations both in taking any decision to sell or where a trust intends to purchase. The general duty of a trustee is to act prudently and cautiously and not take risks. Thus, trustees who sell will need to be seen to have taken every precaution to ensure that the best price is obtained and have obtained full professional advice. Trustees who purchase will also need to have taken advice to ensure that they are paying an appropriate price.

Trustees may have to sell where the purposes of the trust have come to an end, for example where a beneficiary has died. Trustees who purchase may do so as an investment or for the occupation of a beneficiary under the trust, in which case they will need to consult with the beneficiary and ensure that the farm is suitable for his needs.

Executors are a special type of trustee responsible for administering an estate on death. Usually their main concern will be to dispose of the farm or estate as quickly as possible in order to distribute the proceeds to the beneficiaries under the will, but they must have regard to the orderly winding up of the estate and the disposal of other assets such as plant and machinery. Frequently, landowners will give a specific piece of land or a cottage to a named beneficiary under their will and leave the executors to dispose of the balance of their property. In taking the decision to sell, executors must have regard to the valuation rules for death duties and this may dictate the timing of any sale.

4.6   CHARITIES AND PENSION FUNDS

Charities and pension funds provide special types of trust, or a trust may sometimes be set up through other vehicles such as companies. Pension funds will normally hold land purely for investment purposes and must have strict regard to their governing investment criteria, both in relation to the purchase and the sale of land. Except in the case of a very substantial pension fund, or one designed for the requirements of particular individuals, agricultural land will often be unsuitable because it is a relatively illiquid asset.

A charity may hold land either as an investment, in which case pure investment criteria will govern the decision, or for functional purposes. Thus, an environmental charity (such as the National Trust or one of the innumerable small, local environmental charities around the country) will hold land for its natural beauty or for public appreciation and education. A conservation charity (such as the RSPB) will obviously need to satisfy its particular requirements (such as a good breeding ground for birds). If the land is also to be farmed the charity must be careful that the terms of the tenancy are consistent with its objectives. Land may be given to a charity on special trusts, for example an ancient monument to a heritage charity, and if it proves uneconomic for the charity to retain it subsequently it may have to have regard to special requirements under the Charities Act 1993 for the disposal of land held on special trusts. In any event, any charity selling any land has to go through certain procedures laid down in s 36 of the Charities Act 1993.

4.7   CONSORTIUM

A consortium is a group of individuals connected only for the purposes of a single transaction. It is common for consortiums to buy rural estates in order to put in one bid or have one contract so that they can secure the estate more easily either at auction or through private treaty. They will then divide the estate up between themselves. Consortiums of sellers are less common but may arise where, for example, several pieces of farm land in the same area can be sold for a better price if they are grouped together than if they were to be sold individually. A consortium will need to have an agreement which, in the case of buyers, will indicate how they are to contribute the purchase price and costs and, in the case of sellers, how they are to divide the proceeds.

Purchasing consortiums may wish to conceal the fact that they are acting as such from the seller, particularly where, for example, one of the members of the consortium is a sitting tenant or an adjoining landowner, so that if he knew of that person's interest the seller would feel able to demand a higher price.

4.8 LOCAL AUTHORITIES AND OTHER STATUTORY BODIES

Local authorities and similar bodies can acquire or dispose of land only in accordance with their statutory constitution. There must be a specific justification to take land, and in general there is an obligation to dispose of land that is surplus to requirement. In recent years, many county councils who are smallholding authorities have disposed of farming estates which are uneconomic to hold, but this has been the subject of much political criticism and it is essential that the authority goes through the correct procedure. A buyer will also need to be satisfied that any procedural requirements have been followed so that the sale is not void.

In the past, government departments have been the owners of large areas of the countryside, and bodies such as the Ministry of Agriculture, Fisheries and Food (MAFF), the Ministry of Defence (MoD) and the Forestry Commission have disposed of property on a large scale. In these cases, the Treasury often imposes specific conditions, such as an overage provision (see **26.4**).

4.9 MORTGAGEES

Mortgagees may need to sell land where the owner has been unable to service the mortgage or has become bankrupt. In the case of other properties, such as houses and factories, it will usually be sufficient for the mortgagee to take possession and then sell an empty property. This is not normally an option in the case of a farm because if it is left vacant it will quickly deteriorate. Wherever possible, therefore, the mortgagee will try to co-operate with the owner, in which case the sale will technically be by the owner even though it may be instigated and guided by the lender. Where it is necessary to take possession, for example because the owner objects to the sale of a family farm by the bank, the mortgagee may need to put in a farm business tenant on a short-term basis in order to keep the farm operating. There may be many incidental problems such as the ownership of and right to transfer milk quota, the ownership of live and dead stock and the associated premium rights. Furthermore, a mortgagee will not usually be familiar with the land and the buyer may therefore need to carry out detailed surveys which would not always be necessary if there had been a co-operative owner ready to answer enquiries. Where the buyer takes a mortgage, the mortgagee will usually need to have regard to the same issues of valuation and incumbrances that would affect a commercial buyer.

A mortgagee will not usually wish to take possession if it can be avoided because the person in possession of land may be subject to liabilities as occupier. Mortgagees therefore normally appoint a receiver (who is treated under the Law of Property Act 1925, s 109 as the agent of the mortgagor) and this may add to the difficulties of a buyer in getting answers to enquiries or even finding someone to provide information about the land.

Chapter 5

LOCAL VARIATIONS

5.1   INTRODUCTION

As England and Wales together comprise a relatively small area, most of the issues affecting sellers and buyers of land are the same throughout. There are, however, many local distinctions arising out of non-legal matters which can have varying legal implications in different parts of England and Wales and an adviser must acquire all the relevant local knowledge of the area in which the land is being bought or sold.

5.2   FARMING ACTIVITIES

Most types of farming are found in most parts of the country where climate, soil and geography permit. There is, however, a broad distinction between the pastoral west and the arable east. In the west, farmers are concerned with herds of cattle and sheep and the associated quotas, environmental problems arising from silage and slurry, and problems about milking parlours and roads fit for milk tankers. In the east, there is more concern with drainage ditches, arable area payments and set-aside, pollution from nitrates and chemical sprays, and the activities of Internal Drainage Boards.

Many farming activities are determined by the prevailing local features. Sugar beet requires certain types of soil and climate and needs to be produced within a reasonable distance of a sugar processing plant. Market gardens tend to be found on rich soil on the outskirts of large towns. Some parts of the country, such as Wessex, with an abundance of listed ancient monuments, are best suited for grazing or pasture land.

5.3   ASSOCIATED ACTIVITIES

5.3.1   Mining

Mining activities produce many local variations. In the deep mining areas, such as the lead mines of Derbyshire and the tin mines of Cornwall and, most particularly, in former coal mining areas, there can be major problems of subsidence and, very often, pollution from mine tips. Other parts of the country may not have these problems but may instead have limestone, or sand, or gravel excavation, which is usually from surface quarries and these can have problems of restoration, conversion of flooded former workings, and fencing round quarries (either working or abandoned).

Mineral rights and responsibilities may be particularly sensitive to local custom and methods of operation. The terms of a mining lease can vary considerably from area to area and special care must be taken in examining mineral leases where the approach and terminology is unfamiliar.

5.3.2   Tourism

Tourism is a growing activity, especially in attractive and accessible areas such as the West Country, and is having an increasing impact on the operation of estates. There is, however, a distinction between areas with good communications to centres of population which are developing general leisure industries such as pubs and short-term hotels, and more distant areas where people come to stay for a week or a month. This, in turn, has an impact on the type of lease of tourist facilities generally in use.

Of increasing importance is the issue of weekend cottages and residential farms. Such premises are normally situated in an attractive part of the country, are in reach of, but not too close to, a motorway or major road, and are often listed buildings or of considerable age. Where an estate includes buildings of this nature, it can have an impact on the method of sale and the price obtained, especially if it is possible to include enough land to provide sufficient surroundings but not too much that the buyer (who will frequently not be a working farmer) feels unduly burdened. Some buyers of substantial houses will wish to take ownership of additional land but not have the responsibility for running it, and will therefore make some arrangement with a local farmer. It is therefore a growing practice for such properties to be offered for sale with a small amount of land but with the possibility of taking an additional area, either freehold or on lease, if the buyer so wishes. In a private treaty sale, this is straightforward and is a matter for negotiation. However, such properties are often difficult to value and the seller may wish to dispose of them by auction or tender. In that case, it is common for the sale document (which will, by definition, be to an unknown person) to include an option exercisable within, for example, two months to take up the additional land either freehold or on lease.

Sellers, who will normally be familiar with long-term development prospects for their own areas, may wish to retain land or rights over it for overage purposes, as discussed in Chapter 26. The location of the land, for example on the edge of a village which is capable of expanding, or close to a large, prosperous town, can therefore have an important impact on the method of sale. Provisions for overage will not normally be suitable for land situated in the heart of the countryside, in a specially protected area (eg an area of outstanding natural beauty), or on the edge of a declining settlement because of the chance of planning consent is remote. If, however, there is a prospect in the medium term of improved communications, such as a new major road, a railway or even an airport, this can have an impact on the medium-term value of the land. Such considerations should be borne in mind not only by the seller, who may wish to protect himself against any increase in value accruing to the buyer, but also by the potential buyer when making his bid.

5.4 COAST, HILL AND RIVER

In certain areas of the country, particularly along the south coast, the sea view is highly valued. On the other hand, coastal farms on certain parts of the east coast may actually be liabilities, as erosion is proceeding at an increasing pace and some land is literally disappearing into the sea. It is important to have some idea of coast protection policy since in certain areas local authorities are trying to protect the coast from erosion, possibly retaining even isolated farm land in order to protect built-up land further along the coast. In other cases, a decision may have been taken on economic or environmental grounds to allow erosion to take place at its own pace. There is a network of public paths along many stretches of coast and many of these paths are well used, especially in summer.

Uplands have their own special issues. Many uplands are designated as attractive areas and are therefore subject to tight planning controls. Indeed, many are within national parks or areas of outstanding natural beauty (AONBs). Even where planning controls are not in force, special economic incentives, such as payments to hill farmers and the conferment of a European Union Less Favoured Area status on the land, may attract subsidies or favourable treatment. Areas of open moorland are likely to be subject increasingly to public rights of access, whether these are given voluntarily by landowners subject to pressure from government or subsidies under access agreements, or are introduced compulsorily. This may be attractive for tourist-related uses, but there can be problems with litter, gates which are left open allowing animals to stray or, if there are abandoned mineshafts or other dangers on the land, public liability risks. If the land is suitable for a shoot (Chapter 12), public access rights can reduce its value.

Much valuable farm land is located in river valleys in attractive countryside, which may be subject to tight planning control. Increasingly, the Environment Agency is on the alert for pollution and much of this comes from farms, for example from fertilisers spread on the land and passed into streams, from pollution by animals or from chemicals stored on the farm which are allowed to leach out. However, not all flowing streams behave in the same way. The effect of pollution on a fast-flowing stream in the hills may be quite different from the effect on a meandering river across flat country and this should be considered when advising on the impact of pollution and liability for it.

Much of this is common sense and does not depend on special legal or other expert knowledge. However, lawyers practising in a particular part of the country will normally be aware of the special problems that arise in their area and will either alert their clients on selling or raise questions on buying which may not always be evident to lawyers who normally practise in a different part of the country.

Chapter 6

THE PROFESSIONAL TEAM

6.1 INTRODUCTION

Buyers and sellers of agricultural land will need to rely on the assistance of a number of advisers. Wherever possible these advisers should co-operate and be drawn together at an early stage because one type of problem (such as a tax liability or a restrictive covenant) may impact on another issue (such as timing or a proposed change of use). Some buyers and sellers like to maintain control of their business affairs so that they know what is going on and in order to minimise costs. The adviser will need to work to a budget and professional fees will be an important part of that, particularly where a sale is being made to realise a specific sum or where finance is needed for a purchase. Normally, the professionals will be prepared to estimate on the basis of full information given at the outset, and it is therefore important to establish precisely what advice each of them is expected to give, and in what circumstances.

6.2 THE RESIDENT AGENT

Historically, it was the practice for landed estates to have a resident agent who was an employee of the owner. That is now less common, although larger estates may still employ a resident agent or use the services of a surveyor, who may devote most of his time to a particular estate. Other estates may use the services of a local firm, which may have handled small sales (such as paddocks, extensions of gardens or road widening), tenancies, rent reviews and other routine matters over the years. The agent is normally consulted about a sale, but even if his advice is not requested on the policy it will be essential to involve him at all stages in the selling process because of his knowledge of the estate and the associated problems. Agents are not usually involved in this way in relation to working farms, unless the owner is not personally involved in running the farm, in which case the agent may represent him in his dealings with the farm manager or contractor. The agent will normally have a great deal of information which will be needed in the preparation of sales particulars and in reply to enquiries made by the buyer.

6.3   THE SURVEYOR AND TRANSACTION AGENT

When a decision to sell is taken, the farm or estate will be put into the hands of a selling agent who is usually a member of a firm of surveyors. The firm will advise on the best method of sale, including lotting, advertising and timing. It is common practice, particularly for large farms and estates, for at least two firms to be involved, one of which will be locally based and can handle specific enquiries, and the other of which may be a national firm with international contacts. The firms will carry out a survey of the land to be sold and will normally prepare a schedule of areas and a sale plan. They will generally obtain from statutory undertakers, details of any wayleaves and the existence of pipes, cables and other plant. They will assemble other information such as milk quotas, IACS forms and woodland grants, and may also assemble a cropping and production history. In the case of charitable landowners, there is a legal obligation to provide a very detailed report in a specified form, about the land and all buildings on it. There are also certain reporting formalities in relation to public authorities. In the absence of any legal or official requirement on this, it will normally be sensible to assemble the same information.

A buyer may need the help of a surveyor, both to report on the quality of the land and on whether the price is right. In addition, there may be many matters to negotiate such as dates of occupation, boundary responsibilities, the terms of any covenant, the purchase of live and dead stock and related matters. Where the buyer intends to resell part of the land, the advice of a surveyor will be needed in the same way as a seller needs such advice.

6.4   THE ACCOUNTANT

The decision to sell or buy will often be dictated by financial considerations but, even if this is not the case, these will still be relevant. On a sale by most private individuals or companies, the impact of taxation is often a very important consideration. This is particularly true if the proceeds are to be reinvested in some other venture, or to be used to pay off liabilities. The occupation of farm land attracts many significant tax reliefs and special treatments and liabilities can frequently be postponed until they are crystallised by a sale. Apart from tax, however, there may be various other financial issues built into the sale, for example the timing may be critical in relation to the disposal of crops, and the assistance of a professional in drawing up a cashflow will often be useful.

For a buyer, it may be helpful to have accountancy advice on the overall costs, including several hidden ones, and, particularly if the buyer is intending to embark on a new venture (such as diversification or organic farming), help may be needed in seeing how the figures work out.

6.5 LAWYERS

It is normally wise to employ solicitors for the sale or purchase of farms and estates. Although licensed conveyancers, barristers and notaries are legally entitled to carry out this work, few will have the necessary specialised experience. The relevant issues are discussed throughout this book and it is important for both buyers and sellers to know that their legal adviser is familiar with these issues. Previously, much of the routine work was regularly carried out by legal executives or other persons who had experience but no formal qualification. Today, such practice is unusual and most work is done by qualified solicitors, although the solicitor who handles the conveyancing may be a specialist in the firm and not necessarily be the client partner consulted by the landowner. Owners of substantial areas of land may, of course, use may their own in-house solicitors, although, except for the largest institutions, it is unusual for in-house solicitors to have the necessary expertise. Different specialties may be needed in relation to straightforward conveyancing, environmental law, employment issues and other aspects which may be relevant, such as matrimonial or European law.

It is unusual for counsel to be involved in sales or purchases of agricultural land unless there are particularly difficult issues of title or contract. Counsel may, however, be involved incidentally, for example where it is necessary to take proceedings for possession against a farm tenant or cottage tenant, or where the sale arises out of a divorce settlement.

6.6 THE FARM MANAGER

Most working farmers will operate their own farms with the assistance of farm employees, but where a farmer has a number of farms many miles apart, or where the owner is elderly or for some other reason does not wish to be directly involved in running the farm, he may employ a farm manager. The manager will usually not be directly concerned in the details of the sale, but it will be important to consult with him particularly over timing issues. The farm manager will need to know about early entry and holdover, and will be involved in the disposal of live and dead stock as well as relations with employees. He will usually have completed the IACS forms and will be familiar with drainage patterns, water supplies and other practical issues on the ground.

Some working farmers instead employ farming consultants. They will not normally be needed to advise a seller, but where a buyer is taking on a new farm the consultant may be able to advise on the best method of cropping or stock raising, related issues which will be relevant to the management of the farm being acquired, and generally on whether the farming business is likely to be viable.

6.7   SPECIALISTS

A large range of specialist advice may be needed for particular transactions. Where environmental issues exist, for example slurry or silage draining towards a watercourse, or flooded quarries and gravel pits, a buyer may need the advice of an environmental consultant on any possible liabilities and on the statutory requirements to deal with these. Where a farm has mineral deposits, the value of these and the possibility of obtaining planning consent will be relevant to the price, and advice may be needed on any element of value to be placed on the future exploitation of these deposits. Similarly, where the farm includes substantial areas of woodland, especially those which are managed commercially, this will be relevant to price. Quite apart from commercial value (usually in the form of conifer plantations) amenity woodland can add to the value of a residential farm, and woodland is normally essential for the exercise of sporting rights. Accordingly, specialist woodland advice may be needed.

If diversified activities such as caravan sites, farm shops, paintball games or other ventures are planned, a seller may need advice on the value and best means of sale, and a buyer may need advice on future prospects. Caravan sites, in particular, need special treatment because of the variety of licences and statutory requirements.

Chapter 7

THE LAND

7.1 ASSESSING THE WORTH OF LAND

Farm land is sold by the acre. There is a growing tendency, especially where a government department or other official body is involved, to sell it by the hectare, but most farmers and landowners still think in terms of acres and most prices quoted in the farming press are by reference to the old measures. The price will, of course, be affected by matters other than the simple extent of the land. MAFF has classified farm land into grades, so that the most productive and versatile land (Grade 1) typically found in East Anglia or in certain river valleys will be worth many times more than stony moorland (Grade 4). Land which has been well cultivated and drained and maintained will normally be worth more than land which has been allowed to run down, and this may be relevant to claims against departing tenants. The existence, convenience and modernity of farm buildings and other equipment will affect values, and a major factor in recent years has been the existence of attractive farmhouses in good situations, especially if they are conveniently situated for national communications. Other factors will include the presence of woodland, the degree of public access, including rights of common and footpaths, location in relation to a town or the seaside, and numerous other elements. Nevertheless, it remains true that the basic measure of bare open farm land without buildings will relate primarily to its area, and if it turns out that title to part of the land is not good, this can give rise to a claim for damages, which will normally be based on a straightforward acreage calculation.

It is rare nowadays that there is confusion over whether a particular field or house is included with the farm or estate. There may be problems, for example, if for many years the owner of a farm has rented some immediately adjoining land and has removed the hedge between the two areas, combining them into a single field, but reference to old title deeds will usually overcome even problems of that sort. For most of the twentieth century the practice has been to include plans both on title deeds and on tenancy agreements, and even if these are not available there will usually be a schedule of areas by reference to an edition of the Ordnance Survey map. As such, in practice there is normally little confusion over ownership of the substantial areas. There can, however, be doubt over the ownership of smaller, uncultivated pieces of land, such as roads, rivers and hedges, and buyers may need to investigate these. For that reason, unless the extent of the land is clear (for example, because it comprises the whole of the land in a registered title or all the land clearly defined in a title deed) it is sensible to attach a plan to the contract. Where part of a registered title is transferred a plan must be used under the Land Registration Rules 1925, r 98.

7.2 BOUNDARIES

In pastoral areas, boundaries are vital to prevent livestock straying onto other land or escaping onto the highway, and to prevent incursions of livestock from adjoining land. A farm may include several miles of boundary, which can be expensive to maintain, whether the physical boundary comprises a hedge (sometimes on top of a bank), fence, wall or line of barbed or electric wire.

Where land previously in common ownership is sold, it is usual to impose boundary obligations. Some of these are old and date back to enclosure during the eighteenth and nineteenth centuries, about which there is currently a good deal of public interest. Many of the Inclosure Acts laid down boundary responsibilities between adjoining farmers, and the provisions are still enforceable only by the owners of the land on either side. Other provisions of these Acts can be of wider public importance, for example where a hedge adjoins a highway, and there is a growing tendency for members of the public to seek to enforce such provisions to protect historic hedges.

Where a boundary obligation has been imposed by a landowner selling part of his land, this will constitute a positive covenant and, as such, will be enforceable only against the person who has entered into the obligation. Although various devices (including estate rentcharges and rights of re-entry and restrictions on the register of title) can be used to seek to make these covenants binding on future owners, they are untested and of uncertain scope. However, even the existence of an unenforceable positive covenant will be evidence of responsibility for the boundary and if the boundary falls into disrepair and animals escape, this may point to liability. It is standard practice for buyers' solicitors to make enquiries as to boundaries. In the case of farms, these should be considered with care because of the obligations involved. In particular, under the Animals Act 1971 there is a general liability on landowners to prevent their animals straying onto the highway and causing an accident. There is also a custom (as in *Egerton v Harding* [1975] 1 QB 62), sometimes re-enforced by statute (for example in the Dartmoor Commons Act 1985), for the landowner adjoining common land to fence his land so that livestock does not stray. Such provisions may need to be investigated.

Where land is being sold, it may be sufficient to provide that the buyer will erect (or, where boundaries already exist, maintain) 'good and sufficient stockproof fences'. However, it may be necessary to specify this in more detail, for example, by stipulating the height of the fence, whether it is to be post and rail and, if so, how many rails, the frequency of post supports, and other factors.

Many hedges are now protected under the Hedgerow Regulations 1997, SI 1997/1160 made under the Environment Act 1995. These may include internal hedges within a farm as well as boundary hedges. The Regulations provide that hedges of a defined length (usually 20 metres) may not be removed or cut through without prior notice to the local authority, which can object on defined grounds such as historic or scientific interest.

There is a general rule known as the 'Hedge and Ditch Rule', which may be applied to ascertain the ownership of certain boundaries. Derived from the days when most land was open and unfenced and where a landowner was able to assemble enough land to be economically worth defining, the rule presumes that the owner started to dig a ditch with the outer lip on the boundary of his land, throwing the soil behind him to form a bank. A hedge was often planted (or grew naturally) on the bank and therefore the law presumes, in the absence of evidence to the contrary, that where a boundary feature is a hedge on a bank with a ditch on one side of it the legal boundary will be on the far lip of the bank. However, this is not invariable and very often parties will have adopted a different procedure. In particular, where land was in common ownership and parts sold off, the parties may sell by reference to an Ordnance Survey map or a map that shows the position of the hedge. In *Alan Wibberley (Building) Ltd v Insley* [1998] 2 All ER 82, the Court of Appeal held that where the landowner had bought his land by reference to a plan which showed the hedge as the boundary, that should be assumed to be the boundary even where the two sides have not been in common ownership. Usually the farmer on the ditch side of the hedge will have carried out acts of ownership such as dredging the ditch, and this may have given a possessory title if it has been carried on for more than 12 years.

In many areas of the country which are predominantly arable and where stock is not kept, fences are unnecessary and the land can stretch for miles without any barrier. Boundaries between farms may be indicated by drainage ditches or by some feature not obvious on casual inspection. For example, two, low, concrete posts, perhaps 100 yards apart, with no connection between them, will mark either end of the straight-line boundary. Where even such basic indications are absent, it may be necessary to carry out a survey on the land by reference to maps.

As most freehold land becomes the subject of compulsory registration of title, boundaries will often be ascertained by reference to the Land Registry plan. That is subject to r 278 of the Land Registration Rules 1925 (the general boundaries rule), which provides that unless an elaborate procedure to fix a special boundary has been followed, the exact line will be left undetermined as to, for instance, whether it includes a hedge, wall or ditch, runs along the centre of a wall or fence on its inner or outer face, or how far it runs within or beyond it. Thus, the Land Registry plan cannot be relied on to give a detailed analysis of the precise position of the boundary, although in practice most parties will accept it for the sake of certainty. In the case of farm land, it is unusual for the precise position of a boundary to be important to the last few inches (as it may often be between houses and gardens) since the farmer is more likely to be concerned with the cost of maintenance rather than the precise position. However, where there is potential uncertainty over an area of yards, this can affect IACS payments and buyers may therefore need to investigate this in some detail.

Where land is conveyed by reference to unregistered documents (or where the general boundaries need to be clarified by reference to pre-registration deeds) it may be very difficult to reconcile old plans (particularly if they have been drawn by hand) with the position on the ground. It should also be noted that the position of hedges can move over the years. In the 1960s and subsequently, government grants were available for grubbing-out hedges. It remained economically worthwhile to do so into the 1990s, even though by that time there were moves to protect hedges, and grants were available for planting new ones. Where a hedge once existed and was grubbed-out, and a subsequent owner decided to plant a new one, it was often convenient for the old hedge and the new to be in a broadly similar position. However, that position might vary by several yards, and the matter must be considered with care on a purchase.

7.3   RIVERS

Where the boundary of a farm adjoins a river, the legal presumption in the absence of evidence to the contrary is that the boundary goes down the middle of the stream. Where an island exists which clearly belongs to one party, the boundary will be drawn between the island and the far bank. Where a river has changed its course slowly and imperceptibly over the years, the boundary will move with it, but where the course has changed suddenly, either as a result of a flood or, for example, by an ox-bow being pinched off, that will not affect ownership. In the 1960s and 1970s, many previously meandering streams were straightened by river boards and water authorities in the interests of land drainage. Where the old meandering stream was previously the boundary between two farms, this action by the authorities left many isolated pieces of land cut off. In practice, many farmers affected have not had the legal position rectified, eg by deed of exchange, but with the passage of time a possessory title may have been acquired. It should be noted, however, that although time runs against an absolute owner after 12 years provided there have been sufficient acts of cultivation (which will not always be the case with a former riverbed), if a different title arises, for example, under the Settled Land Act 1925, to land on one side, 12 years may not be sufficient, as a result of s 28 of the Limitation Act 1980.

Where rivers are valuable in their own right, they may be in separate ownership. Very often, where fishing is of importance, a previous owner may have sold the riverbed (possibly together with the banks) or excluded it from the sale of adjoining land. This is still common practice. Fishing as an incorporeal right may, in any case, be retained separately from ownership of the riverbed. Where the fishing rights are to be kept out of the sale, it will be necessary to define with care precisely where the boundaries are between the farm land and the fishing land and what rights, such as the ability to stand on the bank or to cut weeds, belong with the fishing.

It can happen that the riverbed was previously have been part of a manor and is still owned by the lord of the manor, even though the land on the bank belongs to a farmer (see *Tilbury v Silva* (1890) 45 ChD 98. In such cases, the boundaries and the rights between the owners of the bed or the bank may be governed by ancient law.

Where a canal has been cut through a farm, the rights will normally be governed by the Act of Parliament which authorised the making of the canal, although in some cases these rights have been modified by agreement between the canal company and the landowner. In particular, it must be clear whether the adjoining landowner has rights of fishing or boating on the canal and the extent of private or public rights over the towpath (see *Staffordshire and Worcestershire Canal Navigation v Bradley* [1912] 1 Ch 91). Canal walls can be expensive to maintain. There has been a revival of interest in maintaining old canals even where they are no longer of commercial importance, and where canals are being repaired and revived it is essential to be aware of the rights. It follows that anyone purchasing land adjoining a canal needs to investigate such matters with care.

In certain parts of the country, for example in the Fens, public drainage schemes exist and some of these go back many centuries. A variety of practices and customs have arisen, and in some cases Internal Drainage Boards have rights to enter and maintain drains even where they do not own them. In such cases, there is usually a drainage rate payable by all farmers for common contributions to the cost of the maintenance of the drainage system.

7.4   ROADS

Where farm land adjoins a public or private road, a grass verge will usually be situated between the land and the metalled carriageway. The ownership of this verge is important in terms of liability, for example trees may fall down and cause damage to passing cars, weeds may spread to farm land, and casual travellers may camp, often for long periods of time, and cause a local nuisance. Ownership of the verge may also be important if planning consent is granted for an access or for the construction of houses. There is much law on the ownership of highway verges, and specialist books should be consulted where applicable.

The general rule is that where land adjoins a public or private track, in the absence of evidence to the contrary the adjoining landowner owns the land up to the middle of the track. Where the way is a highway maintainable at public expense by the highway authority, the surface of the highway (both the metalled part and any other part, subject to highway rights such as the verge) is vested in the highway authority. This may be a few inches or a few feet deep, but it will not go to any great depth. This general presumption is, however, subject to numerous exceptions.

An obvious exception is where the road was constructed under special powers and the highway authority has acquired the freehold of the road. In that case, a normal freehold will extend down to the centre of the earth and up to the sky. Even where that is not the case, many highways have been the subject of dedication (see Chapter 9). Dedication agreements often contain a commitment on the part of the landowner that, if asked to do so, he will convey the freehold to the highway authority without further payment.

Where the road (whether public or private) was laid out under the provisions of an Inclosure Act or award, that Act or award will often contain provisions as to ownership and maintenance. Where this is not the case, certain presumptions are made. These are, broadly, that if the lord of the manor took part in the allotment under an Inclosure Act, the soil of the track belongs to the owners on either side, but if the lord of the manor did not take part, he will have retained ownership of the soil. In any event, where there is an ancient highway the roadside verge will usually belong to the lord of the manor even though he may not own the enclosed farm land beyond. As a result of special local practices or customs, however, the verge may become vested in a variety of other bodies, such as a local charity. Where land on a large estate was sold off, it may be that the terms of the conveyance would have included the farm land but not the road or track. This is particularly likely to be the case if the owner of the farm was given an express right of way over the track (see *Pardoe v Pennington* (1976) 75 P&CR 264).

A particular problem relates to field entrances from the highway. These are often set back a little way and, frequently, title deeds do not specifically show the ownership of the farm gate and associated turning area. This can be important where the entrance needs to be maintained or improved, or where access from the field to the highway is needed for development, possibly some distance away, but with access obtained along a track. In such cases, a detailed historical investigation may be needed to ascertain ownership.

7.5   THE COAST

Special rules apply to ownership of coastal land, including land along the edge of tidal rivers and estuaries. The general presumption is that foreshore (the land between high water mark and low water mark of tide) as well as the seabed below low water mark belong to the Crown. In many cases however the Crown has conceded or granted title over the foreshore to the owner of adjoining land, sometimes by medieval charter. However, many surveys were undertaken in subsequent years and, particularly in the nineteenth and early twentieth century, numerous conveyances and sales were made by the Crown to private landowners, which were intended to clarify doubts over title. The Crown has sold much foreshore since then. Foreshore is a peculiar type of ownership because in most cases it can move if, over the years or centuries, the position of the coast moves. This derives from a presumption of law which can be excluded by agreement, and it was held in *Baxendale v Instow Parish Council* [1982] 1 Ch 14 that, where there is a conveyance of land which at the time was foreshore, but which is sufficiently defined and detailed to make it clear that what was actually intended to be conveyed was a specific portion of the earth's surface, that will remain the case even though the position of the foreshore has moved. Much will depend on the precise interpretation of the conveyance. In a few cases, the Crown has granted parts of the seabed, particularly over the river estuaries, to private landowners, normally in association with the grant of fishing rights.

7.6   COMMON LAND

Common land cannot be fenced under s 193 of the Law of Property Act 1925. As such, the precise extent and ownership can often be a matter of uncertainty because common land is usually of very little value and therefore not worth a great deal of legal time and trouble to ascertain precise boundaries. Under the Commons Registration Act 1965, Parliament directed that the ownership of all common land be registered, and this register will provide an answer to most issues of ownership. However, the Commons register was not prepared following detailed investigation, and is therefore not conclusive of ownership in the same way as registration under the Land Registration Acts 1925 to 1997. It will, however, be strong evidence. Accordingly, as mentioned in Chapter 24, a Commons search should be made in respect of rural land not registered under the Land Registration Act 1925. Many plans of common land were prepared on a very small scale where a single line may represent the width of several yards, so that, again, there may be doubt as to precise boundaries. Encroachments on common land occur regularly, particularly where adjoining house owners extend their gardens imperceptibly over the years. After 12 years, owners will normally obtain possessory rights, although such encroachment will not remove rights of common and s 193 will continue to apply.

The nature of ownership of common land is in some doubt. In *Brackenbank Lodge Ltd v Peart* [1996] EGCS 134, the House of Lords had to consider rival claims by the individual who claimed to be the owner of the land, admittedly subject to rights of common in favour of local farmers, and the farmers who collectively claimed to be the owners because of their joint interests. That case decided in favour of the claimant as landowner, but there are many commons known as beastgates, regulated pastures or other names, where the land may belong collectively to a number of commoners. Frequently, title deeds may be inconsistent and in many cases no title deeds exist at all, especially where the land has belonged to the Crown, the Church or some other institution for many centuries. The purchaser of common land in such cases needs to investigate the title with special care.

Chapter 8

THE TITLE

8.1 INTRODUCTION

The buyer and mortgagee of land will, of necessity, make a large financial outlay as a result of the transaction. As such, both must be satisfied that they are obtaining value for money. The seller therefore has to satisfy the buyer, and the buyer has to satisfy the lender, that he has a good title to the land, for example, the right to go into physical occupation or the right to receive income in the form of rent. There are two main ways of proving title, one in relation to registered land and the other in relation to unregistered land. Under the Land Registration Act 1925, s 123, it could be made compulsory to register title to land on sale in specified areas of the country. In 1990, this was extended to the whole country. Under the Land Registration Act 1997, it became compulsory, after 31 December 1997, to register titles following most other transfers of ownership including gifts, transmissions following death, exchanges and other transactions as well as mortgages where the lender takes the title deeds.

Under English law, all titles to land are relative and comparative, so that in general there is no absolute title to land, although where the proprietor is registered with absolute freehold title, that is very nearly as good. The significance of title is that the person claiming it in a dispute in court can show that he has a better title than any other party to the dispute. Thus title, and particularly unregistered title, is a matter of showing the best available evidence on the balance of probabilities, rather than proving ownership beyond reasonable doubt.

Most titles other than those of the Crown are derivative, in the sense that all land is held from the Crown or some other person. Most freehold land is held direct from the Crown and the owner is, in strict law, a tenant in fee simple. Leasehold land is held from the landlord. In the case of leases and tenancies the obligations between landlord and tenant are significant. In the case of freehold land, this is usually of little practical importance although there can be matters relating to various ancient payments and other obligations, such as maintenance of sea walls, which may be relevant to farms and estates.

8.2   REGISTERED LAND

The law on registered titles is governed by the Land Registration Acts 1925, 1936, 1986 and 1997 and Rules made under them. A system of registering title to land so that evidence consisted of an entry on a government register was introduced during the nineteenth century and became compulsory in London in 1900. Since then, it has been extended progressively to other parts of the country, initially to built-up areas, so that until recently it was relatively rare for titles to farm land to be registered, and title was normally proved by the unregistered method. That is now changing as a result of the spread of compulsory registration. Where a title to land is already registered, the seller will prove evidence by producing copies of the entries on the register and a copy of HM Land Registry filed plan.

The plan will show the land, but this will not be by reference to schedules of acres or hectares. HM Land Registry filed plan can normally be taken as accurate subject to the general boundaries rule mentioned at **7.2**. Normally, where there is any doubt about the boundaries (for example if they do not correspond to existing fields) HM Land Registry will carry out a survey. However, this may not be practical, in which case there may be a note on the plan that the boundaries have been plotted from the title deeds and are subject to rectification in the light of surveys. In any event, the survey is carried out after the completion of the sale leading to first registration and by that time it can be too late to rectify mistakes or misunderstandings. Particularly along unfenced boundaries, subsequent events may show that the boundary was incorrectly shown. Therefore, although the plan is in general reliable, it cannot be taken as an absolutely certain indication of ownership in all circumstances. The buyer should always inspect the land and compare it with the plan.

The remainder of the register is in three parts. The first part is the property register which describes the land in very broad terms, perhaps by reference to the name of a farm or an estate or to the situation as lying, for example, to the north of a particular road. It will also set out various rights relevant to the land as such, including the benefit of rights of way and other easements. The second part of the register, is the proprietorship register, which gives the name of the landowner and may include any restrictions, for example, if the landowner is a charity and needs to comply with the Charities Act 1993, or if a consent to disposal is required. The third part is the charges register, which includes incumbrances on the title. These may be permanent, such as easements and covenants that bind the land, or temporary, such as mortgages including the name of the owner of the mortgage.

The register is not comprehensive, particularly in relation to rights that benefit and bind the land. The register will not always show that the land has the benefit of specific rights, and where these exist they will generally pass automatically whether or not they appear on the register. More significantly, the register is not always conclusive of the existence of rights burdening the land. These are known as overriding interests and are specified in s 70 of the Land Registration Act 1925. They include easements, the fact that the mineral rights may be held by someone else (which is very common in the case of rural land) and various ancient rights, some of which are of little importance but some of which (such as the rights of the lord of the manor) may become significant. HM Land Registry can include only information supplied to it at the time of first registration or subsequently, and very often the title deeds are incomplete. For example, there may be a reference to the land being subject to restrictive covenants but no details are available on what those covenants comprise. Positive covenants may exist which were binding on an original landowner, and although they are not in general binding on later landowners, they may be relevant to other issues. For example, where an original owner undertook to put up a boundary, the obligation to maintain it cannot normally be enforced against later owners, but it may be important evidence of boundary responsibility.

An important class of overriding interest is the rights belonging to any person in occupation of the land. If, for example, a person who appears to be simply an annual tenant or a member of the seller's family also has some other right (such as a right of pre-emption), that other right may be binding on the buyer as an overriding interest, even though the right is of a type which would have needed to be protected by registration if the person entitled had not been in occupation. However, this type of overriding interest is not binding on a buyer if enquiry has been made of the occupier and he does not disclose it.

In general, therefore, while the register is normally as complete as HM Land Registry can make it, buyers should be aware there may be benefits and burdens which are not mentioned on the register and which could affect them, in which case it may be necessary to refer back to the old, unregistered title. It is therefore important that pre-registration title deeds should be preserved safely. Buyers will also need to raise this issue in their preliminary enquiries.

8.3   UNREGISTERED LAND

Because the system of title is comparative, the best method of showing title to land is to produce evidence by way of a collection of title deeds where these are available. Starting with a 'good root of title' (normally a conveyance on sale or a mortgage, which nowadays has to be at least 15 years old and is frequently older), title is then proved by showing a chain of successive conveyances, gifts, inheritances and other matters, as a result of which title passed to the present seller. The precise rules for this are detailed and are set out in standard conveyancing textbooks, but the general concern is to ensure that the documents deal comprehensively with all of the land comprised in the title (and in the case of farm land, which may have been assembled from several different sources, it is important to check that every piece of land is comprised in the title) and that as far as possible all rights binding or benefiting the land are mentioned. For practical purposes this system can normally be relied on because the standard of conveyancing work in the past was generally very high. However, it is not absolutely reliable and it is possible for defects in title to occur. For example, the land may have been held on a long lease at a nominal rent, perhaps for 99 years; in some parts of the country leases of up to 1,000 years were often granted in the seventeenth century. In such cases, the fact that the land was leasehold may be overlooked. The land may be conveyed as freehold and, subsequently, a landlord may assert various claims. More importantly, defects may arise under trusts, as mentioned below. As far as possible, the law gives protection to landowners who appear to have clear title deeds going back for a sufficiently long period and, particularly since 1925, defects in title relating to trusts have been less important. However, where the title goes back before that date, it may be necessary to investigate trusts.

The procedures for examining unregistered titles are designed to detect defects, against which it may be possible to insure. HM Land Registry also has a discretion to overlook technical defects which are unlikely to be of practical importance (such as failure to have acknowledgments for some earlier document) where there is no real doubt over ownership. Although not obliged to do so, the Registry may be prepared to comment on a title before exchange of contracts. As mentioned in Chapter 24, it is now normal practice to deduce title before exchange, and failure to do so can give rise to a suspicion that the seller has something to hide.

Following a sale of unregistered land it is now compulsory to register title. Failure to do so will result in the buyer not obtaining good title. HM Land Registry will investigate the title in the same way as the buyer's solicitor.

8.4   POSSESSORY TITLE

Under s 15 of the Limitation Act 1980, where a person is in possession of land adverse to the interests of the true 'paper' owner and he and people who derive their rights through him remain there for 12 years, the title of the paper owner is extinguished. In many cases therefore it is sufficient for the seller simply to show 12 years' adverse possession, but this is not always conclusive and, in particular, HM Land Registry will not grant an absolute title on the basis of adverse possession but only a 'possessory title', which may be unacceptable to some mortgagees. It is sometimes possible to insure against potential claims by paper owners.

Where possession is against the Crown, 30 years' adverse possession is required (or 60 years in the case of land below high water mark) and the same applies to certain ecclesiastical landowners. Furthermore, where the land is held in trust, then although the interests of any beneficiaries with the right to possession will be extinguished after 12 years, the rights of beneficiaries whose right to possession has not yet arisen will not be extinguished until 12 years after their possessory rights arose. Thus, where land is held in a trust for a father during his lifetime and then for his son, the son's title will not be extinguished until 12 years after his father's death. For example, if the seller was, in the past, an agricultural tenant of a landlord who has died, and since that death the seller has paid no rent and has not recognised the rights of the former landlord's personal representatives in any way, he may claim after 12 years to have acquired possessory title. However, if under the terms of the former landlord's will the land is held in trust for future beneficiaries, or for young children who have not yet attained 18, then possessory title will be ineffective against those persons.

Furthermore, possessory title does not extinguish the rights of third parties. If an easement or a restrictive covenant exists which affects the land, that will still apply, and because by definition a squatter does not have any title deeds, it may not be possible for a person buying from the squatter to find out what rights may exist. In particular, many areas of common land have, over the years, been subject to encroachment and adverse possession, and such possession does not extinguish the rights of people entitled to grazing or other common rights.

8.5 LIMITED OWNERS

An absolute owner of land can deal with it as he wishes and sell it, give it away, lease it or mortgage it, without restriction. Whether or not a person is the absolute owner, the law may impose restrictions on what they can do. As a general rule, any freehold land can be sold, although in some cases the consents of other people (such as beneficiaries under a trust) may be required under s 10 of the Trusts of Land and Appointment of Trustees Act 1925, or s 58 of the Land Registration Act 1925. In practice, such restrictions arise more commonly in relation to trusts.

Historically, trusts of land were of two types. One type is known as settled land and the rules relating to it are codified under the Settled Land Act 1925. It has not been possible to create new Settled Land Act settlements since 31 December 1996 but any existing settlements are capable of running on and may do so for many years. In the early twentieth century, very large areas of the country were settled land, and this is particularly true in the case of country estates. Following the 1925 legislation, it was necessary to prepare a 'vesting deed' by confirming that the freehold was held by the head of the family, who was known as the tenant for life. Many vesting deeds were prepared with great care and often form a very good basis for subsequent titles. The Settled Land Act 1925 contains considerable restrictions on both the method of sale and other powers such as the power of leasing and mortgaging. In broad terms, although the tenant for life holds the fee simple and can contract to sell it, the proceeds of sale must be paid to at least two trustees or a trust corporation, and a purchaser obtains a good title only if he complies with the provisions in the Settled Land Act 1925. A tenant for life can generally grant leases for 50 years and, in certain exceptional cases such as mining and improvement leases, for a longer period. Mortgages can be granted only for the specific purposes laid down in the Act. There are restrictions on the power to grant options and many other transactions. A person dealing with a tenant for life must therefore be aware of the legislation. If the title is unregistered (which will normally be the case), this will be clear from the documents because the document transferring title to the tenant for life will be a vesting deed. In the case of registered land the same rules apply; and the fact that the register specifies that capital money can be paid only to two named trustees or a trust corporation is evidence that the land is settled. It is essential for a person dealing with settled land to be aware of the restrictions and the necessary formalities, otherwise a good title will not be obtained. Settled land is now rare, but the rules are still relevant in relation to country estates.

The more common form of trust is a trust of land (converted from a trust for sale by the Trusts of Land and Appointment of Trustees Act 1996). In general, trustees of land have wide powers of management under s 6 of the 1996 Act and, unlike the position before the 1996 Act, a buyer does not need to be satisfied that a specific power exists allowing trustees to carry out a particular transaction. Once again, however, the purchase money of land held in trust must be paid to at least two individuals or to a trust corporation under s 27 of the Law of Property Act 1925.

Charity landowners are subject to special rules. Many charities are comprised in trusts, where the normal rules for a trust of land will apply; others are comprised in charitable companies, typically a company limited by guarantee. Some charities also hold land by means of an unincorporated association in the names of trustees. Where a charity is intending to sell or mortgage land, the specific procedure under s 36 or s 38 of the Charities Act 1993 must be followed. Provided the conveyance or transfer contains a statement that the charity trustees have power to carry out the transaction and have complied with their obligations under ss 36 or 38, the buyer is protected against procedural defects unless he had any reason to suspect that the procedure had not been followed. If the statement is not included in the document, the buyer is at risk of the transaction being held to be void because, under s 37(3) of the

Charities Act 1993, a purchaser is protected from irregularities only if the statement is made in the sale document. While a maximum of only two persons need give consent in relation to the exercise of certain powers under private trusts, this is not the case under charitable trusts, where the consent of numerous people may need to be obtained. Charities normally have to advertise land and go through other formal valuation procedures.

Universities and colleges are, in some cases, subject to special restrictions under the Universities and College Estates Acts 1925 and 1964, and a purchaser may need to be satisfied that, for example, the consent of the Ministry of Agriculture has been obtained to a disposal.

Local authorities and government departments may be subject to special restrictions. Local authorities can normally dispose of land only in accordance with the Local Government Act 1972 or any other specific power and, in certain cases, may need the consent of the Secretary of State to a sale. Government departments in general do not need such authority, but it should be noted that, under the Crown Lands Act 1702, there is a general prohibition on the sale of Crown or government land and it is therefore necessary to check the precise power under which the department is selling.

Where land is subject to mortgage, the buyer must, of course, be satisfied that the mortgage is cleared off the title. Normally this will be done by obtaining a deed of release or, in the case of registered land, a Form DS1 or Form 53. In some cases, the register will contain a restriction that the consent of a mortgagee is required to a sale, but where Form DS1 or Form 53 is issued, this takes effect as a consent.

8.6   POSITIVE OBLIGATIONS

In order to make a positive covenant binding on the land, there may be a restriction on the register that no transfer is to be registered without the consent of a specified person and that that consent will be given provided the buyer enters into a direct covenant with the person having the benefit of the restriction to perform the obligation. In such circumstances, once the buyer has entered into the covenant, he can then obtain a consent to the transfer and produce this to HM Land Registry.

8.7   LAND WITHOUT DOCUMENTARY TITLE

Much agricultural land historically has belonged to certain bodies such as the Crown, the Church or ancient foundations, and there is no title in the ordinary sense. The Crown does not normally deduce title. In some cases, the Crown will be registered as owner, which is straightforward. Other bodies have, in the past, shown title by producing a statutory declaration from a senior official, such as a bursar, confirming that the body has been in possession or in receipt of the rents and profits for 12 or 30 years, or whatever custom dictates. It is up to the buyer whether to accept this, but there may be no realistic alternative. However, many such institutions have made arrangements with HM Land Registry under which the Registry has issued a letter stating that their title will be accepted without enquiry. This 'title shown' procedure has been extended to various family estates and other traditional landholders who do have title deeds and where the deeds are particularly complicated and lengthy. This is useful where a family estate that has been held for a long period (and where the last good root of title may be 200 or 300 years ago) is to be sold off in multiple lots. To save numerous buyers' solicitors investigating the title and raising requisitions, the 'title shown' procedure can be adopted with HM Land Registry, under which the title is produced to, and the title deeds are lodged with, the Registry, which will then issue absolute title based on those deeds. The details of each title will vary from case to case and the terms of HM Land Registry letter need to be considered with care by each buyer, but this procedure is a very useful short cut.

Where there is some other defect in title and the seller has to give a statutory declaration, such declaration should normally be given by someone who has personal knowledge of the land, for example a farmer, a member of the estate office or a member of the owning family. A statutory declaration is simply a substitute for other forms of evidence, and the quality of the evidence is only as good as the person making the declaration. A declaration therefore needs to contain as much detail as possible, usually by reference to a plan, and should state the length of time the person giving it has known the land, and what has happened during that period.

Chapter 9

ROADS AND WAYS

9.1   INTRODUCTION

The owner or occupier of agricultural land must have access to it, and other people will have the right to pass over it. The existence and type of right of way can materially affect the value of land, and a buyer must check carefully what rights exist or are being created.

Ways are usually classed as carriageways, bridleways and footpaths, and may be either public or private. Much of the law on rights of way is ancient, and both ancient and modern law is confused and inconsistent. Although the basic underlying rules are clear, the application of the detailed rules to particular cases can and often does give rise to argument.

9.2   PUBLIC HIGHWAYS

A highway is land available for use by passage by members of the public at large. Certain routes may be restricted, such as customary ways to a local church which can be used only by local people. Such routes may be found in rural areas, but are rare.

Farms and estates are often crossed or bounded by major public highways such as motorways and trunk roads, which can be a nuisance in relation to the management of agricultural land because of the noise and pollution. Public highways are vested in the Secretary of State for the Environment, Transport and the Regions. Other public carriageways are normally either vested in, or the responsibility of, the local highway authority, normally the county council or unitary council. In broad terms, a highway will be the responsibility of the authority if it is maintainable at public expense and if it was maintainable by the public at large before the Highways Act 1830 (ancient roads) or if subsequently it was adopted by the highway authority (modern roads). The standard enquiries of local authorities before a purchase will reveal what ways are maintainable. Responsibility for maintenance extends the whole width of the highway including the verge, and is not limited to any metalled surface. However, highway authorities are increasingly reluctant to define precisely the limits of the highway following numerous modern disputes over such limits. In addition, authorities try to limit the areas for which they are responsible for budgetary reasons. It can be important for the viability of a farm to know whether the access track is maintained at public expense, and the highway authority is responsible for resurfacing and filling in potholes. For example, many milk processing companies will refuse to send their tankers out on roads that are not adequately maintained, and if the cost of this falls on the farmer it can affect business.

Rural roads can be very narrow and, with modern farm machinery increasing in size, it is important to ensure that it is physically possible for vehicles to travel along such roads. Where a farm is run on a number of separated areas of land and it is necessary for vehicles to get from one area to another along a public road, it is important to make sure that access is easy. Regular use by a slow farm tractor can give rise to complaints and possibly prosecution for driving without due care and attention, particularly along major roads where holiday or commuting traffic is affected. Furthermore, using 'red petrol' (which has a low rate of excise duty and the use of which is therefore restricted) to fuel farm vehicles driven on public roads may attract penalties. Farmers taking on extra land should be aware of these considerations.

Unsurfaced roads will generally be either bridleways or footpaths and the existence of these can be found by an enquiry in Part II of the local authority enquiries (see **25.2**). In broad terms, a footpath can be used only on foot and will usually be obstructed by stiles. A bridleway can be used for horses and bicycles and will usually have gates or cattle grids. In general, the landowner does not have legal responsibility for general maintenance of the surface of footpaths and bridleways, although he must not do anything to break them up; if farm machinery seriously damages a track the landowner must make it good so that it is suitable for public passage. In some cases, a landowner may be made responsible for maintenance, particularly where an old track has been diverted under a diversion order and this is one of the terms on which the order was made.

The Occupiers' Liability Act 1957 does not, in general, apply to public highways. A landowner must ensure that people who walk their dogs along a road do not permit the dogs to trespass, particularly on land grazed by sheep, and special insurance cover may be needed.

A difficult issue relates to tracks known as roads used as public paths (RUPPs) and byways open to all traffic (BOATs) which are in general subject to reclassification under the provisions of the Wildlife and Countryside Act 1981, s 54. In these cases, there may be rights for vehicles to pass even though the track is unsurfaced, and which are popular for use by motorcycle scramblers and others. Such use can cause a lot of damage and landowners need to be aware of the risks. When buying land of this nature, enquiries should be made of the seller.

A particular problem for buyers is where public rights of way are in the course of being acquired. A search of the definitive footpath map will show whether land has been registered as a footpath or bridleway and, if it has, that is conclusive of the existence of such a public right of way – although in certain cases if it can be shown that the map was prepared in error it can be corrected. The map is not, however, conclusive of the non-existence of such a way, and there are many tracks which have been used by the public for over 20 years and where, as such, a highway has come into existence under s 31 of the Highways Act 1980. Furthermore, routes which are marked as footpaths on the definitive map may, in fact, have been used as bridleways and are entitled to be upgraded. This can be relevant to the security and privacy of the farm and, particularly having regard to the growth of rural crime and the increased popularity of hiking, will be material to the degree of control a buyer can exercise.

Many footpaths are located in unusual positions for historical reasons and are either overgrown or lie across ploughed fields. This does not affect their status, and county councils and amenity bodies are increasingly vigilant in protecting them. The Rights of Way Act 1990 (amending s 134 of the Highways Act 1980) governs the position where a footpath crosses a ploughed field, but the existence of such ways can materially affect the commercial management of farm land.

In theory, it is possible to divert footpaths, but in practice this can be very difficult. It will normally be necessary to go through a long and expensive procedure, which involves not only obtaining the agreement of statutory bodies, but also consulting interested local voluntary groups. The landowner will be expected to provide the new route at his own expense, which may include constructing bridges over streams. It may be a condition that the landowner accepts responsibility for the maintenance of the new route even though he was not responsible for the previous route.

'Permissive paths' permitted under s 64 of the National Parks and Access to the Countryside Act 1949 arise from an agreement between the landowner and the highway authority that members of the public will be allowed to use a path. These agreements may last for a fixed period, such as 20 years, or may be terminated, for example, on three months' notice. Such paths are not excluded from the Occupiers' Liability Act 1957, so that if they are not reasonably safe for use by expected members of the public, and, for example, develop potholes into which people may fall, the landowner may be liable for damages. It is therefore essential to check that a public liability policy is in force. A highway authority may accept insurance responsibility, but many are reluctant to do this. It is therefore essential on a purchase to check the status of all tracks, even those which are not official public rights of way, to find out what rights may exist or be in course of acquisition.

Under s 31(6) of the Highways Act 1980, a landowner may lodge a statement and statutory declaration stating what routes are recognised as public rights of way. This may assist in any subsequent dispute, although it is not conclusive. Where the seller has not done this a buyer of newly acquired land should consider lodging such a statement.

9.3   PRIVATE RIGHTS OF WAY

Private rights of way create rights between two landowners – the owner of the land benefited (the dominant tenement) and the owner of the land affected by the way (the servient tenement). These rights are known as 'easements of way', and there are a number of conditions which an easement must satisfy. Normally, it is reasonably clear whether or not a right of way exists, although the extent of the right may be uncertain. In particular, where an area of land is open and unfenced, the precise route of a right of way may need to be clarified.

Private rights may be implied by law or made expressly by agreement, new rights may be created on the sale of part of an estate.

9.3.1   Private rights implied by law

In legal theory, there are a number of ways in which the law recognises rights of way as coming into existence. These include ancient prescription (which are treated as having existed since before 1189), rights of way of necessity and rights of way arising from the doctrine of lost modern grant or under the rule in *Wheeldon v Burrows* (1879) 12 ChD 31. Although these are of theoretical importance, in practice most issues arise over rights implied under s 62 of the Law of Property Act 1925 or under the Prescription Act 1832. The detailed rules for acquisition are dealt with in textbooks on easements and many of the cases are difficult to reconcile. Because of the growing pressure for claimed rights of way where land is subdivided and the pressure to resist them to protect the value of the land over which they are claimed to run, many disputes have been hard fought and confusing.

Rights are implied under s 62 where a single landowner has owned land which has been in more than one separate occupation, for example a cottage which has been let off on a residential tenancy the access to which has reached across a farm let on an agricultural tenancy. If the cottage is sold, s 62 will imply that the sale includes a right of way that was previously enjoyed over the farm, and this will be converted from a practical arrangement between adjoining tenants of the same landlord to a legal right between separate freeholders. Where, in the past, an area of land has been in common ownership, it will be necessary for a purchaser of only part of it to enquire about rights which may have been enjoyed in this way. The law does not imply any converse implication in favour of the owner of the land retained, so that if, in this example, the farm was sold and the cottage kept without any mention made of the right of way, the landowner might discover that the cottage is deprived of its legal access. The standard conditions of sale include a provision that implies such a converse right, but this is sometimes excluded in the contact.

Where land is in separate ownership and the owner of one piece of land has exercised a right over the other, usually for 20 years (or, where there has been some form of consent, for 40 years) a right of way will come into existence under the Prescription Act 1832, s 2 provided the access was not used by virtue of force (including threats), was used openly and not secretly, and was not used by permission.

Where the law implies rights of way, it may be difficult to determine exactly the scope of the right. Sometimes it will be obvious, for example the right to walk or drive to a cottage or to take agricultural machinery to a farm, but where the use has changed over the years this can give rise to difficulties in interpretation. For example, the owner of a field may have had an agricultural access (including farm machinery) for 50 years over an adjoining farm and may then obtain planning consent for the construction of houses, or the owner of a single house with a large garden may obtain consent to build additional houses in that garden. In such circumstances, a great deal of money may be at stake as to whether or not the existing right of way is capable of extending to the new houses. This will often depend on the circumstances during the period in which the right has been enjoyed.

Proof of prescription can be difficult. It is common practice for people to make statutory declarations, but these must be considered very carefully. A standard form declaration taken out of a precedent book is of only limited value, and a declaration needs to set out as much circumstantial detail as possible and should also explain the precise basis of the knowledge of the person who makes it.

9.3.2 Existing express rights of way

The title deeds will usually disclose whether the land being acquired is either subject to a right of way granted in the past or has the benefit of such a right. This is carried out by deed of grant or by a grant included in an earlier conveyance. In the case of large estates, however, copies of conveyances and deeds of grant will commonly not have been kept and it may therefore be difficult to say with certainty what rights exist. Where the express words of the grant define relevant matters, for example the width of the access or the use (for agricultural purposes or residential purposes), that may usually be relied upon as defining the scope of the right of way. Where the terms of an express grant are inconsistent with an earlier use, these will normally be taken as impliedly overriding the provisions of s 62 of the Law of Property Act 1925. However, where a different sort of right of way has been used for over 20 years the Prescription Act 1832 will override the express grant. Thus, even though an express right may have been granted, for example, 30 years ago, over an access 10 feet wide, if in fact the physical access is wider and has been used for large farm machinery for over 20 years then a greater right may have come into existence.

Many older documents do not define rights clearly, and refer simply to rights of way in general terms. It will normally be assumed that for such a right can be exercised for all purposes, unless the circumstances clearly exclude this, for example that the land in question either could be used only for agriculture or is subject to a covenant restricting its use to such purpose.

9.3.3   New rights of way

When a farm or estate is being sold in lots or is otherwise being divided, for example because the seller is retaining part of the land, it may be necessary to create a new right of way either by grant in favour of the buyer or by reservation in favour of the seller. Where a number of lots are being sold at auction, the auction conditions must be drafted in such a way that grants, reservations and newly existing rights are reflected irrespective of the order in which the lots may actually be completed, or to cover the possibility that one or more lots may be withdrawn from the sale. In modern conditions, it is normally sensible to define the right of way as clearly as possible. It should be made clear whether the right is for a specific purpose such as agriculture, for all existing purposes (for example, including storage) or for the existing and any future use and development of the dominant tenement. The right of way should be shown clearly on a plan, and the dominant tenement should also be carefully defined, again usually by reference to a plan. Because one of the rules for an easement is that it must accommodate a dominant tenement which must be capable of benefiting from it, a right of way reserved for the benefit of 'the vendor's adjoining and neighbouring retained land', although in principle capable of being effective, can give rise to disputes over precisely which land benefits.

9.4   MAINTENANCE

Historically, agricultural machinery was relatively light and there was little need to pay attention to the maintenance of the surface of shared rights of way. With modern machinery that is no longer the case. In particular, special machinery such as that used for timber extraction, is capable of causing damage to ground which can be expensive to remedy. Furthermore, increasingly, accesses are shared (for example, on the sale of a farmhouse to a residential occupier or the conversion of redundant farm buildings to offices or workshops) between a variety of different users who may have different requirements. For example, a route that is suitable for passage by tractors will not generally be suitable for a small private car taking children to school, so that different users will have different needs for standard of the access. Various approaches have been tried to overcome this problem. For example, all users may be required to contribute to maintenance up to agricultural standards, but if anyone wishes to improve the track to a better standard, he may do so only on terms that he maintains it for the future. It cannot be said that a satisfactory outcome has yet been reached.

An obligation to maintain or contribute to maintenance is a positive covenant and, as such, is not enforceable against future owners of the covenant (see Chapter 15). However, under the rule of benefit and burden (described at **15.5**), where a right is conditional upon an obligation, the right to use the access may be made conditional on contributing to maintenance. An alternative and more complex approach is to include a restriction on the register of title that no transfer is to be registered without the consent of the owner of the access. That consent will not be given unless the transferee enters into a deed of covenant with the owner of the access to contribute to maintenance. Another solution is by means of an estate rentcharge under the Rentcharges Act 1977. In practice, most people who share the use of an access will see the sense of joint maintenance and will be prepared to co-operate with their neighbours whether or not the provisions are enforceable as a matter of strict law, although, of course, a solicitor drafting the document must be prepared to cover the situation of an obstructive or bankrupt contributory.

Many provisions of the contribution provide that it should be shared 'according to use'. This can be flexible and may be useful where the amount of use can vary, but it can, of course, also give rise to arguments over who uses the access more. This can be accompanied by a specific provision in the covenant that if any one of the users causes identifiable damage (for example, by the use of heavy machinery) then that person must put the damage right. Such provision is intended only to cover general wear and tear.

A more difficult issue can be over the standard of maintenance which can be expected. A farmer selling off a cottage will usually just want to maintain a track to agricultural standards, while the buyer of the cottage may want it to be adequately surfaced for use by a private car. One solution is to provide that there should be a minimum (perhaps agricultural) standard, or the standard no better than the condition of the track at the date of sale (which may have to be recorded by photographs kept with both sets of title deeds). Either party will then have the power to improve the surface of the track at his own cost, but he cannot call on the other for contributions unless the standard falls below that specified.

9.5   DIVERSION

Although diversion is more commonly found in relation to pipes and sewers, it can also apply to rights of way. For example, an existing track may, at a future date be considered to be in an inconvenient position because it crosses two fields which are being combined as one, or crosses land which is being developed as a housing estate or dug as a quarry. In such circumstances the landowner will wish to have the right to divert the track. The precise legal authority for this is unclear because a right of way must generally be permanent in order to exist in fee simple, and one that can be determined is, strictly speaking, only an equitable right. However, a legal right can be granted subject to an option of the landowner to determine it (usually within the perpetuity period of 80 years) provided that, at his own expense, he provides a suitably convenient and satisfactory alternative. Although such provisions are common, they have not been tested in the courts and there must be some doubt as to their enforceability. However, as they are so widespread, it is likely that the courts will try to give force to them.

9.6   GATES AND PADLOCKS

One of the most difficult issues is the ability to obstruct a shared right of way. On the one hand, all persons using it will need to have free access along it; on the other hand, it will be important to prevent members of the public trespassing on private land whether innocently for recreation or with criminal intention. Where animals are kept in adjoining fields it may also be necessary to prevent them straying onto the highway. Increasingly, farmers wish to put up gates and other barriers. This cannot normally be done across public rights of way, although there are provisions for stiles and gates across footpaths and bridleways. There are also provisions in s 86 of the Highways Act 1980, where a landowner has the right to have a gate across a public carriageway, for that to be substituted by a cattle grid. In general, however, where there is a public right of way the highway authority will supervise such obstructions.

Problems usually arise in relation to private rights of way, and frequently lead to lawsuits. The normal solution is to provide gates with padlocks where keys are handed out to all persons having a right to use the access. An alternative, which applies where only two people share the access, is to have a chain with a padlock at each end, one padlock belonging to each user. The existence of such obstructions does, of course, make the use of the access more difficult and, for example, a person who regularly drives children to and from school may be reluctant to get out in the rain in order to unlock and open a gate, drive through it, and then get out again to shut it. This is one of the problems of living in the countryside, however, and has to be accepted as part of rural life.

Chapter 10

SERVICES

10.1 INTRODUCTION

Rural land is crossed by a variety of pipes, cables, drains and other services, some of which benefit the land or are shared with neighbours, and some of which have been installed by statutory undertakers for local or national benefit. The existence of such utilities can therefore materially affect the value of the land through which they run and will need to be taken into account by buyers. Problems include the following: it is not generally possible to build or plant over the line of a pipe; overhead telephone or electricity lines can interfere with crop spraying or the use of large machinery; radio transmitting stations are sensitive to electrical interference from farm machinery; such utilities can prevent development by quarries or housing.

10.2 WATER

In towns and cities, most water is supplied by water companies through public mains supplies, which consist of large pipes, usually leading from reservoirs, with smaller pipes branching off to supply houses, factories and other uses. Wherever possible, these pipes run along public highways.

Many parts of the countryside do not have mains water, but where this does happen, pipes may cut across fields. Very often there is no documentary evidence of this. Pipes may have been laid under an agreement with a former local authority or water company or subsequently the water board, but many pipes were laid under the authority of the old Public Health Act 1936, now s 159 of the Water Industry Act 1991. The normal practice was simply to serve notice on the landowner, or sometimes only on the tenant, which notice was frequently unaccompanied by a plan. The notice consisted of a small piece of paper, often not sent to the solicitor to be kept with the deeds and, where it was, could easily be lost. The route of many public pipes dating from the nineteenth century is unknown and will usually come to light only if the pipe leaks or is damaged by a plough. Records of pipes laid in modern times are generally better, but even here the position of the pipe, as planned and shown in legal documents, is not always the same as the position in which the contractor found it most convenient to lay it in the ground. Because such pipes were generally installed under statutory powers, there are relatively few express restrictions and covenants and the matter will generally be governed by the statutory rules in the Water Industry Act 1991.

10.2.1   Supply and charging

Many farms and farmhouses are served by private pipes running off the public mains. It is normal in the countryside for pipes to be metered and this will be required by the water company where the water is used for agricultural purposes, either to supply troughs for stock or for irrigating crops. Often a single meter will serve a number of farmhouses and farm cottages, especially where these have, in the past, existed under one tenancy or ownership. Where these dwellings are sold off separately, it will be necessary to make arrangements to collect the appropriate proportion of the metered cost (for example, through a submeter) and also the cost of the maintenance of the pipe, which is the responsibility of the landowner. An obligation to contribute to maintenance is a positive covenant but it will usually be possible to make this enforceable under the principle of benefit and burden (described at **15.5**). The best practice is to make one owner, perhaps the farmer or the owner of the largest house, primarily responsible for the system but with a right to collect contributions from the other owners. Water companies usually require separate meters, and in some cases may even require additional pipes to be laid to each separate dwelling. These may be laid in an existing trench, but sometimes new trenches will be needed. Where there is a plan to sell off cottages which have had a shared water supply derived from the mains, it is sensible to discuss the matter well in advance with the water company. Where costs are shared, previously it was common practice to divide these in proportion to rateable value but that is no longer practical and a rough division is usually acceptable. It should, however, be noted that some users may take up more water than others, for example by washing cars, watering gardens or having large households, and this should be taken into account.

If a water meter breaks down, it is good practice to make it a provision that the previous year's consumption is assumed to continue at the same rate unless or until someone can demonstrate that it is different.

On many farms and estates there is a private supply of water from a spring or borehole with pump or a private reservoir which itself may be fed from a collecting chamber or borehole. Many of the same principles will apply to these cases as apply to water derived from the mains. Meters are not necessarily required although they may be useful. In many estates pipes may run for several miles; some are very old and liable to leak, and maintenance costs of the water system are an important head of rural expenditure. Private sources are limited and, particularly in a dry year, may be exhausted, which can represent a threat to health. However, equally farmers need water for their crops and animals and it can be difficult to ration a limited supply. This is particularly important as the climate changes and as increasing quantities of water are taken by the water companies for public use.

Because of these complications the method of governing water supplies is changing. In the past, it was often the practice to give a simple easement in fee simple to take water from a shared source. Because of the complications of shared expenses, it is now more common to have a separate deed of grant, or indeed a licence, which can impose specific obligations on all those who share the supply. This is particularly important because under s 80 of the Water Industry Act 1991, where the supply of drinking water to dwellings which rises on private land is shown to be unwholesome, the local authority can require the owner of the land on which the supply rises to spend money (often a great deal) on bringing it into wholesome condition. Where there is serious pollution, this expense can be very heavy, and it is therefore a growing practice to grant water rights under a licence which can be terminated if the source becomes unwholesome. Other reasons for termination may be where a mains supply is made available to the consumer, where the recipient fails to pay his contribution to costs or breaks some other term, for example by wasting water, or where, for other reasons beyond the control of the supplier, the water supply cannot be continued. Clearly, a buyer will prefer a permanent freehold right to water, but provided the licence is drawn in a form that is fair to all parties and passes automatically on a sale of the property, it should be acceptable.

10.2.2   Reservoirs and water abstraction

A great deal of water is impounded in artificial containers such as ponds, private lakes and reservoirs. Some of these are subject to the constraints of the Reservoirs Act 1975, which provides for regular inspections by qualified engineers where there is an artificial dam or bank maintaining water above the level of the surrounding countryside. There are obvious dangers if such a barrier were to breach and the water were suddenly to be discharged towards adjoining residences.

A water abstraction licence is normally required under s 24 of the Water Resources Act 1991 to extract water from boreholes or rivers. In general, this licence is not required for purely domestic use, although the quality of water for that use may not be up to health standards. The greatest volume of water in the countryside is used for agricultural purposes, as well as by industry, and most farmers will need a water abstraction licence. Since water abstraction licences are difficult to obtain, any existing licence operating when the farm is sold should be transferred with the property and registered within one month; otherwise it will be lost. A single licence may extend to several boreholes and if the land passes into different ownerships, the benefit of the abstraction licence will need to be divided. In general, the Environment Agency is trying to restrict rights to extract water, and such rights need to be strongly defended by landowners.

10.3   DRAINAGE

Few legal issues in the countryside are as contentious as drainage. This contention may extend to surface water drainage, where smelly water from a field which grazes animals flows past a cottage bought by a commuter, or, alternatively, where the commuter washes his car and the water contaminated by petrol flows along a drainage ditch past a field.

The existence of motorways and factories in rural areas can lead to serious problems of water pollution. Equally, slurry from cowsheds or liquid effluent from silage clamps can cause serious harm if it flows into a stream and is capable, for example, of destroying all life in a river. Many of these issues are tackled under the Control of Pollution Act 1990, as amended by the Environment Act 1995, which imposes stringent restrictions on the discharge of any materials into controlled waters – in broad terms, waters which ultimately flow to the sea. Such pollution is also liable to give rise to private rights, particularly in nuisance and negligence. It is therefore important for a buyer of rural land to check the status of any flows of water crossing the land, and any possible sources of pollution.

Foul drainage is liable to cause particular problems. In urban areas, most drainage is dealt with on the mains by publicly maintained sewers usually running under the roads. However, such sewers are relatively rare in the country, although, of course, a main sewer is capable of crossing farm land. More usually, human waste from isolated farmhouses and cottages runs to a cesspit or septic tank where it is treated, and there is an outfall of clarified water. In a few cases, particularly in limestone country or where there has been deep mining, the waste may simply be discharged underground to an unknown destination.

Where drainage systems are shared, the septic tank on the land of one owner may serve several others and detailed rights will be needed to govern discharge, maintenance, cleansing and emptying. As long as the waste is effectively purified, the outfall will not cause a problem, but rights will be necessary to allow it to drain out, usually onto farm land. Technology is developing fast in this area and it is likely that more compact systems of waste disposal will be available in the future. However, the traditional methods will still be found in remote areas for some time to come.

10.4 ELECTRICITY

The line of electricity pylons and cables running overground across most farms will be obvious on superficial inspection. There is a growing tendency for these to be placed underground, particularly in areas of natural beauty, but this is expensive and is usually resisted by the power companies. Most electricity cables are governed by annual wayleaves, which are relatively simple documents and which can easily be lost. However, the power companies normally have good records and the selling agent should make enquiries before a farm is put on the market. Wayleaves typically run from year to year and can be terminated on notice. Where supplies are important, however, the power companies often ask for formal deeds of grant in return for a single payment and such deeds last in perpetuity. Unlike wayleaves, deeds of grant will normally contain restrictions designed to protect the cables, and these conditions need to be observed carefully. Deeds of grant may include lift and shift clauses (see below). In general, rates for wayleaves and the basis of calculation of the premium for an easement are worked out on a national basis on a scale negotiated by the power companies with the Country Landowners Association and the National Farmers Union, but it is always open to a landowner to challenge the rate payable in a particular case if it is thought to be unfair. Wayleave payments are intended as compensation for interference with farming, while premium payments are intended to compensate the diminution in value of land. It should be remembered that the existence of cables, and particularly large structures such as pylons, can materially affect the value of land for mining or building. If it is normal practice to irrigate or spray land from an aircraft, care must be taken when carrying this out close to cables, and if large machinery such as cranes are in use these, again, must be employed with care. A modern practice is for telecommunications equipment to be wrapped around cables (see below). The powers of the electricity companies are governed by the Electricity Act 1989. In general, electricity companies prefer not to use their compulsory powers, but these powers are often held in reserve.

10.5 TELECOMMUNICATIONS

Telecommunications is an important and growing area of wayleaves and easements. Originally, the telecommunications market was the monopoly first of the Post Office and then of British Telecom, but it has now been opened up to a great variety of different operators, which may use cables either buried or carried on their own plant overhead, or wrapped along other plant such as electricity lines. Other operators use radio communications, and require leases of areas for transmitting stations, usually located on hillsides. In general, the rights of telecommunications operators are governed by the Telecommunications Code in Sch 2 to the Telecommunications Act 1984. This Code confers on operators reserve compulsory powers, and operators are, typically, ready to use them. In general, operators are only obliged to deal with the occupier of land, so that if land is subject to a farm tenancy the landlord may not receive any benefit. Where communications supply farm land, for example a line to the farmhouse, it is possible that no payment will be made in return for supplying the service. If the tenancy ends or a farm is sold, the new occupier will be entitled to terminate the arrangement, but the operator may be entitled to have a new one put in place with the power to apply to the county court to fix the compensation. Much telecommunications equipment is sensitive to interference and this can be important if the farmer is intending to operate machinery near a line, or particularly near a transmitting station. Furthermore, where the farmer uses a satellite system to assess land quality or crops or otherwise to survey his land, interference may again be an issue, and a buyer who is proposing to introduce such equipment may need to check whether is it compatible with the secure use of the existing telecommunications plant.

10.6 GAS AND OIL

Many farms are crossed by gas pipelines, which are normally laid under the provisions of standard term agreements, formerly with the Gas Board and subsequently with British Gas or its successors. Pipelines are generally governed by detailed deeds of grant, the general terms of which have been negotiated with the Country Landowners' Association and the National Farmers' Union and, on the whole, are acceptable to landowners. Particular points should be considered. For example, where the deed of grant contains a restriction, it should be ensured that the restriction applies only to the line of the pipe and a few yards either side, and does not extend to the whole farm or even the whole estate. If the covenants are drawn in a form that remains enforceable against the person who originally granted the rights, the seller will need an indemnity from the buyer, and it is better for covenants to be drawn in the first place so that they do not bind owners who have sold. Furthermore, the lift and shift clause (discussed below) must be examined carefully.

Other energy lines may not be governed by such satisfactory documents. In particular, many MoD oil pipelines are laid across the country, often incompletely documented and, because of the security implications of keeping the routes secret from possible sabotage, information about which may not always have been supplied to solicitors and therefore may not be evident when the deeds are produced for a sale. As the pipes are normally buried, even later landowners who may have inherited the land may be ignorant of their existence.

Some pipelines have been laid under the provisions not of an easement (where there is doubt as to whether there is any land capable of benefiting) but of a lease of the strip of land through which the pipe runs. Such a lease will have been granted for a premium and not a rent, and the terms need to be examined in the same way as any other lease.

10.7   LIFT AND SHIFT

Where public or private services are laid across land they have, as mentioned above, the potential to interfere with subsequent productive use. For example, a landowner may wish to quarry away the surface of the land, plough land that was previously in pasture, construct farmbuildings or obtain planning consent for residential development, or put the land to some other use which is inconsistent with the service. In addition, although there is no clear evidence of a health risk from overhead power lines, many people are concerned where these pass close to dwellings.

Where the service is governed by a wayleave, notice can normally be given to the operator to terminate the wayleave agreement. As mentioned above, in some cases the operator has statutory powers to have the agreement renewed, but those powers must be exercised reasonably and responsibly and there is normally an appeal to a public body such as the Secretary of State or the courts. Even where legislation does not apply, a decision by a public body to install or retain equipment will be potentially subject to judicial review.

Where a permanent easement has been granted it is clearly more difficult to have the position reopened. In certain cases (such as under s 185 of the Water Industry Act 1991), there is a statutory right for the grant of an easement to be reassessed. In other cases, it has been possible, either on a national or individual basis, to negotiate a provision that if the continued existence of the plant is inconsistent with a proposed development the operator can be required to move the plant or alternatively, pay compensation. Normally, the landowner will have to meet the removal costs but this is usually acceptable. The main problem arises over the basis of compensation. Many deeds provide, on the face of it, a generous provision that compensation will be equal to the difference in value between the land with and without the cable on the basis of the proposed use, but two points need to be taken into account. The first is that this may have to be ascertained as at the date the plant was laid not at the date the development is proposed. If, for example, land values have moved substantially over 30 or 40 years, or inflation has materially changed the basis of compensation, the sum ascertained under the deed may be derisory. The second point is that it may be possible for an operator to object to a grant of planning consent on the grounds of the existence of the plant, particularly if it consists of major equipment such as a high voltage electricity cable or a large gas main. If it resists the application for planning consent by the landowner and consent is refused, an operator may then argue that there is no basis for compensation even though, in the absence of that plant, the land could have been put to a more valuable use. The terms of any deed need to be looked at carefully in this light, especially where a buyer has proposed an alternative use.

In the case of private easements such as water pipes and drainage, it is usually much easier to build in a lift and shift clause, but there is a technical problem with this which is mentioned briefly in connection with moving rights of way in Chapter 9. Generally, the owner of the land in which the service exists will have the responsibility for providing a suitable alternative and will usually be prepared to do this. However, the owner of the land benefiting from the service will have to enter into a deed surrendering the existing rights in return for taking new rights on some other terms. Such an obligation is a positive covenant and suffers from the associated problems. It may be possible to draft the deed in a form that either constitutes a licence, which can be terminated in return for a new one, or in a form that gives, for example, a right of drainage or a right of way but does not specify a route permanently, provided the route can be changed on reasonable terms. However, care needs to be given in relation to this. Such cases rarely come before the courts because where landowners wish to re-site services there is normally no objection, provided the alternative is satisfactory; as such, the legal position has yet to be fully tested.

10.8   STANDARDS

All services are potentially subject to fluctuation and changed circumstances especially in a fast-changing countryside. For many years, it has been the practice to provide, in relation to water supplies, that the grantor does not warrant the quantity or quality of the water, although this must be read subject to s 80 of the Water Industry Act 1991, mentioned above. Increasingly, however, rights to drain and rights to maintain plant and equipment under land may be subject to variations in circumstances or subject to increasing risks of accidental damage. Clearly, this particularly applies where the position of the utilities is not known. It will be a matter for negotiation between the parties how much protection the beneficiary of the right receives, and how far the grantor can contract out of liability for damage. It should be noted that the normal restrictions on exemption clauses designed to protect consumers do not, in general, apply to rights in land.

10.9   UNKNOWN SERVICES

As mentioned above, many services are situated underground and are invisible on inspection. Many were laid years ago and their position is not now known. When a farm, or particularly an estate, is being sold it is normal practice to provide in the contract that the sale is subject to any rights of this nature which may exist, and that while the seller will disclose any rights of which he is aware, he will not warrant there may also be other rights. Such rights may not only serve third parties but where part of an estate or farm is being sold they may benefit the land retained. Where necessary, a reservation either by reference to s 62 of the Law of Property Act 1925 or in wider terms, where land has not been in separate occupation, should be considered in order to protect unknown services benefiting retained land. This is, however, very much a last resort. Wherever possible the services should be identified and specific provisions included to cover them. This is particularly important at auction, where a person who is bidding without necessarily having had an opportunity to make full enquiries will be taken to have knowledge only of those things which can reasonably be discovered. If it turns out that there are other services in the land and these affect the value of the property being bought, a buyer at auction may have a claim for damages. While this is less likely to occur on a sale by private treaty, it can, in principle, still apply.

Chapter 11

COMMON LAND AND OPEN SPACES

11.1   INTRODUCTION

Much rural land, particularly in the west and north of England and in Wales, comprises open uncultivated land, a great deal of which is subject to the rights of the local farmers to graze cattle and sheep. Other land, especially in the lowlands, is also subject to these common rights. There is growing pressure for public access to open country, and many agreements have been made to provide for this. Buyers of rural land need to be aware of the existence of these rights.

Rights of common are centuries old and, historically, formed an important part of the rural economy. In addition to grazing rights, the local community had other rights such as taking turf, pasturing pigs in the woods, digging sand, and taking fallen branches. Most of these rights are now obsolete or of very little importance, but grazing rights can be essential to the viability of a farming business, especially in the uplands. Because of the age of the rights and changes in farming practices much uncertainty existed, and Parliament passed the Commons Registration Act 1965. Under that Act, three registers were established, one to describe common land itself, one to describe the rights exercisable over it, and one to specify the owners. This was intended to be the first part of a two-stage change in the law, but stage two has never taken place. The registers now comprise all common land (because land which was not so registered has lost its status) and a great deal of uncultivated or wasteland which is not subject to rights of common, although not all such land has been included on the register. The registers are open to public inspection and it is normally essential to carry out a search of these on purchase. It will not always be evident from the title that the land is common.

11.2   RIGHTS OF COMMON

A right of common is exercised in common with other people and, strictly speaking, refers to a freehold right. Similar rights can exist as leasehold for a term of years. Where the tenants of the owner of common land put out their animals on waste belonging to their landlord, which is not included in the farm tenancy, this is not, strictly speaking, a right of common. However, many long-standing tenants did in fact register under the Commons Registration Act 1965 and if the tenanted land was subsequently sold separately from the common land a legal right may have come into existence under s 62 of the Law of Property Act 1925. The register required details of the number of beasts that any commoner could put out on the common. This could be by reference to a specific number of cattle or sheep. In practice, many farmers work by reference to livestock units (LSUs) which are defined in the EEC Council Regulation No 2078/92 which sets out a table comparing capacity of land for given numbers of cattle, sheep, goats, horses and ponies. The register also required details of the land having the benefit of the right and it was assumed that all rights were 'appurtenant' to a particular farm. Historically, this was probably correct because rights were limited to the number of beasts that could be put back on the farm over the winter (levancy and couchancy). However, the effect of specifying the number of beasts in order to enter them on the register seems to have had the effect of converting what was previously a right appurtenant into a right 'in gross', which is a right for a defined number of animals. In principle, such a right can be bought and sold separately from the land. In many cases, farmers who had these rights and did not need to use them, sold them to other farmers who wished to exercise them. This has not generally been favoured by local conservationists and many county councils have refused to accept such transactions. In some cases, such as under the Dartmoor Commons Act 1985, the practice has been prohibited. However, the Court of Appeal has held in *Bettison v Longton* (1999) *The Times*, 11 March that such severance from the land is effective, at least outside Dartmoor.

In the case of some rights appurtenant, if the owner of the farm having the benefit of the rights also becomes owner of part of the common land over which the right is exercised the rights will be lost over that part of the common which the buyer does not then own. The present status of that rule is unclear, but if a farmer who has important and valuable rights of common is considering buying parts of the common land this will need to be checked (see *White v Taylor* [1969] 1 Ch 150).

Most functioning commons have active commoners' associations and enquiries should be made of the secretary of the association about any special regulations and conditions. Every common has different rules. Some commons are open only to certain times of the year ('lammas land' or 'shack land'), and, for others, nineteenth-century regulations (either local or national), made under the Commons Act 1876, may, for example, restrict uncastrated animals or may seek to control disease. Special rules may apply where farmers try to put out too many animals for the carrying capacity. Many commoners' associations work well, but some can run into problems as a result of local personality clashes or political issues, and a farmer intending to buy land with common rights may need to investigate the situation with some care.

11.3 THE LAND

Traditionally, common land belonged to the lord of the manor, and much of it still forms part of a local estate. Unless a public right of access is conferred then, apart from the existence of common rights, the rules that apply to the common are exactly the same as to any other land, save that under s 194 of the Law of Property Act 1925 it is unlawful to put up a fence or enclosure around or across common land. The owner of the common enjoys rights provided they are not inconsistent with the rights of other people. Thus, he will own any growing trees (if they have survived centuries of grazing) and any minerals (although he may not open a quarry since that would deprive the commoners of a grazing area). If the total of the common rights exercised does not utilise the total area of grass, an owner can put out his own animals to eat the surplus. If public access exists he can give permission to people to carry out sports such as hang-gliding, or to trade such as selling ice creams. Many owners of common land which is used by the public derive an income from charging for car parks. On the other hand, the owner is responsible if, for example, rubbish is fly tipped on the common. If new age travellers seek to stay on the common, it is the owner's responsibility to remove them. In general, common land is worth only a fraction of adjoining land which is not common even if physically they appear to be in the same condition.

On land known in the north of England as 'beastgates' or 'cattlegates' and in other areas, for example, as 'regulated pastures', persons collectively having grazing rights may also collectively own the land, which will be held by them jointly under a trust of land. When a buyer of a nearby farm is buying an interest in the land in this way it will be essential to obtain a transfer of the equitable interest under the trust of land, otherwise title to that area may remain with the previous owner.

11.4 PUBLIC ACCESS

Much common land, moorland and other open country is unfenced and increasingly this is seen as part of the heritage and as a recreation resource. As a result, for over 100 years there has been a growing move towards public access. This began in urban areas with provisions such as the Metropolitan Commons Act 1866 which applied to London and was extended, by s 193 of the Law of Property Act 1925, to give a right of access to any land within the area of an urban district. Although these districts were abolished in 1974, the rights in relation to those commons were preserved. Section 193 provided that a landowner could voluntarily grant a similar right of access to land in a rural district and a number of such rights were granted, although they are few. Provisions were also made under several nineteenth-century statutes for public access, but these were generally made by regulation and the owner of the land had a right of veto. As a result, legal rights of access were rare. An attempt was made to remedy this in the National Parks and Access to the Countryside Act 1949 which allowed for the creation of access agreements with a local authority. A number of such agreements exist but, again, have not been taken up by many landowners. Public access to large areas of open country is frequently tolerated where it is not formally regulated. Some amenity charities such as the National Trust also allow or encourage public access, subject, in some cases, to by-laws.

The Government has now proposed a formal public right of access over mountains, moorland and heaths, but this will need to be ratified by an Act of Parliament.

A major problem facing landowners who permit public access is occupier's liability. The joint effect of the Occupier's Liability Acts 1957 and 1984 and the Unfair Contract Terms Act 1977 is that in general a landowner who does not operate a business of charging for public access and who does not fall under certain other categories, such as an educational body, can agree to allow public access on terms on which he will not be liable if the person entering the land suffers death or injury. The precise conditions under which this liability can be excluded may depend on personal or special circumstances, and where it is not effectively excluded the Occupier's Liability Acts will provide that the landowner is responsible for seeing that the land is reasonably safe for the purpose for which he permits people to be present. In the case of large areas of open country, which may include cliffs, worked-out quarries, old mine workings, bogs and other dangers, this can be a serious deterrent to landowners who would otherwise be prepared to permit public access. It is, of course, essential that such landowners have in force an adequate public liability insurance policy.

In some cases, a right of access has been extended by statute, for example, under the Dartmoor Commons Act 1985, which excludes the common duty of care.

Even where a general right of access over the whole land is not necessarily agreed, many landowners have entered into access agreements under the 1949 Act.

A buyer of open country therefore needs to enquire as to any rights which may exist or which may have been exercised. In general, it is not possible for members of the public to acquire a legal right of access, and although in a few cases there may be a customary right for local people this is unlikely. Where the buyer of land, such as a charity or a benevolent estate, is considering tolerating public access a survey to ascertain the risks for insurance liability is vital.

Chapter 12

WILD CREATURES, SPORTING AND CONSERVATION

12.1 INTRODUCTION

Wild creatures cannot be owned. Unlike cattle or horses, wild creatures such as deer, foxes, grouse, pheasant, salmon and trout cannot be confined within the boundaries of any property. Ecological systems, rare insects and migrating birds depend on an ecosystem which may spread across large areas into the land of different owners. Historically, the right to kill animals was valued greatly and although associated with the ownership of land was not confined to it. Increasingly, the conservation of wild species is now valued as something apart from the ownership of the land on which they live.

The right to hunt or kill is often a valued element on the sale of an estate. A farmer may have concerns about rights of access over land under crop. Restrictions may exist on what can be done with the land as a result of laws to protect endangered creatures. All these matters need to be investigated and may need to be dealt with separately on a sale.

12.2 SPORTING RIGHTS

Sporting rights can, broadly speaking, be described as the right to kill living, wild creatures and retain ownership of their bodies. Such rights are usually exercised for the purposes of sport. Even where, as with pheasant, venison or salmon, the prey can be eaten, commercial production for the supermarket is dealt with very differently from sporting rights managed for entertainment. Similarly, although fox-hunting plays a part in reducing numbers of vermin, that is rarely the overriding motive for running the hunt.

The origins of the law go back a long way to the modifications made by the Norman kings to the practice of their Anglo-Saxon predecessors. In some parts of the country, such as the New Forest, these ancient rights may still be of importance, but as a result of the Wild Creatures and Forest Laws Act 1970, the ancient laws were radically simplified. There are still certain remnants of the ancient law particularly where the lord of the manor may claim sporting rights over land that was previously part of the manor under para 12(5) of Sch 12 to the Law of Property Act 1922, but nowadays these have little practical importance. Most of the rights enjoyed by lords of manors were rights of warren and chase which were abolished by the 1970 Act so that what remain are largely rights to kill smaller and less important creatures.

Unless there is a specific grant or reservation of sporting rights (which is very common), the general rule is that a landowner (or tenant) has the right to do what he wishes on his own land (subject to constraints on the general law on firearms and conservation). Furthermore, he is in principle free to kill any wild creatures on his own land, but has no legal right to go onto another's land and can be restrained from trespassing. A landowner has no right of 'hot pursuit' over another's land, nor is there any right to enter onto another's land, for example, to recover the fallen body of a bird shot while flying over the owner's own land. The general rule is that property ownership is paramount. This applies not only to the hunting of mammals and the killing of birds, but also to fishing. If the riverbed is owned separately from the bank, the owner of the bank has no general right to fish. As a special exception, where the owner of the bank owns up to the middle of the bed, he has the right to stand on his own land and cast his rod as far as he can reach and if this involves catching a fish which is actually swimming above his neighbour's half of the bed he is entitled to take it. This is, however, a special exception borne out of convenience.

This basic rule is modified in a number of ways. Historically, sporting rights were commonly reserved with or without a power of entry. Sporting rights separated from the land over which they can be exercised technically comprise a profit. This is a servitude similar to an easement and is part of a larger group of profits, which includes grazing rights, such as rights of common, and mineral rights. Profits in the form of sporting rights are governed by much the same rules, normally subsisting in gross, ie they can be bought and sold separately from the land which they originally benefited, although, in certain cases, a profit may be attached to land. For example, the owner of one piece of land may have the right to recover fallen birds which have been shot on his neighbour's territory, and it is possible that that right cannot be separated from the land to which it belongs.

Sporting rights can be separated from land either by reservation on sale (where the land is sold but the rights are kept back by the seller) or by grant (where the rights are sold but the land is retained). They can subsist as legal interests either in fee simple or for a term of years. Where the situation is straightforward and all that is required is the right to shoot and to come onto the land (eg on a given number of days in the year or between specific dates), stand guns and recover birds, this will generally subsist as a freehold. Where, however, the arrangements are more complex, and particularly where they involve positive covenants such as the maintenance of roads and hedges, the planting of trees and game cover and the removal of obstructions, it may be preferable to grant a long lease of, for example, 99 or even 999 years. Such grants can, in principle, be registered under r 50 of the Land Registration Rules 1925, although registration is not compulsory, but it is wise, where the land is registered, to enter a notice of sporting rights on the register.

Shorter arrangements may be entered into, and leases of sporting rights often accompanied with gamekeepers' cottages are common for periods of five or 10 years. These will usually produce a rent and may include an obligation that the landowner will be entitled to take part in the shoot, usually in return for a contribution to the costs. Because sporting rights are incorporeal hereditaments, even a grant for less than three years must be made by deed. Where a farm or estate has to be sold unexpectedly and quickly, a sporting lease or licence will commonly continue to run for some time after the land has changed hands. In such cases the buyer will need to investigate carefully these rights and ensure that his plans for managing the land, felling trees and ploughing fields, do not prejudice rights of other people. It is especially easy to overlook such rights because they may be exercisable only at limited times of the year and the land may be free from access by sportsmen for most of the year. As they are usually of considerable value, such rights are capable of giving rise to disputes.

In view of the political climate and changing attitudes to the countryside, in recent years it has become more common to reserve hunting rights. The precise nature of these rights is untested and in particular it is unclear whether the simple reservation of a right of hunting to a seller on a sale includes the right to come onto the land with a large group of huntsmen, hunt followers and dogs in order to exercise the right. The occupier has the right to kill hares and rabbits under the Ground Game Act 1880 and the Ground Game (Amendment) Act 1906.

12.2.1   Tenanted land

The general practice in most standard agricultural tenancy agreements is that sporting rights are reserved to the landlord. However, this is not universal, and if these rights are not specifically reserved the normal rule is that the tenant farmer acquires the rights. This gives the tenant farmer a veto on the exercise of sporting rights by the landlord and any others. Conversely, he may authorise sporting rights against the landlord's wishes. This has given rise to problems where tenant farmers have supported hunting, but their landlords, perhaps the county council or an environmental charity, have been opposed. Where no written tenancy agreement exists, the implication is that the sporting rights are included, although it may be possible in the case of an agricultural tenancy for a landlord to apply to an arbitrator under s 6 of the Agricultural Holdings Act 1986, to have a sporting reservation incorporated in the written terms of the tenancy if that was agreed originally and has been omitted from the formal agreement.

Since game can cause a lot of damage (eg damage by pheasants to crops) the tenant is given a right under s 20 of the Agricultural Holdings Act 1986, to claim against his landlord for compensation for the damage done. The procedure is not straightforward. Before 1984, this right extended to cases where someone other than the landlord had sporting rights but now applies only to cases where the rights belong to the landlord. The claim can be made against the landlord for the time being. As such, a buyer of the farm subject to tenancy may need to be aware of pending claims. There is no corresponding provision for farm business tenancies but the parties may incorporate one if they wish.

12.3   CONSERVATION AND ANIMAL HEALTH

There are a growing number of laws designed either to protect animals from unnecessary cruelty or to conserve rare species. The main provisions are set out in the Wildlife and Countryside Act 1981, but others appear in statutes such as the Deer Act 1991, the Protection of Badgers Act 1992 and The Wild Mammals (Protection) Act 1996. European laws such as the Birds Directive 1979 (Council Directive 79/409) and the Habitats Directive 1992 (Council Directive 92/43) have also introduced laws to protect animals. Furthermore, the designation of land as a site of special scientific interest can be relevant to the preservation of wildlife. This area of law is changing fast and interacts closely with environmental provisions. Landowners, in exercising their sporting rights, are also constrained by other laws such as the control of traps and firearms.

Where public rights of access exist over land, either on footpaths and bridleways or under the general provisions of public access discussed at **11.4**, any private sporting rights must clearly be exercised in a way that does not cause danger to members of the public or interfere with their use of public rights. This can often present a major problem for the management of a shoot or hunt, and such problems are frequently exploited by those politically opposed to such activities. Again, therefore, the prospective purchaser of a sporting estate must examine carefully what rights may exist. Private rights can, in theory, operate similarly; for example, rights of common could interfere with shoots over moorland, and a private right of access to a cottage sold off the estate could interfere with a shoot. In practice, because most people living and working in the countryside understand these issues, disputes are rare, but where they do occur they can be particularly bitter. Again, a prospective purchaser of an estate needs to bear this in mind.

Another threat to game is poaching. Since wild animals cannot be owned, taking them is not theft. There are a variety of nineteenth-century Acts, known collectively as 'the Game Laws', which are designed to deal with this issue. Historically, these were very important, and can still be invoked today. Other provisions such as ss 4(4) and 32 of the Theft Act 1968 can also be relevant.

The buyer of a sporting estate will also need to be aware of rights and remedies in relation to other types of interference, for example where pollution is caused to a river by the actions of another landowner, where the construction of a road may interfere with the free passage of animals, or where there may be organised interference by those opposed to hunting or shooting. These problems are not specifically associated with buying and selling, but the possibility of such damage or interference is a factor which needs to be taken into account on a purchase. Although land itself is difficult to destroy, where a substantial part of the value rests with the sporting rights this can be vulnerable to interference.

A buyer will also need to be aware of the restrictions and duties imposed under the designation of land as a site of special scientific interest and under management agreements, as discussed in Chapter 17.

Chapter 13

TREES AND TIMBER

13.1   INTRODUCTION

Woodlands are an important part of the landscape and can add substantial value to an estate. Some commercial woodlands consist largely of softwood conifer trees grown as a crop; other woods are managed for sporting purposes. Trees can also be grown to hide an ugly view or enhance a pleasant one. On farms, trees are primarily grown along hedgerows as shelter belts to provide protection for stock and to discourage erosion.

The UK has a smaller proportion of forest cover than any other part of Europe, but it also has an exceptional number of ancient trees of over 200 years old. Much of the original woodland cover has been cut down over the centuries, most recently during the two world wars. As a result, there has been strong and consistent government support for forestry, and more recently this has been combined with the environmental movement. Buyers of estates and farms therefore need to be aware both of the physical state of any woodland and any financial or legal conditions attached.

13.2   COMMERCIAL WOODLAND

The pattern that developed after 1945 was to encourage woodland in one of two ways. Although policy has now changed, both of these methods still affect many estates. The first was for large areas to be leased to the Ministry of Agriculture, Fisheries and Food (MAFF) for management by the Forestry Commission, typically for 999 years at a nominal rent of £5 per year on standard terms. Landowners agreed to this partly because woods were often planted on unproductive agricultural land, there were strong moves towards nationalisation of land and public access to open country, and there was a perceived need to replace the wood cut down for the war effort. Normally, sporting rights were reserved to the freeholder so that Forestry Commission plantations enhanced the value of the surrounding estate. Leases were freely assignable and, following a change of government policy in the 1980s, many woodlands have been sold off and passed into the hands of private forestry operators, although in some cases freeholders bought out the leases. The result on many estates therefore is that the owner of woodland has a virtual freehold of the woodland save for sporting rights. Where the woodland is intensively managed for conifers, these rights may be of limited value, but where broadleaf trees have been allowed to grow they can often encourage birds. The growing numbers of wild deer, however, present a threat, particularly to young trees, and have encouraged owners of woodland to fence their plantations effectively.

The second method was to encourage landowners who wished to manage their own woods under a dedication scheme. This had two aspects. The landowner entered into a restrictive covenant, which would bind his successors so that the land in question would not be used for any purpose other than woodland. Coupled with that was a positive agreement (which could not be binding on successors) to manage the woods, with an undertaking by the Forestry Commission to pay grants on an agreed scale provided certain minimum standards of planting and maintenance were observed. Since 1980, the Forestry Commission has not made any new dedication agreements and has been negotiating the termination of existing ones, but a great many such agreements remain in force. In general, the positive obligations have been replaced by the grant schemes mentioned below, since for most landowners the scales of grants do not compare favourably with those under other schemes. However, many landowners hold land where the restrictive covenants still apply, although it is usually possible to negotiate their release without difficulty.

13.3   THE WOODLAND GRANT SCHEME

The most important schemes to date have been the Farm Woodland Scheme, which was run in association with setaside under the Common Agricultural Policy (see Chapter 21) and, more significantly, the Woodland Grant Scheme, which applies not only to working farmers but also to owners of woodland. These agreements are usually entered into for 20 years with MAFF under which the landowner is paid planting and maintenance grants in return for carrying out an agreed woodland programme. The scheme is subject to regular inspection and supervision. Problems arise where woodland is sold while such a scheme is running because the scheme contains a condition that if the terms are broken during the 20-year period MAFF can recover the sums paid from the person to whom the payment was made. A person selling woods subject to such a scheme therefore needs protection against the risk that the buyer will not carry on with the scheme, as MAFF will seek to recover the grants from the seller. Most buyers will be prepared to give an indemnity and will normally also commit themselves to negotiate with MAFF for a release of the old agreement in return for their entering into a new one. The seller cannot be sure of this, however, and may seek to have a charge over the land to protect the indemnity. Buyers will normally resist giving a charge and it will be a matter for negotiation as to what protection the seller is given. Releases and variations are normal practice and the Forestry Authority will readily make them. The effect is to make the buyer directly accountable for all grants including the possible repayment of those paid to the seller over the period before purchase.

13.4 PLANNING

The use of land for forestry is outside the scope of the Town and Country Planning Act 1990 and, as such, the actual growing of trees does not require planning permission. However, commercial forestry cannot be carried on without involving other major activities, including fencing, levelling of the ground, construction of forestry roads, and other engineering works which may themselves need planning consent. Furthermore, under Council Directive 85/337, major afforestation (which is not specifically defined) requires an environmental assessment. It is therefore prudent that a buyer who is proposing to convert land to woodland consults closely with the local planning authority. Because of the impact that major woodland may have on the environment and the locality, it is also wise to consult with other local bodies such as the county council and parish council, and possibly with voluntary groups. Where woodland is opposed by local people, the risk of vandalism should not be ruled out.

Where the landowner is prepared to allow a degree of public access, grants may be available for planting in conjunction with car parks and permissive paths.

A local planning authority has the power to make a tree preservation order, usually on an individual basis, although in some cases clumps of trees will be designated. Any major works to trees under an order require the consent of the local planning authority, although minor works of maintenance and emergency works in the case of dangerous trees are exempted. In conservation areas, all trees automatically have the same protection as if they were subject to a tree preservation order. Otherwise, a system of control operates under which a Forestry Commission felling licence is necessary, which will normally be granted on commercial grounds, although increasingly it is used for environmental purposes.

Woodlands frequently comprise sites of special scientific interest (SSSIs) and will be subject to the protection conferred by the Wildlife and Countryside Act 1981. In consequence, a buyer of land who intends to fell trees on that land and convert it to agriculture, should be aware of special constraints. The use of land for agriculture and therefore the conversion to such use, like forestry, is not treated as development and therefore does not require planning permission as such. However, by reason of the various protections given to trees, the effect is often similar.

Certain woods are formally designated as ancient woodlands. This by itself does not confer any direct legal status, although most ancient woodlands will be covered separately by a special control such as an SSSI. However, the existence of ancient woodlands will be a relevant planning consideration where planning consent is required, for example for the construction of a road or housing.

The protection given to hedgerows by the Hedgerows Regulations 1997, SI 1997/1160 made under the Environment Act 1995, will, of course, apply to trees growing in those hedgerows, just as it applies to bushes.

13.5   LIABILITY FOR TREES

Although woodland is normally seen as an amenity, trees can become dangerous and cause a threat. Several cases have related to claims against highway authorities for trees growing in the highway verge which cause damage, or where branches fall and damage a passing motor car. These cases have applied largely in urban areas, but the same principles will apply in the countryside, and a roadside verge will usually be the responsibility of the local estate, especially where trees are growing on land beyond the limits of the highway but overhanging it. A highway authority has certain powers to compel adjoining landowners to keep trees in a safe condition and free from obstructing the highway. This applies not only to carriageways used by vehicles, but also to footpaths and bridleways, where a landowner may be liable either if somebody using the public highway is injured or where the growth of vegetation has caused an obstruction to a footpath. It is therefore important that the buyer of a farm or estate which is crossed by any form of public highway is aware of the need to keep trees under control.

Where a tree falls over a boundary onto a neighbour's land, the owner of the land on which it grew may be liable in negligence or nuisance, particularly if the dangerous condition of the tree was known or ought to have been known. Similarly, if woodland is likely to cause a fire risk, which could spread to adjoining land, the owner may be liable. It is therefore good practice when buying land to carry out a survey of any trees, as well as any buildings.

Chapter 14

MINES AND QUARRIES

14.1   INTRODUCTION

Farms and estates may lie over valuable mineral deposits, or in areas where minerals have been worked in the past. Mineral rights will usually have been separated from the surface, either under the general law or by a grant or reservation. Where this is not the case, however, the parties may, on a sale and purchase, agree to divide them.

Many estates include quarries or are subject to mineral options or leases. Where a farm is located in an old mining area, there may be a risk of subsidence, and the buyer should make appropriate surveys and searches.

14.2   MINERALS

A mineral is, in broad terms, any material substance naturally occurring in the ground which can be profitably worked and is recognised by commercial people as being a mineral. Certain minerals belong to the Crown, including gold, silver, coal, petroleum, natural gas and radioactive substances. These are governed by their own special rules and there is little that the parties can do to change this position on a sale.

Where land was previously copyhold of a manor then, as a general rule, the lord of the manor owned the mineral substances in the land, although he did not generally have the right to work these without the consent of the surface owner. These rules are subject to numerous exceptions and, where they apply, a buyer must investigate the situation in detail. In other cases, it was the practice down the centuries that when land was sold, particularly by ancient institutions such as the Crown or the Church or by family estates, and especially in traditional mining areas, the mineral rights were reserved to the seller. As between successive owners of the surface and the minerals, the rights will be determined by the express provisions of the reservation. In particular, different rules apply depending on whether or not surface entry is permitted. In the case of substantial institutions, the mineral owner can usually be identified, but where minerals were reserved to a particular family, or the head of that family who happened to own the estate for the time being, or some other owner such as a company, it may have become virtually impossible to trace the present owner of the minerals. Sellers did not usually keep copies of the conveyances reserving minerals. Consequently, if the estate has been broken up and the family have lost contact with the locality, they may be completely ignorant of any rights they may have, or the rights may have become divided, for example among the great-grandchildren of the original seller. Where land is being purchased, for example by a mineral company with a view to working the minerals, it may need to consider carefully whether there is a realistic chance of a claim to ownership of minerals being asserted, and whether it is worth covering the possibility of a claim by insurance.

14.3   SURFACE ENTRY OR UNDERGROUND WORKINGS

Traditional mineral rights related to substances which were recovered by deep workings such as coal (before nationalisation), tin and lead. Others, such as ironstone or brickearth, were worked by quarries. In modern conditions, more important minerals are sand, gravel, granite, limestone and clay, which are obtained by open quarrying. The obvious difference is that if sufficient supports are left, deep mining can be carried on without disturbing farming on the surface, except for restricted areas needed for shafts, mine buildings and possibly waste dumps. However, there is always a risk of subsidence, and this can happen not only at the time the mine is being worked but also possibly many years later, as wooden pit props rot or pillars of the natural substance are eroded by flowing water. In such circumstances, the issue is not so much who can claim the benefit of working the minerals and the right to charge mineral royalties to a mining company, but who is liable for the damage resulting from the subsidence.

Where the separation of mineral rights from the surface depends on the fact that the land was copyhold of the manor, the void left by removal of the minerals belongs to the surface owner and not to the mineral owner (*Eardley v Granville* (1876) 3 ChD 826). In most other cases, where severance has been effected by act of parties, either by grant or reservation, the effect is to change the ownership of a specific volume of the earth represented by the minerals. In some cases (and particularly in relation to coal), this might be a defined geological stratum; in other cases, it might be everything below the topsoil. Here, the ownership of the minerals and the airspace after the minerals have been removed remain with the mineral owner. This rule may not apply to quarries which are intended to be open to the air. Again, the position depends on the circumstances. There may be an express right to compensation for surface damage but, if there is not, such right will normally be implied. Whether or not that is the case, there may also be an obligation to restore the surface, in which event the surface owner simply owns the volume previously occupied by the surface and everything above it. However, it is possible that

PART 1
NARRATIVE

the surface owner may, if reinstatement is not contemplated at the original level, become entitled to the new surface represented by the bottom of the quarry after the minerals have been removed.

Material extracted from a mine or quarry, once it has been separated from the original stratum, is converted from being land into a chattel, and retains that status even though it is piled up, for example, as a sand heap or spoil tip. However, if, over the years, it settles into and appears to be part of the land and, for example, becomes overgrown, it may once again become part of the surface. In practice, if the surface owner has exercised rights of ownership for over 12 years he may have obtained title to the new surface by adverse possession, whether the land in question forms part of a quarry floor or a spoil tip. However, he will not necessarily become entitled to the minerals within that surface because a mineral reservation will apply as much to minerals within the tip which has become part of the land as it applies to the original land.

The position is further complicated by planning requirements. In general, mineral planning authorities require reinstatement and impose obligations on the mineral operator to carry this out, although, since they are planning conditions, they will attach to the land as such. The mineral operator may retain obligations in relation to the former quarry even after extraction has ceased, and these may, in turn, prevent the acquisition of a possessory title. In other cases, the mineral planning authority will not require reinstatement but may be content to see the land remain, for example, as a lake for fishing or boating. The owner of the former surface may still own the volume of air immediately above the water level but may not necessarily own the bed of the lake.

Mineral rights without surface entry can be reserved even though the mineral can only be dug from the surface. This may be intended to create a stalemate situation so that if, at some time in the future, it becomes possible to work the minerals, the surface owner has to go to the mineral owner and the royalties may be shared. Alternatively, a former landowner may use the right to minerals as a means of controlling development similar to a restrictive covenant. Ownership of the minerals without surface entry will give him a veto on extraction of minerals, and this may be used, for example, to protect a view from a house that is retained.

14.4 POLLUTION

One of the main concerns arising from old mineral workings is contamination of land surface and pollution of controlled waters, which can arise from many sources. Old underground workings can build up large quantities of water which contain metals and other substances in solution. These may be restrained by only relatively fragile barriers, which may break and flood adjoining land.

Liability can arise under statute or common law. Common law liability can arise under the headings of negligence or nuisance, including *Rylands v Fletcher* (1868) LR 3 HL 330 (which case concerned the flooding of a mine from a neighbouring mine).

Water can itself cause damage (and endanger life) and the resulting pollution can affect soil quality. Many old mineral workings, particularly quarries, have been used as rubbish dumps, which may be domestic, if they are close to houses, industrial, involving chemicals, or used for inert substances such as builders' materials. Mineral workings are now subject to very tight controls following the Control of Pollution Act 1990, but before that controls were less strict and in some cases did not exist at all. Substances are capable of leaching away from old workings and can give rise not only to pollution but also to personal injury, for example, as a result of chemicals in the soil. Under the amendments to the Control of Pollution Act 1990 made by the Environment Act 1995, liability primarily attaches to the person who caused, or at least knowingly permitted, the pollution. This can include a landowner who granted a mineral or tipping lease. There is, furthermore, a fallback against a person who simply owns or occupies the land, even though he is in no way responsible for the pollution. This is subject to various safeguards, but the residual liability exists and may need to be protected. A buyer of land on which there have been old mineral workings will therefore need to investigate this carefully.

Under the Control of Pollution Act 1990, as amended by the Environment Act 1995, there are onerous provisions governing abandoned mines. Most of the provisions affect mines abandoned after 1999, and are intended to be enforced against mineral operators who cause the abandonment and any consequent environmental damage. In broad terms, where such abandonment takes place the former operator, and, in some cases, owner, remains liable for pollution, even if it occurs long after abandonment, and there are procedures to notify proposed abandonment in advance. These are issues that any owner of a disused mine will need to cover.

14.5 MINERAL LEASES

The purchaser of an estate may buy the land with an ongoing mineral operation. Quarries are capable of generating large incomes for landowners, and therefore constitute a valuable capital asset. The buyer of the freehold subject to a mineral lease should carry out investigations as to the mineral reserves, and the income flow. In particular, it should be noted that most quarry leases include a shortfall clause under which a regular minimum royalty is paid each year. If in any year the materials extracted exceed a given threshold, a royalty will be payable in addition. However, as part of this agreement, a mineral operator will usually request that where in any year it produces less than the threshold then, although the standard minimum royalty will be paid every year, the shortfall can be carried forward against excess production in future years. Thus, the value of the unworked reserves may, in practice, be reduced, since the mineral operator will already have paid in advance for the extraction of some of those reserves. Mineral leases vary greatly in their provisions and should be examined carefully. In particular, older leases do not usually contain adequate provision to protect the landowner against breaches of planning control or against liability for pollution.

14.5.1   New grants and reservations

A mineral operator will usually wish to take a mineral lease, but in some cases it may be more convenient to take a freehold mineral interest. Until the 1960s, for tax reasons the mineral rights in land were commonly conveyed freehold to a mineral operator and a 999-year lease was granted either of the surface, or of various defined rights over the surface. Although tax incentives ceased to apply as a result of changes in the tax laws, the practice may still be useful to suit the convenience of the parties. Under such agreements, the surface, including grazing and sporting rights, remain with the owner of the estate.

Where there is no immediate intention to work the minerals, it is the policy of some estates to reserve certain rights over the minerals. Although many standard forms of mineral reservation are available, these may be adopted without properly considering the precise intentions of the parties. The first issue is whether the reservation is intended to protect the real possibility of mineral working, and, as such, whether or not it is to include surface entry or whether access will be obtained from adjoining deep mines. Where surface entry is intended, compensation must be paid to the landowner for depriving him of the use of the surface since the law does not permit a person to sell land while also having the right to dig away and destroy what he has sold without paying compensation. A procedure should be put in place for lodging claims in respect of surface damage with an arbitration clause in case the claim is disputed. The terms of the mineral reservation may go into great detail about precisely what work can be carried out, including constructing buildings, roads and mine railways etc. Exactly what is required will depend on the type of mineral under the ground and the manner in which it is likely to be worked. A seller may reserve the right to open a quarry, again subject to compensation, and subject also to a reinstatement clause whereby the surface will be reconstructed. However, it should be remembered that it may be very difficult to restore land to the same agricultural quality it enjoyed before it was worked.

A reservation of minerals without right of surface entry and without any real intention to work the minerals is easier, especially where this is intended to create a stalemate and to give the seller the right to share in future profits as a form of overage.

It should also be remembered that under the Mines (Working Facilities and Support) Acts 1923 and 1974 there is power for a mineral operator to apply to the Secretary of State for authority to work minerals, even though the owner may be unknown or may refuse consent. Although rarely used, most mineral operators are aware of the existence of the power and may raise it in negotiations.

Mineral rights must be viewed in a long-term context. Minerals have been laid down over millions of years and once they have been removed they have gone forever. However, the consequences of mining them, both in relation to the countryside and problems such as pollution, can give rise to long-term complications. Mineral workings are often planned many years ahead, so that if the prospect of working a mine is no closer than, for example, 30 years, a working farmer buying land may not be affected in the short term by mineral options or reservations, but these may affect future generations, and any change of ownership must be considered with this in mind.

Chapter 15

COVENANTS

15.1 WHAT IS A COVENANT?

Land being sold may be subject to or have the benefit of existing covenants. The seller and buyer may also agree that new covenants will be imposed.

A covenant is a formal promise contained in a deed. In the case of farms and estates, the deed is normally a conveyance or a transfer, but it may be some other document such as a forestry dedication or an easement for a pipe.

The function of covenants in leases is to regulate the relations of landlord and tenant. The function of covenants in freeholds is to govern relations between neighbours. Local authorities also use covenants, for example in planning agreements, to reinforce agricultural ties in conditional planning consents.

Covenants may be either positive or restrictive. A positive covenant is one that in substance obliges the person giving it (the covenantor) to spend money either directly, for example, making a contribution to the cost of repair of a common road, or indirectly, for example keeping a fence in repair. A restrictive covenant limits something that can be done on the land bound by it, for example that the land can be used only for agriculture or that no buildings can be put up without the consent of the person entitled to the benefit (the covenantee).

Covenants found elsewhere in the law relate, for example, to trade and employment and charities, but in the context of farms and estates covenants must relate to land. The covenant must be binding on a specific piece of land and must be taken for the benefit of another identifiable area of land, which must be capable of benefiting. This benefit will normally be presumed by the courts if there is an area that might benefit. However, if the covenantor or his successor in title applies to the Lands Tribunal for a release or variation, the covenantee may need to prove a clear benefit in order to keep the covenant in force.

Positive covenants can be enforced only against the original covenantor. There are devices discussed below for passing on the burden of a covenant, but these are not easy to operate. A restrictive covenant, on the other hand, provided it is either registered at the Land Charges Registry or on the Register of Title, binds the land of the covenantor and any successor in title.

15.2   USE OF COVENANTS

Covenants were originally developed in the context of nineteenth-century housing developments (before the emergence of the modern system of planning control) to control the size and positioning of houses, restrict areas to residential or professional use, and prevent undesirable practices that might be offensive to neighbours. The rules are therefore devised to protect amenity. Although covenants are used in other contexts, they can be adapted only with difficulty.

In the context of farms and estates a covenant may, for example, protect a view. The owner of a large house with a view across farm land may impose a covenant to restrict any building on that land without consent in order to protect the value of the house. Similarly, on the sale of a house in an estate village, a covenant may prohibit unsympathetic extensions.

Covenants can be used to protect business. For example, a farmer selling some fields may provide that no cattle may be grazed on the fields being sold which have not been accredited as free of brucellosis. Where a farm name is important as a trading asset, a covenant could prohibit the purchaser of part of it using a similar name. A covenant may also be used to prevent competition, for example a seller who keeps a farm shop or a caravan site on retained land, may want to prevent the buyer from competing. Such covenants must be drawn in a way that complies with the general rules of law affecting commercial competition.

Covenants may also protect valuable equipment. For example, British Gas, when taking easements for gas pipelines across farm land, invariably imposes a covenant to prevent building over the line of the pipe or damage to it.

Covenants may be used to protect other rights of property. For example, if land is sold subject to a mineral or sporting reservation the seller may impose a covenant not to dig minerals or fire guns. If a watercourse is reserved, there may be a covenant not to pollute it, or if a right of way is granted over the retained land of the seller, a covenant could be imposed not to obstruct it. Sellers often impose general covenants not to do anything on the land sold which could be a nuisance to the retained land. These covenants do not add very much to the rights they are designed to protect, but it may be easier to enforce rights by an injunction for breach of covenant, than by a claim based on the law of nuisance.

Positive covenants are more rare. A common example of a positive covenant is to provide for the erection of a new boundary structure and for the future maintenance of boundaries. If the land sold subsequently changes hands, the covenant is of little value except as evidence of boundary responsibility. However, there may be a covenant on the buyer to put in a new access or drainage system. Another type of positive covenant is to contribute to the cost of maintenance of common services, such as the repair of a water pipe.

15.2.1 Existing covenant

If a farm or estate is sold and existing covenants are binding on it, these must be disclosed to the buyer as a matter of title. If a covenant was imposed on unregistered land after 1925 and was not registered before a subsequent sale, it will not normally be binding on a later owner even if that owner knew about it. In the case of registered land a covenant will be binding if it is referred to in the Charges Register.

Assuming that a restrictive covenant is binding, however, in the case of unregistered land it should be referred to expressly in the conveyance. If the seller is the original covenantor and the covenant is drawn in a form that remains personally binding after sale, or if the seller had already given to a previous seller a covenant for indemnity, the seller should obtain from the buyer a covenant for indemnity to observe and perform the covenant and to indemnify the seller. In the case of restrictive covenants this will depend on the wording. Positive covenants cannot be binding directly on successors and normally therefore can be enforced only by a chain of covenants; indemnity covenants will be invariable. The buyer should be aware of the terms of the covenant and whether it is likely to prevent any proposed activity. In practice, covenants are often unenforceable (see below) and it may therefore be a matter of judgment whether to take indemnities or to take out insurance or to seek a release if it is considered that they are likely to cause only theoretical problems.

The buyer should investigate who has the benefit of a covenant. This depends on the wording of the covenant and the extent of the land to which that benefit was attached.

15.2.2 New covenants

Where the seller retains land, the parties will often agree on the imposition of a new covenant. Many estates have a standard form of covenant which is applied as a matter of policy on sales but, in other cases, covenants have to be adapted to the particular circumstances of each sale. In drafting a covenant, the seller should consider:

(a) the purpose for which it is being imposed. A covenant that is drawn too widely or in an uncertain form may be unenforceable and may not make clear its purpose. This can complicate a sale or operate to reduce the price;

(b) how long it should last. The normal practice is to draft covenants to last forever. As a result, many titles are incumbered with obsolete nineteenth-century covenants. Some covenants are designed to last for only a limited time. For example, on the sale of part of a dairy farm which had milk quota (see Chapter 21) attached, but where the seller is keeping the quota, a covenant may be imposed on the buyer not to use the part sold for milk production for five years. Alternatively, on the sale of a site for building the seller may wish to approve the design of the initial houses, but not wish to approve later rebuilding or extensions; as such, the covenant to approve designs could last until the site has been first developed or for a defined time such as three years;

(c) the area to be benefited. It will usually be appropriate for the covenant to benefit all the retained land of the seller, but that may be inconvenient or not desired. In particular, a covenant can be drafted so that it benefits only land which the seller retains (so that the benefit does not pass automatically to the purchaser of another part of the estate) or a person to whom the benefit is expressly assigned. That person must, of course, have land capable of benefiting;

(d) the land to be bound. A covenant may apply to all the land sold or only to part, or different covenants may bind different areas, so that, for example, the conveyance could specify that a house can be used only as a residence, an area near retained cottages should not be used for keeping pigs, and certain fields should not be built on or be used otherwise than for agriculture.

The buyer should check that the covenant covers everything that has been agreed and should ensure, if it is a restrictive covenant, that it is drawn in a form that cannot be enforced against the buyer personally after he has resold.

15.2.3   Personal covenants

The benefit of a covenant may be limited to an individual. It must still benefit land (otherwise an injunction will not be granted and only nominal damages can be awarded), but the buyer may, for example, agree that as long as the seller personally continues to live in a particular house he will not use the land otherwise than for agriculture, or will not obstruct a view.

15.3 VARIATION AND REMOVAL OF COVENANTS

If a buyer acquires land subject to an existing covenant which needs to be removed or varied there are a number of steps open to him.

(a) He can simply disregard the covenant on the basis that any person entitled to it either does not know or does not object. This carries risks, but such risks can be protected against by indemnity insurance. This is also unlikely to be acceptable to a mortgagee unless the breach is so trivial that it does not affect the value.

(b) He can obtain the release or consent of persons entitled to enforce the covenant. If the covenant is taken for the benefit of defined land, persons entitled to enforce a covenant will generally be the present owners of that land. If the covenant was taken for the benefit of the whole of the estate many years ago, a large number of people could be involved and obtaining the consent of all of them may be difficult. If the covenant is recent, or only benefits a small area of land, it may be possible to obtain a deed of release from the persons having the benefit. This will not by itself cancel the covenant, but it will mean that those persons cannot enforce it or can only do so in a varied form. Such a deed should be noted on the Register of Title.

(c) He can apply to the Lands Tribunal under s 84 of the Law of Property Act 1925 for an order releasing or varying the covenant. This can, however, be a lengthy and expensive course of action, although it is probably less expensive than a court trial.

(d) In certain cases, it may be possible to apply to the court for an order that the covenant is not enforceable, for example on the grounds that the covenantee has no land to benefit. Alternatively, the buyer may invite anyone (such as adjoining landowners) thought to have the benefit to take proceedings if they wish. If they fail to do so they may lose their rights.

(e) He can obtain a deed of release or variation from the covenantee. If the covenant was imposed recently, there is no doubt as to which land has the benefit and all the owners of that land agree, such a course of action can be effective, simple and cheap. However, this may be risky if the benefit has passed to a person who has not consented; as such, the Land Charges Registry and HM Land Registry will cancel a covenant on the register only rarely.

15.4 BUYING LAND WITH THE BENEFIT OF A COVENANT

If the sale is of land that already has the benefit of an existing covenant, or if the seller is giving a covenant over his land for the benefit of the buyer, the options discussed above are reversed. If the covenant is old, the buyer may need to check that it has been registered. The benefit of the covenant is annexed to land automatically, but it is good practice in the case of unregistered conveyancing to assign the specific benefit of the covenant. A personal covenant should be assigned in any event.

15.5   MAKING POSITIVE COVENANTS BINDING

Following the decision of the House of Lords in *Rhone v Stephens* [1994] 2 AC 310, it is difficult to make positive covenants binding on land. However, this may be achieved as follows:

(a)   conditional grant (the rule in *Halsall v Brizell* [1957] Ch 169, as interpreted in *Thamesmead Town Ltd v Allotey* (1998) 37 EG 161. This applies where the burden of the covenant (eg to pay a contribution to the cost of maintenance of a track used in common) is closely connected to some other right (such as an easement to use the track). In this case, the size of the right may be made conditional on performance of the obligation so that if the contribution is not paid the track cannot be used;

(b)   restriction on the register with chain of covenants. The procedure here is to apply to HM Land Registry to include a restriction that, except under an order of the Registrar or of the court, no transfer of the land burdened is to be registered unless a condition is satisfied – usually obtaining the consent of the person entitled to the benefit of the covenant. There will be an obligation on the covenantee to give such consent if the purchaser from the covenantor enters into a positive covenant in the same terms as the covenantor had done. If the covenantee cannot be traced or unreasonably refuses consent, the Registrar or the court can authorise the registration of a transfer;

(c)   estate rentcharge and right of re-entry under the Rentcharges Act 1977. The procedure here is to impose a nominal estate rentcharge of, for example, £1 on the land of the covenantor with the right for the covenantee to re-enter on that land if the covenant is broken. Where works need to be carried out, for example, fencing, this may be coupled with a provision that the covenantee may re-enter simply for the purpose of remedying the breach and carrying out the works; the rentcharge will then be enlarged to cover the cost of doing the work;

(d)   not dispose of the freehold but grant a lease. This is the main reason why flats are normally sold leasehold in order to make positive covenants of repair, shelter and support binding, and the same applies to positive covenants affecting farm land.

Chapter 16

PLANNING

16.1   INTRODUCTION

Agriculture generally is outside the scope of the planning laws, but many agricultural activities and types of development associated with country estates fall under the scope of planning and, as such, need to be considered carefully on any purchase.

The general rule is that the owner of land is entitled to do whatever he wishes on that land. Certain breaches of planning control, particularly related to the heritage and the environment, can be criminal offences, but most types of development are not unlawful unless the local planning authority serves an enforcement notice, for example where an activity defined as 'development' has been carried out without planning permission. Many types of development affecting rural land do not need planning permission and in many other cases planning permission is automatically treated as having been granted. Where development is carried out which would otherwise need planning permission, the local planning authority can serve an enforcement notice within a given period of time (usually 4 or 10 years). If it does not do so, the development is thereafter immune from enforcement procedures, although it does not actually become a lawful use, and would be vulnerable if there were a further change of use.

There are two aspects to development. The first is operational, which comprises building, engineering, mining or other activities in, on, over or under land; the second is a material change in the use of land. Slightly different rules apply to the two aspects; in particular, the period within which an enforcement notice must be served is four years in the case of operational development, and 10 years in the case of change of use.

Certain activities are totally outside the scope of the Planning Acts, and these include the use of land for agriculture or forestry, although it should be noted that any operational works (such as the laying-out of a road to extract timber or the construction of a barn adjoining a highway) may themselves need planning consent. Furthermore, as mentioned below, certain activities may need to be preceded by an environmental assessment.

Under the Town and Country Planning (Use Classes) Order 1987, SI 1987/764, a change of use within a designated class is not a development. These are not in general relevant to agriculture, although they can be to associated activities such as farm shops or the treatment of animal products.

More important is the Town and Country Planning General Development Order 1988, SI 1988/1813 which gives planning consent for certain specified types of development automatically. Under art 4 of that Order, a local planning authority can make a direction which (if confirmed by the Secretary of State) will provide that the permission is withdrawn within a particular locality for certain types of activity. However, if a landowner suffers loss as a result, the authority must pay compensation; as such, these orders are rare.

Special controls over the construction of agricultural buildings apply to land within a National Park or Areas of Outstanding Natural Beauty and other designated land, which do not apply elsewhere in the country.

Certain types of permitted development are particularly important for agriculture, and are specified in the parts of Sch 2 to the Order. These include (subject to various conditions) the construction of a fence, wall or gate, the use of land for any purpose for not more than 28 days in any calendar year (eg letting out a field for car boot sales), and demolition of certain buildings. In relation to farms and estates, the most important are listed in part 7, which deals with forestry buildings and operations, and part 6, which relates to agricultural buildings and operations.

Under class A of part 6, the carrying-out on land comprised in an agricultural unit of five hectares or more of the erection, extension or alteration of a building or excavation or engineering operations is permitted, subject to various conditions, provided it is reasonably necessary for the purposes of agriculture. Such activities cannot be carried out on a separate parcel of land less than one hectare, do not include the construction of, or alterations to a dwelling, or structures exceeding 465 square metres in area or more than 12 metres in height. Works within 25 metres of a trunk road or classified road, or which relate to the accommodation of livestock, slurry or sewage if it is within 400 metres of a residence other than one connected with the farm, are similarly excluded. The person carrying out any development must notify the planning authority in advance, which must state within 28 days whether it wishes that person to apply for formal consent.

Under class B of part 6, development is permitted for the carrying-out on an agricultural unit of not less than 0.4 of a hectare but less than five hectares, of certain specified types of development including works to agricultural buildings, the creation of a hard surface, repairing ponds and other matters which are subject to various conditions.

Under class C of Part 6, the mining and working of minerals on land occupied with agricultural land is permitted provided the activities are reasonably necessary for agricultural purposes, again subject to certain conditions, notably that the minerals must not be taken outside the unit. The details of permitted activities and conditions are set out in full in the Order and must be considered carefully.

Under the Town and Country Planning (Assessment of Environmental Effects) Regulations 1988 SI 1998/1199, introduced to give effect to a Council Directive 85/337, it is necessary, before certain types of activity are instituted, to provide an environmental assessment to the local planning authority. This may be obligatory or at the discretion of the authority. Discretionary activities include various rural operations, including water management for agriculture, poultry rearing, pig rearing and certain fisheries. Other activities include certain mineral and waste disposal operations, including dumping in worked-out quarries, and other water activities such as the construction of a dam, and afforestation as mentioned in Chapter 13.

16.2 PROTECTED AREAS

Certain areas are subject to special controls, either under the Planning Acts or associated with them. These include National Parks designated under the National Parks and Access to the Countryside Act 1949, Areas of Outstanding Natural Beauty (AONBs) and various informal designations adopted by local planning authorities, such as heritage coasts. Under the Ancient Monuments and Archaeological Areas Act 1979, various ancient monuments can be made subject to special controls, under which it is a criminal offence to damage such monuments. Under the Town and Country Planning (Listed Buildings and Conservation Areas) Act 1990, individual buildings or built-up areas can be protected. Individual farmhouses and other structures such as dovecotes and barns may be listed. Many villages have been declared Conservation Areas and the designated area usually includes adjoining farm land. Sites of special scientific interest (SSSIs) may be designated under the Wildlife and Countryside Act 1981, and these include areas which need to be protected for their flora or fauna and therefore where certain agricultural activities, such as spraying or cutting, may be controlled. Under the Wild Birds Directive, Council Directive 79/409, and the Habitats Directive, Council Directive 92/43, certain other areas are also subject to special controls in the interests of habitat protection. The buyer of any land which includes such an area must be aware of the restrictions on future activities.

16.3   FARM COTTAGES

The construction of a new dwelling always requires planning consent. In the interests of agricultural production, consent has been granted for the building of a cottage on the farm to house an essential farm worker, in circumstances where permission would not otherwise have been given for an isolated house. Such consents are usually subject to special controls, particularly relating to the size of the dwelling, but the main condition is always that the dwelling must be occupied only by a person employed (or last employed) in agriculture or forestry or his or her widow or widower. These 'agricultural ties' often cause problems when the dwelling becomes surplus to agricultural needs following changes in farming, and there is no suitable occupier who can take a tenancy of or purchase the cottage. Landowners who own such cottages, have tried to have the tie lifted in order to sell to anyone wishing to have a home or holiday home in the countryside. Generally, such attempts have been resisted by local planning authorities and, and as a result, numerous disputed inquiries and decisions have arisen. In general, the tie will be lifted only if it can be clearly shown that there is no realistic prospect whatever of finding an agricultural occupier, or a purchaser who is prepared to install such an occupier. It must be demonstrated clearly that there is no market for the cottage subject to the tie and that the cottage would therefore otherwise stand empty. In many cases, a change of use will have occurred, and it is now established that where a tied cottage has been actively used for a non-farming purpose (such as an office worker's home) for a continuous period of 10 years, it is thereafter immune from enforcement.

Where permission has been granted for the construction a new cottage the local planning authority may have attached this condition to an existing farmhouse, usually by means of a planning agreement under s 106 of the Town and Country Planning Act. It is therefore possible, even when acquiring an old farmhouse, to find that it is subject to such a restriction.

16.4   DIVERSIFICATION

Where farm land is put to a non-traditional use, planning consent is usually required. Non-traditional use includes, for example, converting redundant farm buildings to offices or industrial units, or the laying out of a golf course, but it also applies to simple changes of use where there is no physical alteration. One of the most common changes of use is where a farmer, for example in order to straighten an irregular boundary, sells a small piece of land to the owner of an adjoining house, as an extension to that owner's garden. In the past, such encroachments were tolerated, but planning authorities are now more likely to view this as a change of use requiring planning consent, which is rarely granted. In a number of cases the new owner has been required to change the garden back to farm land.

A difficulty relates to the use of land for horses. The case-law is not easy to reconcile since cases have arisen in a variety of contexts, including agricultural tenancies and taxation and rating as well as planning. In general, the use of a paddock for grazing ponies is viewed as an agricultural use because the ponies eat the grass growing there. Where, however, the paddock is not sufficient to feed the ponies and it is necessary to bring in fodder for outside sources, this will not usually be agricultural. Other activities, such as the use of land for jumps or gallops, or the conversion of a barn to livery stables, may constitute development depending on the degree. In order to require planning consent a change of use must be 'material'. A particular use for horses may sometimes be agricultural for one purpose, such as whether a tenant is protected under the Agricultural Holdings Act 1986, but not for another, such as rating.

Many of these cases involve a matter of degree and it should be remembered that the local planning authority is not obliged to take enforcement action if it does not consider it necessary. In particular, even where a minor change has taken place, but reversible (for example, where the field does not change appearance) and does not cause a nuisance or arouse local comment, this may be tolerated. However, if a buyer has a substantial change in mind, it is always prudent either to apply for planning consent or apply for formal confirmation that consent to the proposed activity is not necessary.

Chapter 17

THE ENVIRONMENT

17.1   INTRODUCTION

Since farms and estates form part of a larger countryside, activities upon them affect and are affected by other land in the vicinity. One of the motives for purchasing rural land may be its natural quality, which applies not only to individual private buyers but, increasingly, to a range of environmental bodies such as conservation trusts. There are many sources of heritage funding available to assist voluntary bodies to buy rural land for conservation. A seller will need to be aware of that market, as well as the normal commercial farm land market.

Laws relating to the environment, operate using both carrot and stick. The 'carrot' operates by way of grants and reliefs which are available for environmental purposes. The 'stick' operates by way of laws which penalise unneighbourly activities under either the civil law or the criminal law.

17.2   POLLUTION AND CONTAMINATION – CIVIL LIABILITY

Liability in tort can arise under almost any heading, but the most common headings are negligence and nuisance (including *Rylands v Fletcher* (1868) LR 3 HL 330). Broadly, negligence creates a liability where one person has a duty to a neighbour and by an act or omission commits a breach of that duty, and damage results. The negligent person is liable for reasonably foreseeable damage. Liability relates to the act or omission itself, not to the status of being the owner of the property where it took place. Indeed, it is not necessary that the tortfeasor owns any property, and frequently he does not. It follows that if an owner has allowed a state of affairs to arise, for example by neglecting to repair a dam or repair a plug restraining water in a disused mine, or by allowing a fire hazard to arise in woodlands, any resulting damage will be his liability whether or not he is still the owner of the land and even though he may have sold it. This is particularly the case in relation to pollution, which can involve the escape of chemicals over several years percolating through land to adjoining property, which becomes contaminated. Thus, simply by selling land the tortfeasor cannot avoid liability and although a seller in such a situation may ask the buyer for an indemnity this will not usually be given.

By contrast, liability in nuisance depends on the ownership of land. The owner of an interest in the land on which a nuisance occurs, which causes damage, or which interferes with the enjoyment of adjoining land, will be liable simply by virtue of being the owner of that land whether or not the owner was responsible for the nuisance in the first place. 'Owner' here includes a tenant. A degree of fault must be shown, in that liability depends on foreseeability, so that an innocent buyer of land on which a nuisance exists may be able to escape liability. However, in most cases the owner will be expected to take reasonable steps to abate the nuisance whether or not he caused it. Thus, buying land may involve taking on a nuisance and therefore a liability to a neighbour. Nuisances can include, for example, a dangerous tree, an abandoned mine full of water, or an old tip full of chemicals. Liability is to a person having an interest in the adjoining land affected, and does not extend to people who do not have any interest in that land.

It follows that a buyer of land adversely affected by something occurring on neighbouring land may have different remedies in nuisance and negligence, against different people who have caused or adopted the source of damage on adjoining land. A buyer of a large estate may wish to continue with the purchase even though there is a relatively small problem of contamination affecting part of it, and pursue whatever remedies are available against the adjoining owner. Where liability is in negligence, the buyer will not usually be able to take over a claim where the damage has already occurred, although he may, of course, take an assignment from the seller of any damages that may be awarded. He may also be able to take over the right to take proceedings in the name of the seller subject, normally, to an indemnity as to costs and damages. If he has a claim in nuisance against an adjoining owner, it is normally not open to the defendant to argue that the plaintiff came to the nuisance. If a state of affairs constitutes a nuisance, it remains one, even though the plaintiff knew about it when he purchased the land.

17.3   POLLUTION AND CONTAMINATION – CRIMINAL LIABILITY

Criminal liability for pollution and contamination is, in practice, a far more important and serious head of claim. Various statutes are relevant, including the Public Health Acts 1875, 1925 and 1961, and, in the case of dwellings, various housing legislation, but the most important legislation is the Environmental Protection Act 1990, as amended by the Environment Act 1995. The underlying principle is that the polluter pays, ie that the person who caused environmental damage is responsible for putting it right. The Act, however, contains a fall-back, in that if the polluter cannot be traced, has ceased to exist or is not worth suing, there is a remedy against any person who is, for the time being, the owner or occupier of the land which is the source of the pollution. The Act contains numerous safeguards. The standard of remediation required by the enforcing authority (either the local authority or the Environment Agency) must be reasonable in the context; as such, it must not entail excessive cost. There are various opportunities for appeal and judicial review, but ultimately where there is a sufficiently serious or continuing pollution or contamination it must be put right, and this would normally be at the expense of the landowner if no one else can be found.

In this context, pollution normally relates to substances which escape into controlled waters, ie waters in broad terms which ultimately flow to the sea; contamination involves the existence of any substance in land which is liable to cause harm or damage to people or property. In an extreme case, costs can be substantial. For example, where an old quarry has been filled with domestic refuse or chemicals which are leaching away, and over the years the quarry has been filled up with other substances, it may cost several millions of pounds to empty it out and remove the pollution.

Under the Environmental Protection Act 1990, a local authority has various powers in relation to sources of pollution, including, for example, litter and fly-tipped rubbish. The landowner can be made liable for cleaning them up even though the pollution actually occurred during a previous ownership.

One source of problems has been farm waste, notably slurry (largely from dairies and other cattle yards) and silage effluent from silage clamps. After the passing of the 1990 Act and subsequent regulations, a major effort was made by the National Rivers Authority (the predecessor of the Environment Agency) to visit as many farms as possible to make sure that safeguards were in order. Many farmers were compelled to spend large sums of money to rectify problems or were forced to give up their polluting activities. It is essential for a buyer of a cattle unit, or indeed other intensive animal units, to carry out a physical inspection since although there may have been no complaint in the past, there may be hidden trouble. Again, the onus to remedy the trouble is on the owner for the time being, although criminal proceedings can be taken only against a person who caused or knowingly permitted the pollution.

17.4   REGULATIONS

Many potentially polluting activities can, of course, be carried out provided the standard of the activity complies with national regulations. The most significant of these is tipping, and any area on which controlled waste (which is very widely defined) is deposited can be managed only under a waste management licence, which is tightly controlled by the Environment Agency. Under present conditions, compliance with the terms of a licence is normally sufficient, and a buyer of land where tipping has taken place under licence or is continuing to take place can generally rely on that fact as providing an adequate standard. However, it should be pointed out that this does not exclude possible liability for future claims, for example in negligence or under *Rylands v Fletcher* (1868) LR 3 HL 330 where it may be arguable that the activity of depositing waste is itself so inherently dangerous that liability under the civil law could exist even though the landowner has complied with the regulations.

The licence itself is granted to an approved operator, so that a buyer of land who wishes to continue tipping will need to obtain the approval of the Environment Agency or the local authority. The old licence will then be withdrawn and a new one issued, possibly on updated terms.

17.5   GRANTS AND RELIEFS

There is a growing tendency for financial inducements to be made to landowners either to refrain from carrying out activities that are deemed harmful to the environment, such as spraying or deep ploughing, or to carry out good management practices, such as reinstating and maintaining hedges, clearing out ponds and improving the environmental quality. Certain reliefs are available, particularly in the form of inheritance tax reliefs on heritage property, where property may be exempted from inheritance tax provided certain conditions as to maintenance and public access are met. Where such reliefs have been given in the past they may also be available in the future, which may be of interest, for example, to an elderly prospective buyer of attractive rural land.

More important are a variety of management agreements, some operated by MAFF, others by local authorities or national parks, which provide regular payments to the owners and occupiers of land provided certain acts are or are not undertaken. These include management agreements in relation to SSSIs where, in order to protect such a site, English Nature is obliged to offer an agreement with suitable financial terms to an owner as the price of insisting on protection. Payments of this nature can be very substantial and can materially affect the viability of rural land. They can therefore have an important impact on price, and a buyer should investigate any agreements which may exist.

Such agreements typically run for a period of 20 years, and if these are broken the sums paid will be recoverable. On a sale, therefore, the seller will need to protect his interests against a breach of the agreement by the buyer. The authority will normally be prepared to enter into a tripartite agreement, releasing the seller, but only on terms that the buyer accepts responsibility for past breaches. As such, the buyer will need to check there are no such breaches. The principles are similar to those discussed for Woodland Grant Schemes at **13.3**.

17.6   THE BUILT ENVIRONMENT

As mentioned in Chapter 16 on planning, there are a variety of planning controls, including Areas of Outstanding Natural Beauty (AONBs), conservation areas, listed buildings and ancient monuments, which prohibit activities which are considered to be undesirable, for example the construction or alteration of buildings in sensitive areas. These may be supplemented by agreements that go further, for example to maintain drystone walls, including various types of repair grants. It is frequently a condition of such a grant that if the subject matter ceases to exist, for example if the repaired building falls down, the grant will be repayable. Compliance with conditions of a grant may be secured by a charge. At present, public charges (registered as local land charges) of this nature are rare (unlike eg housing grants in urban areas, although housing grants can, of course, also be paid for country cottages), but a number of grants made by semi-public bodies may be secured in this way, for example by an equitable charge, so that if the conditions of the grant are broken the charge may be repayable, whoever the owner is. Normally, this will be evident from the title, and a buyer will have to consider whether to take over the liability or to insist on the seller discharging the charge.

17.7   MOORS AND OPEN COUNTRY

There is growing pressure for access to open country. This has been discussed at **11.4** on common land but it should be noted that, particularly in national parks and similar areas, an access agreement may be combined with a management agreement, so that in return for grant payments, a landowner may be required both to maintain certain parts of the open country in an agreed condition, as well as allowing public access either along defined routes or over a particular area. An agreement which involves restrictions (such as not preventing public access) will usually be binding on future owners. Generally, positive obligations (such as to carry out maintenance works) cannot be made so binding. Section 33 of the Local Government (Miscellaneous Provisions) Act 1982 authorises local authorities to enter into agreements containing positive obligations which can be binding on successors, but the enforcement of such obligations presents practical problems. In most cases the local authority will, under s 33, have power to enter on the land and do work and then recover the cost from the landowner. Where land is subject to such an agreement, however, the buyer will need to consider carefully the implications of any obligations contained in it.

Chapter 18

AGRICULTURAL AND FARM BUSINESS TENANCIES

18.1 INTRODUCTION

Many arrangements are made between the owners of farm land and other persons, for occupation on commercial terms. Various types of tenancy exist, including residential and business tenancies, which are dealt with in Chapters 19 and 20, as well as other arrangements such as partnerships and contract farming, but the most important arrangement involves a commercial tenancy of agricultural land. In broad terms, if the tenancy was granted before 1 September 1995, or granted as a continuation or succession of such a tenancy, it will be subject to the Agricultural Holdings Act 1986 and is generally known as an agricultural holding (AH). If it was granted on or after that date, it will be subject to the Agricultural Tenancies Act 1995, and is known as a farm business tenancy (FBT).

There are four situations where tenancies can be relevant to a sale and purchase: a sale subject to a tenancy which will continue to run; where an existing tenancy is coming to an end and the buyer not the seller will have vacant possession; a sale and lease-back where an owner–occupier raises finance by selling the freehold but remains in occupation; and a sale by way of lease where the seller retains the freehold as an investment and grants a lease to the buyer.

An existing protected tenant will usually be the person most favourably placed to bid for the freehold, and sales to sitting tenants are a special feature. Another aspect that needs to be considered is where the landlord's interest under an existing tenancy is divided typically between the former landlord of the whole and the purchaser of part.

Agricultural tenancies (ATs) are usually in the form of annual tenancies. However, legally there is no need for this, and some have existed as leases for years. The policy between 1947 and 1995 was that commercial agricultural occupiers would have at least lifetime security of tenure and, if the tenancy was entered into before 12 July 1984, security for two successors, making a possible total of three generations. As such, there was no particular need to grant a lease, and the legal rules assume an annual tenancy. An FBT arises where a tenancy is granted after 1 September 1995 unless either it is, in effect, a variation of an existing, pre-1995 tenancy, or it is a succession to such a tenancy on the retirement of the original tenant or a first successor. ATs are governed partly by the terms of the written tenancy agreement, if there is one, but mainly by statutory rules laid down in the Agricultual Holdings Act 1986, most of which cannot be varied. FBTs are almost entirely governed by the terms of the written tenancy, although the Agricultural Tenancies Act 1995 contains obligatory provisions on three topics, namely the length of notice, the method of reviewing the rent, and compensation for improvements.

A tenancy which is granted for more than three years must be made by lease in the form of a deed. The consequences of failure to do this are discussed at **19.4**.

18.2   EXISTING TENANCIES

Most ATs are granted under a written contract, very often in one of the standard forms produced by firms of law stationers or substantial agricultural surveying firms. However, this is not necessary, and a purely verbal tenancy can exist for up to three years or as a periodic tenancy. Historically many farms were simply let on the basis of a handshake. If a written tenancy exists the buyer must, of course, see a copy and if not, he should obtain as much information as possible about any terms which may have been agreed verbally or by letter. It is common for such tenancies to be varied, usually by a more or less informal memorandum which is stapled to or kept with the tenancy agreement. Such memoranda can easily be lost so that even what appears to be a complete agreement may in fact not give the whole story. Under s 6 of the Agricultural Holdings Act 1986, either party can serve a notice requiring an unwritten tenancy (or unwritten terms of a partially written tenancy) to be put in writing.

A good written agreement will describe the land usually by reference to both plan and schedule. Over the course of a tenancy, the land may be added to by way, for example, of extra fields, or removed, for example, for road widening or sold as an extension to a neighbour's garden. In practice, the area at any given time subject to the tenancy will usually be clear because it will be the land actually being farmed by the tenant. If there is any doubt, this will usually have been resolved on a rent review since rent is assessed on a given rate per acre and the tenant will not pay for land he does not occupy. However, there may be odd areas of rough ground, woodland and similar pieces of land whose status is in doubt and a buyer will need to investigate exactly what is included.

18.2.1   Tenant's rights

The tenancy will grant to the tenant various rights, including rights of way, the right to take water and, possible grazing rights over open land. If the seller retains ownership of the land affected by those rights the buyer will normally need to have those freehold rights included in his purchase although in some cases they may simply be continued as personal privileges for the present tenant, in which case the effect on rent needs to be considered.

18.2.2   Landlord's reservations

The tenancy will also contain a long list of reservations to the landlord. These include such matters as minerals, rights to water, timber, antiquities and other matters, but in practice two are most important – sporting rights and easements over pipes, cables and other services. On a sporting estate the value of shooting over let land is an important part of the freehold value, and the terms of the sporting reservation must be considered with care. Section 20 of the Agricultural Holdings Act 1986 deals with compensation claims by an AT tenant for damage by game. There is no equivalent in the Agricultural Tenancies Act 1995, but agreements should include this. The terms of the sporting reservation can also be politically relevant as to who has the power to control hunting over the farm.

An agreement may contain a reservation of the right of the landlord to grant to third parties easements for pipes, cables and other services. If this is not included, the body providing the services may have statutory powers to compel the tenant to allow it to instal its pipes or cables, but such a right relevant to the way in which the compensation is divided between landlord and tenant.

18.2.3   Tenant's obligations

The tenancy agreement will list numerous obligations on the part of the tenant. It is becoming common practice to provide that late payment of rent will attract an interest penalty. Under an AT, if the tenant does not pay rent within two months of it becoming due and being notified in writing, he risks losing his tenancy. There is no similar sanction under an FBT, but, if it is a periodic tenancy, the landlord can simply serve notice to quit, and, if for a term of years, can invoke a forfeiture clause.

Repairing obligations need to be considered with care. Although some full repairing and insuring ATs do exist, and more such FBTs, the normal pattern, particularly for periodic tenancies, is for the landlord to be responsible for main structural repairs and major works, and the tenant to be responsible for minor matters. In the case of an AT, provided there is nothing inconsistent in the agreement, the parties are governed by the Agricultural (Maintenance,

Repair and Insurance of Fixed Equipment) Regulations 1973, SI 1973/1473 ('the Model Clauses'). Again, there is no equivalent for an FBT.

Tenancies usually contain an absolute prohibition on assignment, and this is essential in an AT since if the tenancy is assigned, for example to a company (which clearly cannot die), the tenancy may continue for ever. For this reason, s 6 of the Agricultural Holdings Act 1986 allows the landlord to serve a notice which, at least in the short term, has the effect of imposing a restriction on assignment. Most written tenancies go a great deal further and limit rigidly the identity of the person who can carry on farming activities. Normally, a tenant will be allowed to go into partnership with his own family, but not with strangers.

The agreement will contain a use clause, and, again, in ATs such use is traditionally tightly restricted. In modern conditions, this is not always an advantage because the tighter the restriction, the lower the rent, and where incomes from agriculture are uncertain over the long term this can materially affect the rent payable, especially in circumstances where the tenant might otherwise be able to diversify (see Chapter 23).

A tenancy agreement will contain many other provisions, usually designed to maintain the fertility and good order of the land. In addition, landlords may include provisions for conservation or amenity.

18.2.4   Landlord's obligations

The agreement will list obligations on the landlord and this will usually include repairing provisions. The Landlord and Tenant (Covenants) Act 1995 applies to agricultural leases as much as to any other and although, as mentioned above, the interest of the tenant is not usually assignable, it is relevant for the landlord. Thus, under privity of contract, an original landlord remains liable on the repairing covenant, even though the freehold has been sold, unless the landlord is released under that Act.

18.2.5   Forfeiture clauses

The tenancy agreement will normally include a forfeiture clause. Under the rule in *Coates v Diment* [1951] 1 All ER 890 and *Parry v Million Pigs Ltd* (1980) 260 EG 281, forfeiture clauses which provide for a lease to end automatically without at least one month's notice are void in the case of ATs. As most ATs are annual tenancies and can be terminated by notice to quit on suitable grounds, this is usually irrelevant. It is not clear whether the same rules apply to FBTs, but there is a provision under s 8 of the 1995 Act that the tenant is entitled to remove certain fixtures while he is tenant, and it is therefore possible that a forfeiture clause having immediate effect, which does not give the tenant enough time, may also be void in the case of an FBT. This is important since most FBTs last for a period of years.

18.2.6 Miscellaneous and resumption clauses

Numerous other clauses may be written into the agreement, for example in relation to quotas, giving a landlord a right of first refusal for beef or sheep quotas, or allowing the tenant to sell milk quota. An important clause is an express provision for termination as to part of the tenancy, on short notice, in the event of planning consent being obtained. This must be expressly included since where it is not, it will not be implied, so that a buyer who acquires tenanted land with the intention of obtaining possession of part for redevelopment may be frustrated if the clause is omitted or is drafted incorrectly. Again, at least one month's notice must be given, and three months' is more usual. The effect of failure to include a redevelopment clause may be avoided by a sale of the part which has planning permission to an independent developer, who then serves his own notice to quit in relation to the separate part he then owns; however, it is essential that the boundaries correspond precisely to the area with consent.

18.3   STATUTORY PROVISION

Parliament has intervened to govern the relationship between agricultural landlords and tenants. In the case of ATs, there are a great many of these interventions and for FBTs there are fewer.

In the case of both ATs and FBTs, rent review is governed by statute, namely s 12 of the Agricultural Holdings Act 1986 and s 9 of the Agricultural Tenancies Act 1995. In both cases one year's notice must be given to trigger a review which, in default of agreement, is referred to arbitration. The normal procedure is for reviews to take place at intervals of three years. In the case of ATs, it was held in *Childers Trustees v Anker* (1995) 73 P&CR 458 that the Agricultural Holdings Act 1986 lays down a special formula which, although related to market rent, is not itself a market rent provision. This arises from a compromise between the major landlord and tenant interests recorded originally in the Agricultural Holdings Act 1984. In the case of FBTs, the review is to market rent, unless there is a specific provision in the agreement either that the rent is to be unchanged, or ascertaining precisely what it is, or laying down a formula that does not involve human intervention.

Both types of tenancy are subject to statutory provisions in relation to improvements and other benefits provided at the expense of the tenant, including tenant right and fixtures. In the case of ATs, improvements are specifically defined in the Schedules to the Agricultural Holdings Act 1986. Slightly different rules apply in relation to tenancies granted before 1948, but these are not usually material. In the case of FBTs, improvements are anything that adds to the value of the land, and these may be tangible, such as a barn, or intangible, such as quota rights. In both cases, the Acts provide a method for the tenant to claim compensation at the end of a tenancy by reference to the increase in value of the holding attributable to the improvement. In both cases, the improvement must have had the landlord's consent in writing, and there is provision for a landlord who unreasonably refuses consent to be overridden either by the Agricultural Land Tribunal (for an AT) or by arbitration (for an FBT). The main difference is that, in the case of ATs, it is possible by agreement between landlord and tenant for the amount of the compensation to be fixed, and it is common practice for this to be done by taking the cost of the improvement and writing it down, typically over a period of 20 years, so that if, for example, the tenant quits after two-thirds of that period have elapsed he will receive one-third of the cost as compensation. In the case of FBTs, compensation must be related to the value at the end of a tenancy.

Both the Agricultural Holdings Act 1986 and the Agricultural Tenancies Act 1995 contain provisions for a tenant to be compensated for tenants' fixtures, such as bulk tanks, grain dryers, and even small buildings, and where something does not qualify as an improvement, typically because the tenant has not obtained prior consent, it may qualify as a fixture. Where compensation is not available, the tenant has the right to remove the fixture.

There is also provision for compensation to a tenant for crops, sprays, manurial values and other temporary matters. For ATs, these are described as tenant right matters, and for FBTs they are referred to as routine improvements, the main significance being that they do not necessarily require advance consent.

In the case of ATs, there is also provision for certain other heads of compensation, typically disturbance payments, especially where the landlord gives notice to quit without giving a reason, or for compensation for redevelopment.

18.4   SECURITY AND SUCCESSION

An FBT generally lasts only for the period agreed. If an FBT was granted for more than two years, or is an annual tenancy, the landlord must give one clear year's notice before it comes to an end. In the case of ATs, the landlord can serve one year's notice to quit, but the tenant is entitled to serve a counter-notice so that the notice to quit will not take effect unless it is given on one of the specific number of grounds set out in the Agricultural Holdings Act 1986. The effect of this is that provided the tenant complies with his obligations and pays the rent, and there is no overriding factor such as a grant of planning consent, a tenant under an AT can remain in possession for the whole of his life.

Normally, the tenancy can be terminated on death, but the 1986 Act provides, in the case of pre-1984 tenants or their successors, that following death there can be a succession to a member of the tenant's family, and one further succession after that. This may also apply if the tenant retires. The effect is that pre-1984 tenancies may last for up to three generations. Because of the restrictions on powers of landlords and particularly on rent, and the strong wish of people to farm land themselves rather than buy farm land as an investment, there is a major difference in value between land which is vacant and land subject to an AT. In addition, the age and quality of the tenant is important. Hence, for example, the value of a farm tenanted by a widow in her late eighties with no family, may be very different from the value of the farm which is let to an active tenant in his fifties with a grown son and grandson. A buyer may therefore need to investigate not only the normal matters relating to a tenant, such as whether he pays the rent and carries out repairing obligations, but also the tenant's family situation.

Many farms include cottages which were originally let for occupation by farmhands, whose presence was essential to operate the farming business. Many of these are now surplus. Their fate often depends on the terms of the tenancy agreement, which may contain a strict restriction to agricultural use. In that case, if the tenant wishes to let the cottages, for example to holiday visitors, he will need the landlord's consent, and this may be given either by way of a separate licence at a licence fee, or by varying the terms of the tenancy, so that the rent is calculated having regard to the income potential. However, if a tenant is not willing to do this or terms cannot be agreed, a stalemate may arise which could leave valuable farm buildings empty. The same is true of other buildings that may be suitable for conversion, although it may often be possible for the landlord to obtain planning consent for the conversion, and serve a notice to quit subsequently based on that consent. Sellers and buyers therefore must consider the potential of unused buildings, as well as the current income flow. Where cottages are still occupied by farmworkers or former farmworkers, they may have security as mentioned at **19.9**.

It should be remembered that, as indicated below, many farm tenants are in the market to buy their farms if the landlord wishes to sell. This is such a widespread practice, that some tenants may feel a sense of grievance if they are outbid by an investor buying a let farm or estate. This can affect relations between the new landowner and a resentful, long-established tenant, and the buyer may need to bear this in mind, especially in the first few years following his purchase. A special gesture, such as a new farmhouse kitchen, may help.

18.5   THE TENANCY COMES TO AN END

Where the former tenancy, usually an AT but sometimes an FBT, comes to an end, the landlord may not wish to take possession or relet, but sell with vacant possession when it is available. Indeed, the landlord may be prepared to make a payment to a tenant to bring this about. The reasons for ending the tenancy may be because the tenant is retiring or moving, or where notice to quit has been given either on the death of the former tenant without any successor, or because the tenant has committed a breach of the terms, such as failure to pay rent. Most of the problems associated with the ending of a tenancy under this heading concern the seller. The buyer will simply be aware that he is acquiring a farm with vacant possession, and will not be concerned how that is achieved. However, there may be problems in relation to the tenant's right, or existing buildings or employees, which a buyer will need to investigate.

Where the tenancy terminates under a notice to quit, the rights between the seller and tenant will be governed by the general law and the terms of the tenancy agreement. The tenant may have claims for compensation, as set out above. Where a hostile situation exists, particularly where the notice to quit was served on the grounds of breach of repairs or similar matters, the holding may not be in a satisfactory condition. A hostile tenant may also resist prospective buyers being shown round the farm, and unless there is a specific reservation in the tenancy agreement he has a right to do so. In some cases, although the tenancy is not being ended by agreement, good relations will exist, for example, where the tenancy has ended on the death of the tenant, or in the case of an FBT, where the tenancy has ended in accordance with its terms. However, even in those cases the tenant may be in a position to exploit weaknesses in the landlord's rights, which can affect the marketability of the farm.

The tenancy may be terminated by an agreement by the outgoing tenant to surrender his tenancy, but more often a notice to quit will be given by consent, which is either incorporated in a termination agreement or given separately. Tenants often request a landlord's notice so that part of the compensation payments they receive as part of the terms of giving up the tenancy will not be taxed. It is also good practice for a landlord to require the matter to be terminated by notice, either given by himself (which gives the tenant automatically a tax-free sum equal to five or six times the rent) or by the tenant, on the basis that in the case of notice given by the landlord it cannot be opposed by the tenant after one month has passed, and in the case of notice given by the tenant it cannot be withdrawn (*Elsden v Pick* [1980] 3 All ER 235).

The surrender agreement may simply state that compensation will be calculated in accordance with statutory rules, but will usually go into great detail. It will set out the basis of any payments by the landlord to the tenant, and if the tenant is to share in the purchase price it will set out the formula by which the tenant's payment will be calculated. Most tenants require a formal release of any liability for dilapidations. Other clauses will cover matters such as milk quota, sales of live and dead stock, and the removal of fixtures.

It is usual for tenant-right matters (within the Agricultural Holdings Act 1986) or routine improvements (within the Agricultural Tenancies Act 1995) to be compensated under the relevant Act, but a landlord/seller must be careful that if he intends to recover these amounts from the incoming buyer, the basis of valuation is exactly the same. It is not unknown for there to be one arbitration between landlord and tenant, producing one figure for the compensation payable by the landlord to the tenant, and another arbitration between the seller and the buyer, giving a different and possibly smaller figure to be paid by the buyer to the seller. This may have to be accepted as part of the terms of the buyer's offer, but, if not, the sale contract may provide that the buyer will pay whatever is awarded to the tenant. A buyer who is prepared to agree to this may insist on the right to conduct the compensation proceedings.

Where the outgoing tenant has the right to remove fixtures, this should be notified to the buyer and the sale particulars should be worded in a way which covers the rights of the existing tenant, preferably in the agreement.

Where the outgoing tenant intends to sell milk quota but the buyer does not wish to acquire this, then, unless the quota can be apportioned onto other land before sale (which will frequently be possible where the seller is not selling all the land in the former tenancy), provision will need to be made for tenancies to purchasers of the quota as with an owner–occupier/seller (see **21.3**).

Further rights, which are discussed in other chapters, could be relevant to a buyer, for example: tax allowances in relation to buildings; rights under building contracts where the tenant has put up a new building recently and defects become evident; and environmental agreements or farm woodland schemes, where the tenant entered into the agreement and, as such, is liable to repay any grants if the buyer does not continue with the scheme. In each of these cases, there will need to be some relationship between the tenant and the buyer for the purposes of protection.

Early entry and holdover will need to be covered. The tenancy agreement will usually give the landlord a right of early entry in the last year, but, if it does not, this will need to be negotiated for the benefit of the buyer and the terms may, of course, depend on the crops which the buyer intends to plant. Holdover will need to be specified by the tenant and agreed with the landlord and covered in the sale contract. Holdover in fields is relatively straightforward, but if the tenant retains holdover in buildings, for example a grain store, then, again, it will be important to make sure that a reimbursement of electricity supplies and other matters such as insurance are covered.

One area of difficulty relates to employees, particularly in relation to the Transfer of Undertakings Regulations discussed at **22.2**. The buyer will usually want to ensure that the tenant dismisses, or makes redundant, employees whom he is not taking on. The seller will have no incentive to do this, and may have very limited information, for example where notice to quit has been served on a hostile tenant. The buyer will usually ask for an indemnity from the seller to cover such an event if he cannot gain co-operation from the tenant.

18.6   DIVIDED TENANCIES

A landlord may wish to sell part of a holding, retaining another part for long-term development, or in the hope that in the future it can be combined with another farm. In some cases the tenant may be prepared to assist, either by giving up the existing tenancy and taking two completely fresh tenancies, or by agreeing to a deed of apportionment of the rent. However, where this is not possible, a single tenancy with a single rent will continue. Following *Jelley v Buckman* [1974] QB 488, it is clear that a single notice must be served, for example to revise the rent or in relation to any other matters affecting the tenancy, on behalf of all landlords. It could be in the interests of one landlord to serve notice, but not in the interests of another, depending on their views as to, for example, future levels of rent or their relationships with the tenant. The sale contract should therefore provide that each party will co-operate with the other in doing anything that is necessary in relation to the tenancy.

Where there is a single rent, it is entirely up to the seller and the buyer to agree between themselves how this money payment is to be divided, and the tenant cannot complain if they split it in a way which he finds unacceptable. However, in so far as rent is payable in respect of part of the holding (and this will be especially relevant if he is given notice to quit part), the tenant is entitled to have the rent formally apportioned.

Where there are two landlords, under s 140 of the Law of Property Act 1925, each is entitled independently to serve a notice to quit on his part. Where no provision has been made for notice to quit part in the tenancy agreement, this may be a method of securing vacant possession. For example, where part of the land is granted planning consent for development, notice to quit can be given on the land having the consent, but it is essential that the boundaries of the separate ownership correspond precisely to the land for which consent is given. It is common for land in old tenancies, which do not have such agreements, to be sold to developers subject to tenancies which can be terminated in this way. In some cases, the tenant has the right to expand the notice so as to quit the whole tenancy, but the owner of the land which is voluntarily given up in this manner will not usually have cause to complain. It should, however, be noted that where improvements have been made, the compensation to the tenant may be based on the value which improvements add to the whole farm. This is made expressly clear by s 24 of the Agricultural Tenancies Act 1995, although the position under the Agricultural Holdings Act 1986, s 74 is different.

18.7   SALE TO SITTING TENANT

A common situation occurs where the best bid available to the landlord is made by the sitting tenant. In principle, this is no different from any other sale, although it will usually be simpler since the tenant will not need to raise as many enquiries as a stranger. The sale agreement should cover any possible claims on either side as under s 83 of the Agricultural Holdings Act 1986 there is an irremovable right for either party to serve notice within two months of the termination of the tenancy, claiming compensation. Normally, compensation is payable by or to the existing landlord, to or by the existing tenant, who, by the time the two-month period expires, will be the same person. However, this may not always be the case, particularly where the sitting tenant sells on.

A sale to a sitting tenant may be part of a deal under which another part of the farm is given up, for example, where farm cottages are released back to the landlord, or by exchange, for example by transferring the freehold of the farmhouse to the tenant in return for giving up all the land.

18.8   SALES WITH NEW LEASES

Sales with new leases arise in two circumstances, but the results are very similar. An existing owner–occupier may sell the freehold, usually to an investor, and take back an FBT for his own benefit, possibly for 20 years. Alternatively, the sale transaction itself may be carried through by way of lease at a premium. In the first case, the buyer will, of course, need to investigate title and be aware of all the long-term issues, even though many of them may not concern him directly provided the lease is running. In the second case, if the new lease is over 21 years he will need to register his title at HM Land Registry and will therefore need to have the freehold title available. In both types of transaction the main issue will be the terms of the new FBT, including many of the issues mentioned above.

One special case of sale by long lease, typically for 250 years, will be as a form of overage where the seller wishes to retain future development value, as described at **26.4**.

18.9   ALTERNATIVES TO TENANCIES

In the years up to 1995, when the Agricultural Holdings Act 1986 constrained the freedom of parties to make arrangements, a great variety of alternative commercial arrangements were developed, including farming partnerships, contract farming and share farming, as well as various forms of occupational licence. Many of these are fully justified as proper commercial arrangements although they do not usually affect buyers and sellers. Many were disguised tenancies and some lapsed into actual tenancies. As such, in some cases a buyer will acquire a farm subject to an arrangement that may be treated as a tenancy, even though it was not originally drafted as one. Where, for example, something claimed to be a partnership agreement or a grazing licence has become a tenancy, it will not contain many of the terms and conditions discussed above and may therefore be a less than satisfactory investment. In such cases a potential dispute with the tenant may arise since the tenant will have claimed the tenancy against the will of the selling landlord in circumstances where he originally entered on the basis of what was intended to be an unprotected arrangement, and this will have to be taken into account by a buyer.

Apart from this, where a farm, which on the face of it is in hand and occupied by the owner, has in fact been run not by him but by a commercial farmer, often successfully for many years with good relationships, the buyer similarly may not wish to be involved in the details of farming and the third party farmer may well be prepared to continue running the farm on much the same basis. The most common situations where this arises are contract farming and farming partnerships. Although share farming arrangements exist, they are rare. In the case of a partnership it may be desirable for tax reasons to keep the partnership in existence and substitute the new landowning partner for the old one. The buyer will therefore need to investigate fully the way the partnership is run and all the financial implications. This applies particularly where the partnership arrangement has been made not simply with the local farmer but with one of the large agri-business organisations, which have a great variety of farming partnerships throughout the country and operate on a very large scale. Normally, however, such organisations will be prepared to cancel the old farming partnership and enter a new one.

Where the farm has been operated on a contract farming basis, it will normally be much simpler to terminate the old contract and make a new one.

The legal relationships in these transactions are well understood, but, unlike tenancies, each must be treated as a separate arrangement, and very often the wishes and experience of the changing parties will, in any event, involve a change of emphasis. For example, the incoming buyer may wish to take a greater or lesser part in the management than the seller, have different views on environmental issues, or be prepared to inject more cash into the farming business.

18.10   LET ESTATES

The above discussion relates largely to the sale of individual farms, but the same issues will apply where the land changing hands is an estate subject to numerous tenancies. The buyer must check the tenancy agreement for each farm, and frequently there will have been many supplemental documents and changes over the years as the boundaries between different farms were adjusted and fields were added and taken out. Normally, the estate will have a single standard form of tenancy agreement, which may include provisions reflecting the special concerns of the owner, for example that there be estate signs at farm gates or special terms on sporting. In particular, a private estate water supply may be provided to different farms on a standard set of terms. Many estates have, in the past, been large enough to run their own maintenance departments and, therefore, the landlord has been able to undertake more in the way of repairs than might be expected of a landlord of an isolated farm. In addition, on many traditional family estates there has been an acceptance that sons could follow fathers whether or not they have a legal right to do so, and this often means that formal succession claims have not been submitted. It may therefore be difficult to ascertain whether or not succession rights apply to a present tenant, particularly where there was a change of tenant between 1976 when the succession rules came in, and 1984 when they were removed for new tenancies.

Where estates are being put on the market it is common for tenants of one or more farms to seek to form a consortium to outbid potential outside buyers. However, where the estate includes vacant land a buyer who can join with estate tenants in a joint bid may be better placed to acquire the land in which he is interested, particularly where the estate is being sold at auction.

Chapter 19

RESIDENTIAL TENANCIES

19.1 INTRODUCTION

Most estates and some farms will include residential properties let separately from farms or businesses. The legal rules relating to dwellings are the same whether the lease comprises a great mansion, a surplus farmhouse, houses in an estate village or isolated farmworkers' cottages. Houses with values above a certain limit cannot be Rent Act tenancies or assured tenancies and the basis on which the price is calculated under the Leasehold Reform Act 1967 can vary according to the value. However, apart from such limited exceptions, the rules distinguishing different types of tenancy depend not so much on size or value, as on time, namely the length of the lease and the date on which it was granted.

Discussions of residential tenancies usually include much of the law relating to flats, which are rare in the countryside. It is of course possible that a mansion house has been converted into several dwellings, or in a smaller house the first floor is let separately from the ground floor. However, the law relating to flats, including the rules relating to enfranchisement and rights of first refusal if the landlord wishes to sell, are more appropriate to a treatment of urban property. As such, although buyers and sellers of rural property need to be aware of those rules in rare instances, they are not common.

19.2 DATE OF GRANT

A house or part of a house let as a separate dwelling before February 1989 will, provided certain basic conditions are satisfied, be subject to the provisions of the Rent Act 1977, which governs the right of a tenant to security and the way in which the rent is determined. Where a qualifying worker in agriculture or forestry first went into occupation of a dwelling before that date, his rights will be protected under the Rent (Agriculture) Act 1976. In broad terms, a protected tenant or occupier under the Rent Act 1977 or the Rent (Agriculture) Act 1976 is entitled to lifetime security, and there will normally be one succession to a widow or other member of the family after his death. This security lasts as long as the premises are used as a residence (not necessarily sole or main residence) and the landlord's grounds for possession are extremely limited, largely being restricted to cases where the tenant has failed to pay the rent, broken the terms of the tenancy, or the premises are overcrowded or have been allowed to run down. The landlord can usually obtain possession if he provides suitable alternative accommodation and, if he does so, broadly similar protection will apply to the new accommodation even though the tenancy may have been granted after 1989, although in some cases it may be sufficient to grant an assured tenancy.

Where the tenancy was granted after February 1989 (or the farm or forestry worker took occupation after that date) the rights of the tenant will be governed by the Housing Act 1988 and the tenant will be an assured tenant (or assured agricultural occupier). Under an assured tenancy, a landlord has wider rights of possession, including for purposes of redevelopment, and succession rights are more restricted.

The service of various notices can affect the degree of security to which a tenant is entitled. Under the Rent Act 1977, it was possible to serve certain notices before the tenant went into occupation, allowing a landlord to recover possession. Most of these are not directly applicable to cases where the landlord is buying the interest, although it should be noted that under case 16 of Sch 15 to the Rent Act 1977, where a cottage was previously occupied by an agricultural employee and a notice to that effect was served on the tenant, the landlord can recover possession for the purpose of housing another farmworker. Having regard to the diminishing numbers of farmworkers in modern conditions this is of little practical importance. However, many such notices were served on rural estates in the past, and if a former farmworker claims a Rent (Agriculture) Act 1976 tenancy or an assured agricultural occupancy and a new employee is required to replace him, it may be easier to recover possession of another cottage on which a case 16 notice was served.

In the case of assured tenancies granted between February 1989 and 24 September 1996, provided a notice was served on the tenant that it was to be an assured shorthold tenancy, the tenant has no more security than that granted by the terms of the tenancy or lease. Since September 1996, all tenancies (falling within the other qualifying rules) which are assured tenancies will automatically be shortholds without the need to serve a notice, unless either a notice was served on the tenant stating that it was to be an assured tenancy (with lifetime protection rights) or was incorporated in the tenancy agreement. An exception applies to farm and agricultural employees where, if they are to occupy as shorthold tenants, a notice must be served on them to that effect before they go into occupation. In addition, they must pay a rent of at least £250 a year, which is unusual for such employees. Subject to that they will still enjoy lifetime protection.

Leasehold Reform Act 1967 rights are restricted in the case of certain houses forming parts of landed estates in rural areas. The Housing Act 1996 extended the operation of leasehold enfranchisement, which had previously been restricted to any lease over 21 years at a low rent (as defined), to apply to a lease over 35 years, whatever the rent might be. However, an exception was made under what is now s 1AA(3) of the Leasehold Reform Act 1967 for leases granted before the Act came into force (September 1996) of a house which belonged to a country estate in certain designated areas (which, in practice, comprise most rural areas of England and Wales) even where the lease was over 35 years. Such cases will be excluded from the new rules. Clearly, however, if the lease is at a low rent it will still qualify under the original 1967 rules.

19.3   LEASES UP TO SEVEN YEARS

Section 11 of the Landlord and Tenant Act 1985 provides that in a lease not exceeding seven years the landlord is responsible for main external repairs and structural repairs as well as certain basic services such as drainage, water and electricity. A breach of these obligations is not a criminal offence, although it will give rise to civil liability. Separately, a landlord may be liable in some cases for public nuisance where a house is not fit for human habitation, provided the local authority takes certain enforcement steps. The landlord under a lease not exceeding seven years is also bound to keep a gas supply in good repair under the Gas Safety (Installation and Use) Regulations 1994, SI 1994/1886, breach of which is a criminal offence. For these purposes, a lease will be treated as less than seven years if the landlord has the right to break it earlier, and treated as more than seven years if the tenant is unilaterally capable of extending it, or if it follows an earlier tenancy which was itself outside the scope of these rules.

The parties cannot dispense with these obligations by agreement, but it is possible to obtain a court order excluding the repairing obligations under the Landlord and Tenant Act 1985, although this will usually be permitted only on joint application. The liability for repairs extends to the landlord for the time being, although there may be a continuing liability even after change of landlord under the Landlord and Tenant (Covenants) Act 1995 on the original landlord and, hence, the seller. The landlord is normally liable only if the tenant has drawn his attention to the defect, but if the premises form part of a larger building (for example, a cottage in a terrace) and another part of the building is out of repair, the landlord may be liable even if he was not notified. Thus, it is prudent for a buyer to have a survey carried out of any occupied residences where the leases are less than seven years.

19.4   LEASES OVER THREE YEARS

Under ss 52 and 54 of the Law of Property Act 1925, leases over three years have to be granted by deed, with all the appropriate formalities. This applies not only to residential lettings but to all other leases, including farm business tenancies and business tenancies. In most circumstances, these formalities are generally irrelevant since even an informal arrangement can be enforced between a continuing landlord and tenant. However, where the landlord's interest changes hands such formalities can be very important. Failure to comply with the formalities does not mean that the arrangement is totally void. First, if the tenant goes into possession and pays rent on a regular basis, for example quarterly, a quarterly tenancy will be created. Secondly, the arrangement may be effective to create a contract for the grant of a lease which could be enforced by the tenant against the original landlord who was a party to the contract, provided the contract itself complies with the provisions of the Law of Property (Miscellaneous Provisions) Act 1989. Thirdly, the tenancy may create an equitable lease under the rule in *Walsh v Lonsdale* (1882) 21 ChD 9, which provides that, where what would otherwise be a valid lease is agreed on but does not comply with the formal rules needed to create a legal estate, it may still be enforced under the equitable jurisdiction of the court. However, the second and third arguments take effect only in equity and, as a result, are not enforceable against a bona fide purchaser of the legal estate for money or money's worth. If, therefore, a seller has entered into an informal arrangement (even if it is recorded in writing but not by deed) for a lease to a residential tenant for, say, 10 years, this occurred after September 1996, the tenant moved into possession and pays rent quarterly and, assuming that the written document is sufficient, takes no further steps, and the landlord then sells, the position of the tenant may be weak. Even though the buyer actually knows about the presence of the tenant and may even have accepted rent after the purchase was completed, if the tenant has not registered a land charge against his original landlord's title, if unregistered, or a notice on the register if it was registered, the buyer is not bound by the arrangement. The tenancy will be treated as a quarterly tenancy and the buyer will be entitled to give to the tenant one-quarter's notice to quit. The tenant may, of course, have contractual rights for damages against the original landlord, but that will not be sufficient to allow him to remain in possession.

19.5   WEEKLY TENANCIES

If the tenant of a residence pays rent weekly, the landlord is obliged to provide a rent book under s 4 of the Landlord and Tenant Act 1985.

19.6 LONG LEASES

If the lease was originally granted for over 21 years at a low rent and the tenant uses the property as his sole or main residence, the tenant will be entitled after three years to acquire the freehold. Different rules apply for the purposes of calculation of the price, depending on various factors. If the lease was for over 35 years then, subject to the exception for houses granted before 1996 out of rural estates (discussed above), the tenant is entitled to enfranchise irrespective of the amount of the rent. In a lease granted for over 40 years in consideration of the tenant making improvements, which contains a covenant against assignment without the landlord's consent, the requirement for consent is replaced, for assignments previous to the last seven years, by an obligation to notify the landlord after assignment.

If the lease was granted for more than 300 years at a rent of less than £1 and there is no forfeiture clause, the tenant is entitled to enlarge the lease into a freehold. A number of such leases werer granted in the sixteenth and seventeenth centuries, many of which are still running. The interest of the landlords under such leases is normally of no value, but buyers may find that the title to part of an estate consists of such a lease. Unfortunately, in the absence of a written document (which may have been lost centuries ago), it may not be known whether or not there was a forfeiture clause and, therefore, whether the lease was eligible for enlargement.

19.7 BLOCKS OF FLATS

As mentioned above, it is not normally appropriate to discuss the details of law relating to flats in relation to rural estates. It should, however, be noted that if a house is divided into more than one unit the tenants may, in certain circumstances, have right of first refusal. Furthermore, under the Landlord and Tenant Act 1987, it may be a criminal offence to sell the freehold over the heads of the tenants without giving them an opportunity, in accordance with the Act, to acquire the landlord's interest. Frequently, country estates include a considerable number of houses which have been large enough to convert, perhaps under a sub-underlease of which the freeholder may have no direct knowledge, and it will therefore be essential to check every dwelling on the estate which is being sold to ensure that the Act does not apply. Under the Leasehold Reform Housing and Urban Development Act 1983, some tenants have a right either to extend their individual leases or collectively to acquire the freehold.

19.8   NOTICES

On a change of landlord, it is necessary under s 3 of the Landlord and Tenant Act 1985 to serve notice on the tenant. Under ss 46 and 47 of the Landlord and Tenant Act 1987, rent cannot be recovered lawfully from a tenant unless a notice has been served giving the name of the landlord and an address for service in the UK. In addition, if a service charge is payable (eg a contribution to cost of maintenance of a common track or water pipe) that cannot be recovered unless a similar notice is served. These latter provisions do not apply to business tenancies under the Landlord and Tenant Act 1954, but they do apply to agricultural holdings and farm business tenancies. In practice, a new landlord will normally wish to serve formal notice on all tenants as soon as possible, notifying them of his purchase and requiring them to pay rent to him. In certain cases, however, where the management will continue in the hands of the same agents and where the landlord may not wish his acquisition to be known, there may be a tendency to secrecy. However, this does affect a landlord's right to claim money from his tenants.

19.9   NATURE OF TENANT

Many of the rules set out above apply irrespective of the nature of the tenant. However, certain provisions apply only where the tenant (or at least one of the tenants, if there is more than one) is an individual. This applies particularly to rights under Rent Act 1977 tenancies where the premises must be a residence (not necessarily the only one) of the tenant, and to rights under assured tenancies and under the Leasehold Reform Act 1967, where the residence must be the sole or main residence of at least one of the tenants. Clearly, a company cannot be resident in the above sense, and this explains the reason behind many company lets in the past, although since the introduction of assured shorthold tenancies such lets have become less common.

Similarly, where premises are let to one person for occupation by another (such as an employee), rights to protection do not normally attach either to the tenant (who is not resident) or to the occupier (who is not the tenant). However, in the case of Rent (Agriculture) Act 1976 tenancies and assured agricultural occupancies, if an arrangement exists between the landlord and some other person for accommodating the employee, the occupier will be entitled to protection. This is qualified by the fact that the employee must be employed in agriculture, not necessarily employed by his landlord, even though, in practice, that is the most common situation.

Problems may arise where tenants divorce or separate. The divorce court has a wide jurisdiction to make a property adjustment order as between husband and wife, whether the tenancy was granted to them jointly or to only one of them.

The landlord is normally entitled to make representations, but will not usually be consulted over the application to the divorce court for a property adjustment order, and many divorce courts do not insist on the landlord being notified of any application.

In most cases, where a tenant is protected his spouse has a similar right to protection after his death. The buyer of an estate subject to residential occupation may therefore discover that a tenant who was married to the tenant to whom the tenancy was granted, perhaps many years later, may be entitled to remain in occupation either following her spouse's death or on divorce, and this must be taken into account, in terms of that tenant's right to protection.

19.10   PENSIONERS AND LICENSEES

As well as current employees, rights may also be enjoyed by previous employees. In *Binions v Evans* [1972] Ch 359, the occupier of a cottage had worked for her employer on an estate for many years and, on retirement, was told that she could remain in occupation for the rest of her life. The estate was subsequently sold, and the buyer claimed to evict her on the basis that she merely had a licence to remain. The court held she was entitled to protection and, although the basis of the decision is not entirely clear, it is probable that the decision was reached on the basis of a trust under the Settled Land Act 1925, which conferred on the occupier lifetime occupation rights and the right to have the freehold transferred to her. However, following the Trusts of Land and Appointment of Trustees Act 1996, the decision would not now extend to future arrangements.

When employees are taken on, they may be informed that they can expect to have accommodation for the rest of their lives. Where this commitment can be treated as part of the terms of employment, it was held, in *Ivory v Palmer* [1975] ICR 340, that even though the occupier cannot insist on actually remaining in the cottage for his life (unlike a normal agricultural employee), he is entitled to damages for breach of contract of employment. Furthermore, where a buyer is treated as taking over the contract of employment under the Transfer of Undertakings (Protection of Employment) Regulations 1981, SI 1981/1794 (discussed at **22.2**) this claim may form part of the head of damages under a claim for unfair dismissal.

Chapter 20

BUSINESS AND OTHER LEASES AND LICENCES

20.1 INTRODUCTION

Although agricultural and residential tenancies are the most significant forms of arrangement between owners and occupiers on farms and estates, there are a variety of other arrangements which may confer more or less protection on the occupier and which may remain in force following a change of ownership of the land. Of these, the most important are business tenancies within the Landlord and Tenant Acts 1927 and 1954. In order to attract protection, there must be a tenancy and the premises must be used either for the business of the occupier or for an activity carried on by a group of persons.

20.2 LICENCES

Not all arrangements for occupation of land give rise to a tenancy, and many will merely be licences. A lease or tenancy is a right of property; it creates a legal estate in the land which can be specifically enforced by the tenant not just against the landlord but against any other person. A tenancy may last for a given period of time or it may be periodic and, as such, brought to an end on a relatively short notice to quit. However, a tenancy will exist for a defined term, except for the unusual case of a tenancy at will. A licence, by contrast, is primarily a personal arrangement. It is personal to the occupier, cannot be transferred to anyone else and will not usually be enforceable if the person who has granted the licence sells his interest. There are exceptions where, for example, a licence is 'coupled with a grant', such as where the licensee has spent money on the land, in which case the licence may be specifically enforceable.

The principal test laid down in the House of Lords' decision in *Street v Mountford* [1985] AC 809 provides that where there is an arrangement for exclusive possession of land for a defined or periodic term in return for the payment of a rent, that will create a tenancy unless there are special reasons (such as an arrangement arising out of a family relationship or the terms of an employment) to interpret the arrangement as a licence. Where these facts are absent, a licence, not a tenancy will exist, although a tenancy may be granted for a single premium instead of a regular rent, and there can be a degree of sharing of occupation where certain rights are reserved to the landlord. The status of the arrangement is a matter of law and although the parties may choose to put a label of 'lease' or 'licence' on the arrangement, that is not conclusive. However, the courts will have some regard to the parties' intentions when the arrangement was entered into.

An agricultural example relates to grazing arrangements. If one person allows another to put animals into a field in return for payment, that could create a grazing tenancy or a grazing licence. The distinction can be important, for example on transfer of milk quota, where a tenancy is essential. If the arrangement creates a tenancy, the tenant has the right to possession, so that, for example, if a field is invaded by trespassers looking for a place to camp, the tenant has to take proceedings to evict them. Where a tenancy exists, the tenant has all the rights of an owner except those rights specifically reserved to the landlord. If there is merely a licence, the occupier simply has permission to be there for the specific purpose of the arrangement. This distinction may be important to buyers, who, for example, have other plans for the land or, indeed, need to occupy it for tax purposes.

Where a tenant allows another person to use a field or other property and the terms of the tenancy prohibit sub-letting but do not prohibit sharing occupation, the nature of the permission may be relevant to whether the landlord can determine the tenancy for breach.

20.3   BUSINESS TENANCIES

Where a tenancy exists and where the land is occupied either by a tenant carrying on a business or by a body of persons carrying on an activity (which does not need to be a business), the tenant is protected under the Landlord and Tenant Act 1954, unless the tenancy has been excluded by a court order made before the tenancy was granted. This means that, subject to the landlord's right to recover possession on certain limited grounds (for example redevelopment or, in some cases, for his own business occupation, although this does not apply to recent purchases), the tenant has the right to remain in occupation indefinitely, provided a proper rent is paid. The Act lays down a detailed procedure for protecting the tenant's interests, and a buyer will not usually be able to recover possession for his own purposes. If the arrangement does not amount to a tenancy, or if it is an unprotected tenancy, then, subject to any specific agreement, the buyer will be able to recover possession in due course.

The Act is primarily aimed at urban conditions such as shops, offices and factories and has relatively little application to rural land, although the transaction may include, for example, a village shop, pub or a craft workshop in a converted barn.

It may be difficult to determine precisely whether a protected tenancy exists. If a farmer has allowed someone to operate a caravan park and the operator has, in turn, allowed people to buy caravans and live there, the caravan operator may be protected as a tenant if he is providing sufficient services to show that he is clearly in occupation. However, it is possible in those circumstances for the occupiers of the caravans or, on similar facts, chalets, themselves to be tenants protected under the Rent Act 1977 or the Housing Act 1988 (*Elitestone Ltd v Morris* [1997] 2 All ER 513). In *Graysim Holdings Ltd v P & O Property Holdings Ltd* [1995] 4 All ER 831, the plaintiff operated a market under the terms of a tenancy and granted to stallholders rights to run their stalls within the market. The House of Lords held that the stallholders had business tenancy protection but, even though the plaintiff provided various services for the market as a whole, the plaintiff did not have such protection. On the same basis, if land is let out to a person who runs a car boot sale or a weekly market and he, in turn, sublets plots to individual stallholders, it will be a question of fact whether a business tenancy protection applies to the operator or to the stallholders.

The fact that occupation may be intermittent is no argument against the existence of a tenancy. For example, a tenancy which applies only on Wednesday afternoons in alternate weeks, may be a perfectly valid legal lease.

20.3.1 Clubs and voluntary groups

Business tenancy protection can also apply to clubs and similar voluntary groups. The leading case is *Addiscombe Garden Estates v Crabbe* [1958] 1 QB 513. In that case, a tennis club was held entitled to business tenancy protection even though it was an amenity club for its members. The same principles would apply to a football or cricket ground. If, for example, a local football club had always been entitled to use a particular field on Easter Monday, and made a payment of £1 for the privilege, that might create a legally binding commitment. Consequently, if a buyer were planning to plough the field so that it was unsuitable for playing football, he may be prevented from doing so even though the field is used only one afternoon a year.

A seller who claims to sell land with vacant possession will be liable to the buyer for any loss suffered if it transpires that there exists some right which affects the land.

20.4 DIVERSIFICATION

A farmer who undertakes diversified activities, as discussed in Chapter 23, will usually do so through the mechanism of a tenancy. Where the tenancy is granted to an unconnected third party, this will be a clear business arrangement, clear to both buyer and seller, and the land will be sold subject to that arrangement. Where the farmer carries out the diversification himself, or through a member of the family, the position may be less clear-cut. In particular, if he sets up his own company, for example, to run a farm shop or to operate a golf course, he may grant the company a tenancy. In such circumstances, it will usually be desirable, for accounting or tax purposes, to have a rent paid, which will create a protected business tenancy. Provided the parties are aware of the position it will be relatively easy to bring the tenancy to an end on the sale. However, the fact that the shareholders and directors of the company are the same people who sell the freehold of the farm does not necessarily mean that the rights of the company itself are ended by the sale; as such, the seller will need to make sure that the appropriate steps are taken to deal, for example, with accounting and tax issues on termination of the tenancy.

20.5   MINERAL AND SPORTING TENANCIES

Mineral and sporting were considered in Chapters 12 and 14. Minerals will normally be extracted under the terms of a lease. Although the mineral operator is carrying on a business, mineral leases are expressly excluded from protection under the Landlord and Tenant Act 1954 and, as such, come to an end when the contractual arrangement ends. In the light of planning requirements now being imposed on environmental grounds, many mineral operators will need to have licences to have access to the land after extraction and infill has been completed, in order to ensure that the terms of any waste management licence are complied with. It will be a question of the terms of the licence in each case whether they are binding on a purchaser. It is likely that the law would view such licences as being coupled with a grant. This is because the mineral operator has a legal interest in making sure that the site restoration conditions are complied with, otherwise it may have liabilities under the Environmental Protection Act 1990 as a person having caused pollution. It is therefore probable that these licences will be enforced against a buyer provided they are protected by entries on the Register of Title or the Land Charges Register.

Sporting leases relate largely to incorporeal hereditaments (unless they also include, for example, a gamekeeper's cottage). Provided the arrangement has been created by a valid lease by deed, it will be binding on a buyer of the freehold, but provided it does not include any land, the tenant will not have security under the Landord and Tenant Act 1954 even if he runs the shoot as a business.

20.6   AMENITY ARRANGEMENTS

There are a large and growing number of arrangements for access to land by special interest groups. These include, for example, the activities of hang-gliding groups, occasional access by motorcycle scrambling organis- ations, camping by youth groups and village fêtes, among others. Such arrangements usually exist under the terms of a brief licence, which will be granted every year. As such, they will not generally be binding on a buyer who will, as a matter of law, be free to decide whether or not to grant them afresh. In practice, access arrangements are made with local people who have a long-established interest in their regular activities. If a new owner offends local feelings by refusing permission for such activities to continue, he may meet fierce opposition in the community. This non-legal sanction can often be far more powerful than any legal rights.

20.7   PUBLIC UTILITIES

The arrangements for pipes, sewers and similar matters have been considered in Chapter 10. Electricity pylons will generally be governed by a wayleave or easement, but telecommunications towers, for example, will more often be governed by a lease. Some of the documents produced by telecommunications operators are drawn in the form of licences for a fixed period of time, although as a matter of law they probably take effect as business tenancies. A buyer must check the terms of such arrangements carefully. In view of the sensitivity of telecommunications equipment, the lease may contain a restriction, for example, on using electrical equipment elsewhere on the farm which might interfere with the activities on the premises and which could, for example, restrict the farmer's use of certain types of vehicle or satellite equipment.

Similarly, electricity companies have numerous sub-stations across the countryside, usually comprising an area of only a few square yards, where the rent is minimal. As such, these may be easily overlooked, and a buyer may be unaware that he is acquiring the freehold subject to such a tenancy, possibly assuming that the sub-station is constructed on highway land. However, all the normal rules between landlord and tenant will apply.

As mentioned at **10.6**, some pipelines are laid under the terms of a lease where they cannot be in the form of an easement. Such a lease will be a business tenancy if the undertaker is in occupation.

Public utilities, as with easements and wayleaves, will normally have compulsory powers to acquire land for their plant usually under a tenancy agreement, although, if terms cannot be agreed, possibly under a freehold.

20.8   ALLOTMENTS

In the period after the First World War, many areas of land, both on the edges of towns and in villages, were set aside for allotment holdings for people to grow crops. Many were managed by local authorities and, in some cases, an authority acquired the freehold of the land in order to create allotments. In other cases, however, the freehold was retained by the local estate, which either let the land on a long lease to the local authority, which, in turn sub-let to allotment holders, or dealt directly with the allotment holders themselves. Allotment gardens are often now in areas which are suitable for building.

In general, allotment holders do not have security. If the allotment is being used for the purpose of a trade or business in agriculture (for example if the allotment holder grows vegetables to sell in the local market), this is capable of being an agricultural holding or farm business tenancy because there is no minimum size for land to comprise such a holding or tenancy. Usually, however, flowers and vegetables grown will be for the personal consumption of the allotment holder. The Allotment Acts 1922, 1928 and 1950 confer certain limited protection, chiefly relating to the dates on which a notice to quit can expire. The Acts do not confer any long-term protection. A buyer who has plans to recover possession of an allotment will again, however, need to consider non-legal issues. An active group of allotment holders may, for example, have a considerable local voice and if their allotments are threatened they may write to the local press, contact their MP and be capable of causing considerable inconvenience. Where a buyer is considering recovering possession of an allotment, it is usually sensible to discuss the matter with the allotments committee first and, perhaps, provide an alternative site.

Chapter 21

GRANTS AND SUBSIDIES

21.1 INTRODUCTION

Commercial farming cannot be carried on without assistance from government sources, either directly from the UK, usually through the Ministry of Agriculture, Fisheries and Food (MAFF), or from the European Union. A variety of payments are available, which are under constant review in line with changes in policy, new political pressures and economic and fiscal forces. The approaches of the UK Government and the European Union are not the same and, increasingly, there is also pressure from world sources, particularly the World Trade Organisation (WTO) and environmental treaties. The position is made no easier by the inconsistency of many of the policies. On the one hand, there is pressure for more efficient farming with greater production at lower cost, which leads to the amalgamation of small farms into big ones, and small fields into larger ones, and the application of fertilisers and pesticides. Large farms tend to be operated with advanced, modern machinery, which reduces the need for numbers of partly-trained agricultural labourers and places more emphasis on a small number of highly trained operators. Against this, is the policy to retain strong rural communities with large numbers of small farms, and to keep up high levels of agricultural employment among the rural poor and uneducated. There is also a growing move for conservation, the retention of hedges, coppices and ponds, and opposition to deep ploughing and the pollution of watercourses by the run-off from nitrates. One illustration is the recent replacement of grants for grubbing out hedges by grants for planting new ones.

As a consequence, the system of grants and subsidies and the legal structure is changing fast. It is likely that a new system will be brought into force throughout the European Union in, or shortly after, the year 2000, but this may subsequently have to be modified as a result of obligations to the World Trade Organisation. What follows, therefore, is an outline of the main features at the date of writing, and it will be essential for farmers and landlords to check the position at the time of purchase. As these payments are crucial to the financial viability of an economic farm, the matter needs to be investigated with care.

21.2 COMMON AGRICULTURAL POLICY

Before the UK joined the Common Market in 1971, assistance to agriculture was largely through a system of subsidies to farmers designed to keep food prices low in the interests of consumers. That was replaced by the Common Agricultural Policy (CAP), already developed on the Continent, which encouraged the viability of small farms by the system of intervention. The basis of this was that farmers were normally expected to sell their produce on the market, at the so-called 'world price'. However, the European Community established a safety net of a minimum price at which farmers could be guaranteed to sell their produce into intervention funded by the European Economic Community. The intervention price for each agricultural product was fixed by agriculture ministers every year. In practice, it tended to be above the world price, and as a result farmers were able to produce what they wished, with a guaranteed market and at a price that would give them a proper return whether or not produce could be resold. The result was the building-up of large surpluses, the so-called 'grain and butter mountains' and 'wine and milk lakes'. The process was also encouraged by the development of sprays and fertilisers which led to dramatic increases in production.

21.3 MILK QUOTA

21.3.1 In general

In 1984, the European Community modified this system in relation to dairy produce by introducing milk quotas. A system already existed which compelled dairy farmers to sell their milk to specified companies (with limited exceptions for door-to-door sales subject to close regulation). A limit was put on the total milk production in the Community, and the total number of litres was divided up among the Member States. Each State, in turn, divided this figure up, and in the UK a quota of a given number of litres was allocated to each dairy producer. If a dairy farmer produces more milk than he has quota for in any given quota year (ending on 1 April), and if the national production is above the national quota, he is subject to a levy which operates as a fine. Quota therefore has a considerable value because the more quota a farmer has, the more he is able to produce.

Quota is attached to land, and, throughout the European Union, remains with the land to which it relates. However, the UK has developed a highly sophisticated market in quota, based on a special interpretation of Council Regulations 3950/92 and 536/93, which allow quota to be sold freely only on the basis it is being managed.

The total area of a producer's land (whether owned or tenanted) used for milk production is known as his 'Euroholding', which may be the same in area as the land in a single freehold ownership or a single tenancy. The area of land may be smaller if part of that land is used for arable production, or may be larger if a single registered producer uses land in several ownerships for dairy purposes, for example his own freehold as well as various tenanted pieces of land and, possibly, land occupied on other terms. The land to be taken into account has been widely interpreted by the courts (*Puncknowle Farms Ltd v Kane* [1985] 3 All ER 790) and includes land actually occupied by the milk-producing herd, as well as land used by young stock, land on which fodder crops are grown and buildings such as dairies. Under European law, the test is *occupation*, not the nature of the *interest* in land. If the producer gives up occupation of part of his Euroholding (by surrendering or assigning the tenancy or the land) then, unless steps are taken to the contrary, there will be a transfer of all or part of his milk quota to the new occupier of the land, and this is determined according to the areas used for milk production over the preceding five years under the Dairy Produce Quota Regulations 1989, SI 1989/380.

21.3.2   Quota and sales of land

Quota may affect sales in various ways.

(a)   Where the whole of the Euroholding comprises the seller's freehold land and he is selling all of it to one buyer who wishes to take on the quota: the quota will automatically pass with the land.

(b)   Where the seller is selling only part of his freehold land, he may wish to divide the quota in proportion to the areas used for production: in practice, it would normally be easier for the parties to agree a division than to rest on the terms of the Regulations.

(c)   Where the seller is selling only part of his Euroholding and is either keeping all the quota or is including all the quota in the sale: the parties will likewise have to agree this.

(d)   Where the seller is a landlord whose tenant was a dairy producer and the tenancy comes to an end at the time of the sale: in these circumstances, if the tenant's entire Euroholding comprised the tenanted land and the buyer wishes to take on all the quota, this will again pass over with the land, although the tenant may be entitled to compensation from the seller under the Agriculture Act 1986, s 15 and Sch 1.

(e)   In the same circumstances as above, but where the tenant occupied other land, whether rented from the same or another landlord, or owned by the tenant: the quota will have to be divided. Sometimes it is also agreed that instead of the tenant being paid money compensation for his share of the value of the quota, part of the quota itself will be transferred to his other land.

(f)   Where the seller is a landlord and the tenancy remains in force, and the tenant stays in occupation: the rights of the tenant will not be affected but the buyer will, of course, need to know what quota will attach to the land (even though the tenant is the registered producer) as this affects the value of the land when he gets vacant possession. He will also need to know what compensation rights the tenant may have.

(g) Where the sale is of bare land without quota because either the buyer does not want it (eg, he is using the land for horses), is not prepared to pay for it, or has his own quota (possibly with a different butterfat content) on other land which he is proposing to import to the land being bought: the quota will need to be disposed of, and if there is no other land to which it can be transferred the seller will have to sell it by granting a tenancy as mentioned below.

21.3.3   Sales of quota apart from land

Nominally milk quota remains attached to land and the method of sale of quota apart from land is that the farmer in occupation (whether as owner, occupier or tenant) of land to which quota is attached agrees with the buyer that the buyer will take a tenancy of at least 10 months of part of his farm. Both parties can then agree an apportionment of the quota to the let land at a rate of no more than 20,000 litres per hectare. The land must not be used by the buyer of the quota for milk production, and the normal practice is for the buyer to engage the seller to manage the land on his behalf, typically for grass keep, by paying a management fee equal to the amount of the rent which the seller charges the buyer under the tenancy.

If the quota is sold to one person and the land to another, the buyer of the land will become the landlord, manage the land and, of course, need to check that the terms of the tenancy and the management agreement are acceptable.

At the end of the 10 months, the buyer of the quota can then apportion all the quota over to his own holding which may be hundreds of miles away. Where a former dairy farm is sold but the buyer of the land does not wish to acquire the milk quota, it is normal practice for such tenancies to run for 10 months after completion of the sale of the land. Buyers of former dairy land no longer used for milk production will need to take this into account since their ability to use the area allocated to the sale of quota will be restricted.

21.3.4   Other points on quota

Quota is registered in the name of the producer, but remains attached to land and belongs to the landowner. Where an agricultural tenant was in dairy production before the introduction of quota in 1984, he will have had quota allocated to him. If he gives up the farm, the quota will pass either to his landlord or to the new tenant, but the old tenant will be entitled to compensation under s 15 of and Sch 1 to the Agriculture Act 1986. In broad terms, the value of the quota is divided between landlord and tenant according to the formula laid down in the Act, and the tenant is entitled to compensation.

Although quota can be transferred permanently only by way of a formal sale accompanied by a tenancy, it is possible to lease out quota in any given quota year, and if a farm changes hands during the course of that year, although there may be quota attached to the land, it may not be available for the buyer if the owner or tenant has leased it out. A buyer also needs to check whether any quota is 'clean', ie unused, if he acquires during the quota year. In the case of any quota, the buyer also needs to check that the butterfat content meets his needs. This will depend on the type of product (such as drinking milk, yoghurt or ice cream) to be produced from the milk.

Where quota is attached to an area of land, and only part of the land changes hands, the quota must be apportioned in accordance with the areas used for milk production. Such transactions may occur where a farmer sells part of his own land, but usually it is because a dairy farmer has land held from a number of different landlords and one of the tenancies comes to an end. 'Land' is interpreted widely to include not just grazing land and the land on which the dairy parlour is situated, but any land used, for example, for followers, young stock or forage crops. If all parties affected by the transfer, including landlords, mortgagees and trustees, as well as occupiers, all agree on an apportionment within one month of the change of occupation then notice can be given to the Intervention Board of an agreed apportionment, and that is binding. However, if this is not agreed, the matter must be referred to arbitration and the arbitrator apportions the quota by reference to the areas used for milk production over the last five years. This could present a problem where quota is initially attached to one area of land but, because of the pattern of the dairy business, it is subsequently 'massaged' onto another area, for example from tenanted land to owner–occupied land. As such, a buyer who is purchasing land occupied by a farm tenant who also occupies other land, should investigate what quota is attached to the land being purchased.

21.4   INTEGRATED ACCOUNTING AND CONTROL SYSTEM (IACS)

Production of cereal crops, beef cattle and sheep come under a system of control which was introduced in 1992. Unlike milk, there is no restriction on sales of these products, but the intervention price (and the market price) remain low, so that it is not economically possible to produce them without a subsidy. The subsidy is paid out of EU funds to farmers who satisfy certain conditions. In the case of cereals, the land originally had to be in cereal production when the controls were introduced, and must have remained so since then, either in production or set-aside although these rules have since been relaxed. Originally, a relationship existed between land taken out of production and land left fallow, although that relationship has been varied greatly from year to year. At one stage, compulsory set-aside virtually ceased, although voluntary set-aside remained. However, depending on the level of production and international trade, even compulsory set-aside may resume its importance. The precise rules for set-aside are detailed and arrangements will depend on particular circumstances. Special rules apply to small producers. It is essential that a buyer is aware of which land qualifies for arable area payments (including, where applicable, set-aside payments), by examining the IACS form, which must be submitted by every farmer claiming such payments before May in every year. In broad terms, payments are made to the farmer responsible for planting the crop. Since payments are made in cash, normally in October, it is up to the parties to any transaction to agree to whom that money must be paid. MAFF will accept directions for payment to a person who has not submitted the IACS form or planted the crop if that has been agreed between the parties.

The IACS form also includes details relating to beef suckler premium, beef premium and sheep premium. In broad terms, these are subsidies paid in respect of every animal qualifying under certain rules and in respect of which the producing farmer has quota. These quotas are not, as such, attached to land and can be bought and sold freely. However, if they are sold separately from an accompanying transaction involving the transfer of land there will be a 'siphon' of 15 per cent of the quota to the National Reserve, which is then allocated to other producers. It can therefore be to the advantage of both buyer and seller to sell quota with land where this suits their requirements.

21.5   ENVIRONMENTAL AND WOODLAND GRANTS

Under the Agriculture Act 1986, MAFF has power to make grants for various types of environmentally desirable practices, which fall, broadly, into two classes. The first is environmentally sensitive areas where payments are made to farmers for farming in a way that is less than the most economically productive, in order to preserve particular habitats or types of landscape. Although such agreements vary according to different requirements and rules, in general they are made for a period of 20 years (see **12.3**, **13.3** and **17.5**). If, during that period, the land ceases to be managed in accordance with the terms of the agreement, the annual payment is stopped and all payments previously made under the scheme become repayable. Because the agreement is between MAFF (or sometimes another body such as a national park authority) and the farmer who originally entered into the scheme (whether owner, tenant, or otherwise) the farmer is responsible for any repayment. If, therefore, the farmer sells or gives up the land he will need to ensure that his successor will either take on the obligations (usually by cancelling the existing agreement and making a new one) or be able to meet the demand for any repayment if he fails to meet those obligations. The buyer may promise to meet the repayment, but the seller will need to consider how far he can safely rely on the promise if the terms are broken. If the buyer has borrowed heavily on mortgage to finance the purchase, he may not have sufficient funds to meet the liability if it arises. It is therefore common practice for the seller to request a mortgage to support an indemnity, but this is normally resisted by buyers. The decision will largely depend on the amount at stake and the degree of risk as perceived by the seller.

The second class, to which similar arrangements apply, is the planting of trees under the Farm Woodland Scheme and various other woodlands arrangements. These largely replaced the previous system of forestry dedication agreements (see Chapter 13) which, in any event, are not now being renewed with new owners. Arrangements normally run for 20 years and the grants which provide for original planting and subsequent maintenance will be repayable if the woodland ceases to be so maintained.

Chapter 22

THE FARMING BUSINESS

22.1   INTRODUCTION

Most sales of farms and estates comprise the transfer of land and, traditionally, the buyer has (subject to existing rights of tenants and others) been free to do whatever he wished on the land. A growing number of activities which relate to the form of farming business can, or sometimes must, be carried over to the new occupier. This is separate from any continuing arrangements, for example under woodland or environmental management schemes as described at **21.5**. Diversification will be considered in Chapter 23.

22.2   EMPLOYEES

A farming business is an undertaking for the purposes of the Transfer of Undertakings (Protection of Employment) Regulations 1981 made under the provisions of Council Directive 77/187. The Regulations are designed to protect employees where businesses, typically run in offices or factories, change hands. Any dismissal connected with the transferred business will be treated as automatically unfair (and so give rise to a claim) unless the reason for the dismissal is 'economic, technical or organisational' and results in a change in the workforce. The Regulations are complex and their application will vary from case to case. The Regulations may apply to farming operations where the farm changes hands even though no business assets have been transferred.

Thus, for example, if Mr Jones employs Alfred as his shepherd and sells the farm to Mr Smith, Alfred's contract of employment will be transferred to Mr Smith automatically, and he will be treated as being continuously employed. If Mr Smith makes Alfred redundant, because, for example, he is converting to a dairy business and Alfred knows only about sheep, there may be a genuine redundancy. In that case, Alfred would be entitled to claim a statutory redundancy payment from Mr Smith. If Mr Smith is in fact continuing a sheep business but simply wishes to replace Alfred (who he does not know) with John (who has been his shepherd on another farm for many years), Alfred will be treated as being unfairly dismissed. Because the dismissal is a direct result of the transfer and is not within the exception, Alfred would have a claim for unfair dismissal on that basis. For this reason, a buyer of a farm should make full enquiries about employees, their terms of employment, length of service and rates of pay, and other contractual terms. Where employees are not being kept on, arrangements need to be made for the former owner to make them redundant. If, under the Regulations, that is not possible because the employees continued to work up to the date of completion, the buyer will need to arrange that the seller should meet any redundancy or unfair dismissal payments because the claim will be made against the buyer or new employer. Such event may be covered by indemnities but if, for example, Mr Jones intends to emigrate to Brazil to farm there, this may not be practical and it may be desirable for the buyer to retain part of the purchase price in a joint account of the solicitors for the parties, pending resolution of any employee claims.

Where a farm is being sold by auction, information on whether it is intended that former employers will be retained after the sale will need to be made available with the auction information, and this could have a material effect on the bids.

Where the former employer and the new farmer are in direct relationship, as with the sale of a farm by an owner–occupier to a new one, there is no special difficulty apart from the ones mentioned above, although the Regulations still apply. If the sale is by a landlord where a farm is becoming vacant it will be necessary to make arrangements between seller, tenant and buyer, so that the buyer does not have to meet claims by the tenant's former employees. Where the former tenant is leaving willingly and surrendering his holding, perhaps on retirement, this can normally be carried out as part of the terms of the surrender. However, in a hostile situation, for example where the former tenant has fallen behind with his rent and been served with notice to quit, the selling landlord may not have any information on the terms of employment of farmworkers or who has been employed on the farm. The law recognises many people as being employees who at first sight appear only to be casual workers, if that is a correct description of the character of their work.

Where a farmworker lives in a tied cottage, the position will normally be evident and it will usually be possible to make enquiries of that person. The employee will have rights under the Rent (Agriculture) Act 1976 or as an assured agricultural occupier as described in Chapter 19. However, many workers no longer live on the farm and may even live in a nearby town, in which case their presence may not always be evident.

Where the buyer is prepared to take on the employees, he may wish to change the terms of employment. Technically, any change requires the agreement of both parties and if the employee does not accept the change (or accepts the change and subsequently challenges it) he will be able to treat the proposed change as an unfair dismissal. Where, however, the proposed change constitutes the termination of the existing employment and an offer to re-employ on new terms, the employee may be considered as acting unreasonably if he rejects the new terms when it would be proper to accept them.

Continued employment carries responsibilities under health and safety regulations, in relation to PAYE, pensions and similar matters, but in relation to these, farming is little different from other activities.

Similar considerations may apply to other estate workers, for example, woodsmen and maintenance men. The position of gardeners and domestic employees in a private house may alter on change of ownership since their employment is of a much more personal nature.

22.3   BUSINESS CONTRACTS

It is still uncommon for normal business contracts to be taken over on a change of ownership of a farm, although the practice is growing. There may, for example, be security contracts for buildings or stock, supply contracts and occasionally even sale contracts. Normally, these will have to be renegotiated by the buyer with the other party.

Where farms have specialised produce, for example a vineyard, contracts with other aspects of the industry may be of vital importance and the buyer may wish to take them on. This is particularly the case where a product grown on the farm is prized, for example, because of its special taste arising from the nature of the soil.

Organic farming is increasingly important and, in order to qualify, a farmer has to meet the criteria laid down by the Soil Association. Such criteria may include a warranty that chemicals such as sprays, or biochemicals such as antibiotics, have not been used on the farm for a minimum period, typically two years. Some organic products command premium prices and it may therefore be essential to the business plan that the seller has complied with all the necessary requirements. The Association will inspect the farm at frequent intervals to ensure that the buyer is complying with its standards.

22.4   BUILDING CONTRACTS

If a farm building has been erected or a building has been converted, for example, as offices, and the work has been carried out negligently so that damage results, a claim will be made against the contractors, or even the architect. It is therefore essential to ensure that any existing rights in respect of recent work are assigned to the buyer. This may be difficult under the terms of the building contract which will usually be personal to the seller or other person who ordered the work. Contractors and architects may be prepared to give collateral warranties to third parties who are known to be likely to be involved, such as the landlord or a mortgagee, and some contracts and warranties are drawn in such a form that they can be assigned to a buyer. Where this is the case, the buyer should take an assignment of the rights and should notify the contractor. Where this is not the case, it may be necessary for the seller to declare a trust of any damages for the benefit of the buyer. The rules on this are still being worked out by the courts because, once he has sold, the seller will not have suffered any continuing damage as a result of the defective workmanship. It may, however, be possible for the sale contract to include a provision that if the work has been carried out defectively, the buyer will have a remedy against the seller and this may be sufficient to support a claim by the seller against the contractor. A seller will normally be unwilling to give an unconditional warranty of this nature and the matter will therefore be the subject of negotiation.

22.5   FARMING EQUIPMENT AND CULTIVATIONS

A sale of a farm will often involve the sale of live and dead stock. Livestock comprises animals such as cattle and sheep; dead stock is everything else such as tractors, stores and sprays. Other agricultural matters such as residual or unexhausted manurial values and cultivations and growing crops may also be sold. The latter are usually called 'tenant right matters' because, under the Agricultural Holdings Act 1986, when a tenant quits the land, he is entitled to compensation for such things.

The value of the live and dead stock and right of the tenant will vary over time, and especially where there is a long period between the negotiation and completion of the sale it may not be possible to put a fixed figure for them in the contract. Indeed, if the buyer takes on a farm previously subject to tenancy and meets the outgoing tenant's right to claim compensation, it may not be possible to ascertain the figure until it has been settled with the tenant. Instead, the contract will usually provide for a valuation to be carried out at the time of completion. A typical valuation clause will require the buyer to take and pay for at valuation, certain specified livestock, dead stock and tenant right matters. The clause will specify the basis of valuation for different items, such as open market value, consuming value on the farm or value to an incoming occupier, or, in the case of tenant right matters, the statutory basis between landlord and tenant. There will be provision for the parties to appoint valuers and for an independent expert in the event of disagreement. If the figure is not ascertained by the date of completion, there may be provision for a payment on account of, say, half the sum determined by the seller's valuer, and the balance will be payable (with interest) seven days after the figure has been finally ascertained. Value added tax is important since it can apply variably to different items.

Chapter 23

DIVERSIFICATION

23.1 INTRODUCTION

In recent years, farmers have undertaken activities outside agriculture. This has been encouraged by government and made possible largely through increased mobility, which has meant that people can visit distant parts of the country, as tourists or otherwise, and can live and work many miles apart. The traditional estate has always undertaken diversified activities including mining, forestry and sporting, and the main emphasis of diversification has been in the leisure industry. Many farms, particularly in areas popular for holidays, now obtain more income outside agriculture than within it.

Where the seller has established a business or permitted someone else to do so, the buyer may take the land with that business continuing. Equally, a buyer may see an opening for a non-agricultural business, and a farm may be sold specifically with that in view. Many of the factors discussed in other chapters such as planning, employment and the environment, will need to be looked at by such a buyer, but certain specific points need to be considered separately.

A diversified activity may have been carried out by the former occupier, typically as a sole trader, or through a company controlled by him, or carried out by someone else under the terms of a lease or licence, or there may have been a joint venture. All of these have implications on a sale.

A farmer who has built up an enterprise by his own activities, for example setting apart a field as a caravan site or allowing people living in the village to graze their horses in his paddock, may have started from small origins and have built up over the years. As such, he may not have needed to use a separate legal structure (such as a company or tenancy) to distinguish his non-farming activities from those of an agricultural nature. This is particularly the case where there has been no special need to inject large sums of money. Certain activities need special consents. Normally, planning consent will be required, although where a change of use has continued for 10 years it will become immune from planning enforcement. Nevertheless, certain activities, such as a caravan site, will need a special licence. If this activity has added substantial value to the farm, a buyer may wish to continue with it. Alternatively, the farmer may get a better price by selling the pure agricultural land to one person, and the land having the diversified activity to somebody else. In that case, it will be necessary to ensure that all necessary consents and rights are in place. If a field used for camping is to go to one person, and the adjoining field used for grazing is to go to another, there may need to be special arrangements, for example to deter campers from dumping their rubbish in the wrong place. Rights of way will be especially important in this context, and will need to be considered well ahead of the sale so that the physical arrangements on the site can be worked out.

A diversified business which has been built up by some person other than the farmer or landowner, will typically be under the terms of a lease or licence, and a formal document will exist recording the terms. One part of the farm may, for example, have been leased to a local golf club or to someone operating war games for business executives, and there will usually be in place a series of documents governing the arrangements including rent, insurance, repairs and other normal matters. In such cases, the business operator will simply continue with the new landlord. The usual arrangements between landlord and tenant outlined in Chapter 20 will apply.

Problems can arise where the activity has been a joint venture between the farmer and some other person. For example, there may be a pony-trekking arrangement under which the farmer makes available some buildings for use as stables, and provides an area for the trekking to begin, but the rides themselves take place over a large area of country along bridleways and open moorland under the supervision of a guide. There will then be some arrangements for the proceeds to be shared. Such arrangements are normally personal to the parties and amount to a partnership in law between the farmer and the operator. Unless there is a specific provision in a written partnership agreement, the rights of partners cannot be transferred and it will be necessary for the farmer who is selling to make arrangements with the other partner, either to bring the business to an end or to allow it to continue on some specified basis.

23.2 'HORSEYCULTURE'

'Horseyculture' has aroused more problems than any other form of diversification, largely because it is cheap to institute and does not involve any immediate, obvious change to the land. It can also be very profitable, particularly in areas where there has been an increase in residential development, and there is little grazing land available and competition for what there is.

The planning aspects of whether grazing by horses is agriculture have been considered at **16.4**. The cases on these issues are not always easy to reconcile and the matter has been further complicated by decisions in relation to rating.

As a general rule, if horses eat the grass that grows in the paddock, that will amount to agriculture but, if the horses simply gallop over the land or if fodder is brought to them, it will not. The matter can also be affected by associated activities, for example the extent of livery, and every case will need to be considered on its own facts. This is particularly the case if the buyer is acquiring a field simply for the purpose of putting a horse on it, and especially where the buyer is intending to carry on a commercial horse activity.

23.3   BED AND BREAKFAST

Bed and breakfast is a traditional activity for farmers and, for many years, even centuries, farmers' wives have made available spare rooms to visitors. Recently, standards have risen substantially and where a bed and breakfast business is being operated, detailed controls exist which relate to safety (including fire escapes and the fire-proofing of beds and other equipment) and hygiene (especially where meals are provided). Visitors also expect high standards of accommodation, often including their own bathrooms, televisions and other amenities. In order to qualify for inclusion in various registers, operators of bed and breakfast businesses must comply with high standards and are subject to regular inspection.

Where a buyer is intending to continue a bed and breakfast business, he should inspect the facilities closely, and check all consents.

One important issue when a business of this nature changes hands is 'the list', which sets out the names and addresses of people who have visited the farm over the years, many of whom will return frequently. The list is technically copyright as well as an important marketing tool, and, as such, the copyright will need to be transferred on the sale.

23.4   MOVABLE EQUIPMENT

A diversified activity will involve equipment which does not form part of the land, and will therefore be the subject of a separate transfer of ownership. Equipment may include: mobile caravans and even chalets if they can be dismantled (see *Elitestone Ltd v Morris* [1997] 2 All ER 513); stocks of advertising materials; horse equipment and sometimes horses themselves; climbing gear which can be available for hire; catering equipment; and a whole host of other items.

Garden centres can raise special issues. Apart from normal equipment and items available for sale, which will be covered by the sale of the business, there will be growing plants, some of which will have been supplied by contractors possibly on terms that title is reserved until paid for, and piles of rock, topsoil, manure and other items not usually covered by a transfer agreement.

23.5   WORKSHOPS

Many redundant farm buildings have been converted into offices or workshops. These may be occupied by designers, craftsmen, or computer businesses, which have been attracted by the rural environment. It will be important to them that the surroundings are kept clean, especially where they use sensitive material. A buyer should therefore be aware that his tenants will expect a higher standard than may apply in a normal farming situation. If there is material interference with the business of the tenants, even as a result of normal farming activities (eg slow-moving equipment on the farm drive which obstructs access by visitors), the tenants may have a substantial claim for damages for loss of business. Even if there is no express covenant on the landlord, it may be implied from the circumstances and the courts may construe the covenant for quiet enjoyment as extending to such matters. A buyer must, therefore, consider carefully the type of farming that will be carried on.

23.6   OPERATING COMPANIES

The seller may have carried on the diversified business through a separate vehicle, typically a wholly owned company under a tenancy or licence. Where the sale is with vacant possession, it is important that such an arrangement is brought to an end, and assets, such as goodwill belonging to the company as distinct from the individual, must be assigned by the person who owns them.

Similarly, some businesses may be carried on by another member of the family, such as the wife, brother, or child, who owns the business assets. That person will need to be joined into agreement to give warranties and assignments.

In rare cases, it may be agreed that the ownership of the company itself should change and the agreement for the sale of land will be accompanied by an agreement for sale of shares in the company.

Chapter 24

THE CONVEYANCING PROCESS

24.1 INTRODUCTION

The successful sale of rural property will depend upon the completion of a transfer, in the case of registered land, or a conveyance, in the case of unregistered land. The conveyancing process is designed to lead up to these documents and to implement outstanding details after completion. The completion date is the date on which ownership changes hands in return for payment of the money, and in the case of rural property will usually be Michaelmas (29 September or, occasionally, 6 or 10 October) or Lady Day (25 March or 6 or 10 April). The change of occupation of arable farms is normally timed to coincide with harvest and there may need to be flexibility by way of early entry where the buyer is allowed into occupation before completion in order to carry out acts of cultivation, or by way of holdover where the seller is entitled to access for harvesting or storage after completion.

What follows is to some extent an ideal. In practice, the constraints of timing and finance may not allow the parties to go through the full procedure and in many cases a seller will wish to save costs by not instructing lawyers until a late stage. However, this may cause problems later, and increased costs but, particularly where the decision to sell a farm depends on the types of offers received after it is put on the market, the reluctance of sellers to run up several hundreds of pounds of legal costs without knowing whether or not they will sell the land is understandable.

24.2 PRELIMINARY STEPS

Once the decision to sell has been taken, the seller will discuss timing with his farm manager (if any) and will appoint a selling agent, who will consider how to market the property and whether to sell as a whole, or in lots, and whether by auction or by private treaty.

At this stage the seller should instruct his solicitor to carry out preliminary work, which includes assembling the title deeds and checking that there is a good title to all the land being sold. In the case of family farms, ownership may be divided up between various parts of the family or may still form part of the estate of a deceased member. Where a farm has been built up over many years by different purchases, the transactions may have been handled by different solicitors. Often different parts of the farm or estate are mortgaged to different lenders. There may also be areas which have no paper title and where, as such, the seller has to sell a possessory title.

The solicitor will also need to check the title deeds and documents for any existing encumbrances and rights such as rights of way, drainage and restrictive covenants.

24.3   DRAFT CONTRACT

It is generally sensible to prepare a draft contract at this stage. In many cases, the terms of sale will be specifically negotiated, particularly where the seller is selling only part of his land which involves rights of way, covenants and temporary arrangements such as continued occupation of a farmhouse or cottage. Where land may be sold either as a single unit or in separate lots, rights may need to be created over some of the lots for the benefit of others which will not be needed if the land is sold as a unit. Nevertheless, there is a great deal of work which can be done at an early stage, even before a buyer is found, and clauses can cover matters such as title, valuation, tied cottages and other leases.

On any sale of land, it is customary to take a deposit, usually 10 per cent of the sale price. Where a farm is being sold for several millions of pounds, however, it may be appropriate to reduce the deposit, or to provide special arrangements for any interest earned on it since completion will normally depend on the date for possession, typically harvest, while the contract itself can sometimes be made several months earlier.

Insurance should be considered carefully. The normal practice is for the risk to pass on exchange of contracts, but most sellers keep their insurance in place until completion. Normal practice will cover farm buildings, but special arrangements will need to be made in relation to other items including live and dead stock.

24.4   MANAGEMENT

The seller will usually remain in possession until completion and will be responsible for running the farm. The buyer will have a particular programme of cropping in mind and it may be necessary to agree the extent and nature of cultivations and crops in particular fields. Work is also likely to continue with regard to removing fallen trees, clearing ditches and general maintenance.

As mentioned above, early entry and holdover clauses will need to be agreed. Entry may be permitted onto one field while the seller is still harvesting another. The seller may retain occupation of grain stores on holdover for many months until he can sell the grain. This will not usually inconvenience the buyer who will not need the store until his own harvest, but arrangements must be made to cover, for example, the cost of electricity, insurance of the grain and the storage building, and access by grain merchants.

24.5   SEARCHES AND ENQUIRIES

The seller's solicitor will need to consider the extent to which searches should be carried out (see Chapter 25). If these are made too early, they may be stale by the time a buyer is found, resulting in duplication of expenditure. On sales by auction, the seller should always make searches and have them available in the auction room or to enquirers beforehand. It is a matter of discretion whether the seller recovers the cost of the search fee from the buyer's solicitor. This is common practice, although a few hundred pounds in the context of the normal price of a farm or estate may be considered petty.

The buyer's solicitor will raise numerous enquiries, many of which will be standard, filling several pages and covering boundaries, disputes, services and existing rights as well as additional enquiries particularly nowadays on environmental matters and on the effects of the Common Agricultural Policy (CAP). A strong temptation to ask too many questions should be resisted, and buyers' solicitors should try to restrict their enquiries to those matters that are strictly necessary, are in their client's direct interests and which arise specifically out of the title or the terms of the draft contract. Although there is a tendency to ask wide-ranging questions, for example whether the property has ever been subject to pollutants, the seller's solicitor will generally have a prepared reply, so that the ritual dance of enquiry and reply is a pointless exercise.

It is now normal practice for the seller's solicitor to produce his client's title before exchange of contracts. Historically, this was done after exchange because the title usually contained confidential material, particularly before 1925. Registered titles are now available to public inspection. If the title is unregistered, it is a ground for suspicion if the seller's solicitor is not prepared to produce it before exchange. For reasons mentioned above, it may be necessary to include specific provisions to cover defects in title. The buyer's solicitor will need to be satisfied that the title he is acquiring is sufficient to persuade HM Land Registry to give him a registered absolute title, or that his client accepts the risks that go with a title that is not acceptable to the Land Registry. Accordingly, enquiries in the nature of requisitions should also be raised at this stage, although there will be certain specific requisitions particularly about financial matters immediately before completion.

Contracts now normally incorporate the standard conditions of sale. Although these were designed for residential conveyancing and therefore may need to be adapted to rural issues, they generally form an acceptable basis. Again, the temptation on the part of the seller's solicitor to introduce a wide range of variations should be resisted. Variations that may be desired and acceptable include provisions as to insurance, especially if there is a long gap between contract and completion, and provisions as to possession where early entry by the buyer is expected, who may, consequently, be asked to put down a double deposit instead of paying interest.

Once all the outstanding issues have been resolved, the contract can be put into final form and signed. The actual exchange of contracts commits the parties to buy and sell and determines their rights, although it is of course possible (and common) for minor variations to be made between contract and completion. The timing of the contract constitutes a disposal for tax purposes provided the contract is ultimately completed and, of course, the buyer will need to have all his financial arrangements in place before committing himself.

In the past, it was common on sales of estates for a purchaser to contract to buy with a long completion date, on the basis that following exchange he would then seek to sub-sell. Such arrangements have been rare since 1945 since most buyers are unwilling to commit themselves without being sure that they have the finance available. However, sub-sales are still very common where, for example, the true purchase is by a consortium of landowners who have appointed one member to sign the contract, or where the person buying the farm or estate as principal purchaser has certain land surplus to his requirements which he is able to pass on. In residential and some commercial transactions it is common to include in the contract a restriction on sub-sales, but this is less usual for rural property. However, the seller may wish to impose a condition that any sub-sales should not, in total, be made at a greater price than the sale price, since there may be adverse tax consequences if the Inland Revenue considers that the true break-up value of the estate is greater than the price being obtained. This applies particularly on a sale by executors shortly after the death of the owner.

24.6   FOLLOWING THE CONTRACT

As indicated above, the property will need to be managed between contract and completion. One issue that commonly arises on estates is where cottages become vacant unexpectedly, for example on the death of a tenant. Similarly, where a holiday cottage is being sold there may be a succession of changes in the anticipated occupiers. The parties should be ready to co-operate in such arrangements, particularly on isolated farms near motorways and trunk roads, where there can be a risk of squatters moving into empty properties. It is the duty of the seller to give vacant possession where he has contracted to do so, but where a cottage is subject to tenancy the burden of terminating the tenancy and recovering possession from a squatter may fall on the buyer. Security will, of course, be relevant to insurance.

The draft conveyance or transfer is traditionally prepared by the buyer's solicitor and under s 48 of the Law of Property Act 1925, his right to do so cannot be excluded by contract. In practice, especially where there are numerous easements and covenants, it is becoming more common for the document to be prepared by the seller's solicitor and annexing this to the draft contract. Otherwise, the draft should be prepared as soon as possible after exchange, and the temptation to leave it until a late stage in the process should be resisted since, immediately following exchange, the parties will still have in mind the complex provisions involved, whereas several months later, when completion is imminent, these may have been forgotten. Where the sale is of part of the land, a plan must be prepared, whether it is transfer of part or a conveyance. Where the sale is of all the land, a plan cannot be used if it is a registered title. If the title is unregistered, it may be convenient to refer to all the land comprised in a previous conveyance without attaching a further plan, but if there is a clear plan of the estate, it will assist the Land Registry and, of course, make it clearer to the parties what is being conveyed.

It is now necessary in the case of acquisitions by registered companies to state the number of the company on the application to HM Land Registry, which should be included in the conveyance document. The conveyance or transfer should, of course, cover all matters referred to in the contract which need to be reflected on the title. However, it should not, as a matter of course, cover temporary matters such as short-term tenancies, wayleaves and general rights of uncertain nature, for example that the sale is subject to any existing third-party rights, without those being expressly defined. The buyer's solicitor must specify in the application any incumbrances which are not referred to in the document leading to first registration. It is therefore in practice simpler to incorporate these in the conveyance or Land Registry transfer under r 72 of the Land Registration Rules 1925, leading to first registration.

Where the buyers are trustees, statements may be required under the Trusts of Land and Appointment of Trustees Act 1996, particularly if powers are restricted, and it is good practice, although not essential, to refer to the settlement on the trusts of which the land is to be held. This is not possible for registered land or under a r 72 transfer. It can be altered on form FR1 and, if not, an application should be made to HM Land Registry to impose the trustee restriction. Where either the seller or the buyer is a charity, it is necessary to incorporate the wording required under s 37 of the Charities Act 1993 and rr 61 and 62 of the Land Registration Rules 1925, and where the seller is a charity, it will, of course, be necessary to go through the procedure laid down under s 36 and include a statement to that effect. In the rare cases where the buyer is a tenant for life (or a statutory owner) under a Settled Land Act 1925 settlement, the procedures under that Act must be complied with. It may also be evident from the title that consents are needed to the sale and these must be obtained in writing for production to HM Land Registry.

Where the transfer document is a conveyance and the earlier title deeds are not being handed over, it was necessary previously to include an acknowledgment for production; however, that is not usually necessary where the buyer is applying for first registration. The conveyance must, of course, contain other standard provisions such as a certificate for value, where applicable.

24.7   COMPLETION

Once the conveyance has been engrossed and executed, usually by both parties, it will be retained by the seller's solicitor pending completion. In many cases the conveyance or transfer is executed in duplicate where the seller is taking covenants or easements. The buyer will need to raise the purchase money, which will represent the balance of the purchase price after deduction of the deposit.

It is common practice, where the title is uncertain, for part of the purchase money to be held back pending the transfer of an absolute registered title.

Where a payment is made in relation to tenant right matters, then, provided this is an agreed figure, it should be added to the purchase price. Where payment depends on a valuation to be made at the date of completion, it will only be possible for payment to be made in full when the final figure is known, if necessary after an arbitration. However, it is common practice for the contract to provide that a substantial payment on account, representing the minimum value of the tenant right matters, should be paid on completion with the purchase money.

Where land is subject to tenancy, rents may need to be apportioned, although if, as is common, completion takes place on the half-yearly rent day, there may be nothing to apportion. On completion, authorities should be given to any continuing tenants to pay future rents to the buyer. This is usually achieved by a letter from the seller's solicitor, addressed to the tenant, but handed over to the buyer's solicitor on completion.

The old practice of completions attended in person, with the buyer handing over a bank draft at the office of the seller's solicitor (or his mortgagee's solicitors), and examining the title deeds or taking delivery of the deeds along with the conveyance, is now obsolete. Completion usually takes place by post and by means of telegraphic transfer of the completion moneys.

The contract will usually provide for completion to take place by a given time, so that the seller's solicitor is able to deposit the proceeds of sale during banking hours. As early as possible in the morning, the buyer's solicitor should transmit the funds to the seller's solicitor's account. If the buyer is raising the finance by mortgage or some other source (such as from a stock broker or the sale of other land), this may, of course, depend on receipt of funds from the mortgagee or other source, but it is wise for the seller's solicitor to arrange to receive such funds the day before completion. Once the seller's solicitor has received the funds in his account, he will telephone the buyer's solicitor. Assuming that all documents have been executed, any land charges searches certified and any other outstanding matters resolved, the parties will agree a completion over the telephone, and from that moment the seller's solicitor will be under an obligation to send the deeds to the buyer's solicitor or to his mortgagees. At that point, the seller's solicitor will be free to account to the seller or to his mortgagees for the proceeds of sale.

Where vacant possession is given, it may be necessary for an inspection to take place, particularly where the seller is a landlord and possession is being given by a tenant.

Following completion, the seller's solicitor will need to account to his client and provide details to the client's accountant. The buyer's solicitor must pay stamp duty in order to have the transfer stamped, submit the transfer to HM Land Registry and deal with any requisitions it may raise. If the seller's title was mortgaged, the buyer will need to obtain a formal release (on sale of part) or discharge (if the mortgage has been paid off or all the land in it is being sold). Following completion, the buyer's title will be recorded in a land certificate (or, if it is mortgaged, in a charge certificate). It is good practice, however, to retain pre-registration title deeds, particularly in the case of farms and estates since there may be third-party rights, including mineral rights or provisions over boundaries, which are not adequately reflected on the certificate of title.

Where the sale is substantial or the property is one which, because of the interest of the house or the landscape, is of public interest, it is increasingly common to issue a press statement which may include details about the intentions of the buyer, for example to convert the farm to organic production or to put the estate cottages into good order.

Chapter 25

SEARCHES AND INFORMATION

25.1 INTRODUCTION

The buyer will need as much information as possible about the farm or estate he is taking on. Normally it will be possible to raise enquiries with the seller or his solicitor. The seller may have very limited information, for example, if he is an executor selling shortly after the death of a former owner, or is a mortgagee, trustee in bankruptcy or a landlord who has never been in possession. Even where the seller has been a farmer in occupation of land for many years, there may be much information he will not have or have forgotten. The buyer will therefore need to obtain this information from elsewhere.

25.2 NORMAL SEARCHES

The buyer's solicitor will usually lodge a search with the local authority unless the seller's solicitor has already done so and made it available. This search falls into two parts. The first is a search in the register of local land charges which contains certain defined information of public importance which the local authority is bound to keep on a register and to notify to anyone who asks. This includes certain planning information, designation of houses as unfit, certain compulsory purchase orders and similar public information. Separately, and in addition, all local authorities have agreed that in return for a fee (which varies from council to council) they will answer a standard list of enquiries dealing with planning and environmental matters and other issues within their knowledge. A growing number of authorities have computerised these registers. Outside unitary areas, some information is held by district councils and by county councils, and different questions may be answered from different sources.

The standard local authority enquiries are submitted on Form CON 29. Part I of the form covers enquiries relevant to every transaction. Part II covers specialised enquiries of voluntary information which buyers can request for an additional fee. Two particularly important questions which should be raised are whether any footpaths or bridleways cross the land, and whether there are any pipelines.

In addition, local authorities may be prepared to consider other questions in return for a further fee, although they reserve the right to refuse to reply to questions which cannot be answered economically.

A second standard search is of common land and village greens, where there is a possibility that common rights exist (*Ladenbau (G & K) (UK) Ltd v Crawley & de Reya* [1978] 1 All ER 682).

A third standard search, in the case of unregistered land, is a search of the index map to find out if any of the land is registered. It will often be found that large estates with unregistered title have been subject to infringement at the boundaries, and it is important for this to be clarified at an early stage, rather than waiting until the buyer submits his application for first registration only to find that not all the land is available.

25.3   LAND CHARGES SEARCHES

In the case of unregistered land, it is essential to make a land charge search against estate owners on the title. This is normally done immediately before completion, but as it is capable of throwing up unexpected entries, and possibly delaying completion, it is sensible that this search is made well in advance (preferably well before exchange of contracts), followed by a final search against the current estate owners immediately before completion. Such a search will reveal matters such as restrictive covenants, options, second mortgages and similar matters. By contrast, as long as up-to-date office copies of the entries on the register of registered land have been provided during the conveyancing process (or obtained by the buyer's solicitor), it is usually sufficient to put in a Land Registry search shortly before completion. This should not be undertaken too early because the period of priority depends on the date of the search, and, particularly where there may be delays in stamping or obtaining discharge of a mortgage, the buyer's solicitor will need plenty of time before submitting the application for registration to HM Land Registry.

25.4   OTHER SEARCHES

Searches mentioned above are standard and will apply in most cases, although there will of course be circumstances where some searches are not appropriate. The following searches are less usual and will depend on the circumstances of the land.

25.4.1   Coal mining

A coal mining search is standard in coal mining areas, and there are a surprising number of counties where coal mining may have been carried out in the past, even though not within living memory. Such a search will reveal old workings, abandoned or infilled shafts and other matters.

25.4.2   Old mine workings

In certain areas of the country, where old lead or tin workings existed, it may be possible to arrange for informal checks on any known records of mineshafts, subsidence or spoil tips. Some of these are held by local schools of mines. A number of private search agents and environmental consultants have collated information on old mineworkings or can give information as to where surveys are kept.

25.4.3   Agricultural credits

An agricultural credits search should be made where a working farmer is in occupation, whether that farmer is a tenant or an owner. The Agricultural Credits Act 1928 allowed farmers to grant floating charges to banks over live and dead stock and over any compensation rights. Floating charges are unusual in that they can usually only be granted by companies, but an agricultural credits charge can be granted by an individual farmer. A floating charge attaches to assets for the time being subject to it, so that, for example, a farmer can freely sell a tractor or cow subject to a charge and buy another. A floating charge which relates to growing crops can vary with the time of year and the crops actually sown. Such a charge gives the bank security for money lent, and if the bank has registered its charge at the Land Charges Registry a buyer of the land will be bound. Thus, if the buyer takes over the land with crops growing on it, or if he buys the livestock with the land, these may be subject to a bank charge. An agricultural credits search is therefore sensible, and will be essential if a tenant is in occupation.

25.4.4   Boundaries

Various searches can be made to determine boundaries. If the land is crossed by a railway, there may be doubt over the precise extent of the land owned by Railtrack, or indeed one of the other companies derived from the former British Railways Board. These bodies will generally answer enquiries as to the extent of their ownership. Similarly, if the land adjoins the foreshore and there is doubt over ownership, it may be appropriate to raise the issue with the Crown Estate Commissioners, or (in Lancashire or Cornwall) with the Royal Duchies. If the land adjoins a statutory harbour, the harbour authority may be able to provide information as to ownership. Indeed, wherever the boundaries of the land are unclear, it will usually be appropriate to make enquiries of an adjoining owner. Private owners may not welcome enquiries, but by such methods subsequent boundary disputes can be prevented, particularly where the buyer has plans to change the fences or incorporate part of a hedge into a field.

25.4.5   Chancel repair liability

Parts of some estates may be subject to a chancel repair liability. This attaches to land which previously belonged to a monastery or abbey and which was sold off by the Crown after the Dissolution of the Monasteries in the sixteenth century. Such land may be subject to a liability to pay for the repair of the chancel of the parish church, which is potentially a heavy burden. There is no formal method of searching, but some researchers will investigate church records for a fee.

25.5   ENVIRONMENTAL AUDIT

It is becoming increasingly important to check the environmental history of land and any risk of contamination. The Environmental Protection Act 1990 proposed a formal register of contaminated land, but this met with a great deal of opposition and the proposals were never brought into effect. They were replaced by substantive rules which impose liability where contamination or pollution has occurred (see Chapter 17). Although a local authority will have a record of any formal steps taken under the 1990 Act, there is no single, central government-sponsored place where a prospective buyer can enquire about past pollution. A number of private firms have developed to fill this gap in the market. In return for a fee, which will vary according to the amount of work, they will carry out either a 'desktop' survey, with access to certain published or unpublished records, or they may be prepared to carry out a physical survey on site. The expertise and resources of these organisations varies greatly, and a prospective purchaser should ensure that the firm is experienced and reputable.

Although a surveyor's report on the condition of the property is standard in the case of residential or commercial purchases, this is less usual for agricultural land, where most of the value lies in the land itself rather than in the buildings on it. A buyer may, however, wish to have a survey of the farmhouse in which he is intending to live, or of any structures, particularly ruined buildings scheduled as ancient monuments, which could become dangerous. Similarly, if he is intending to convert a barn he will need to be sure that it is suitable for conversion.

Surveys of the land are less common. If land is being bought for woodland, it may be desirable to have it examined by a forestry expert. Similarly, if land is to be used for a particular crop or particularly for organic production, while the buyer's own view of the land will normally be sufficient, he may need specialist advice. MAFF grades agricultural land according to certain classifications and the buyer may wish to check the grading of the land. It should be noted, however, these are prepared on a national basis on a fairly broad scale, and it may be sensible to check the land quality field by field.

The Environmental Authority will answer questions about streams and rivers and land along their banks for a fee.

25.6   OTHER INFORMATION

Much archaeologically relevant information is held in the sites and monuments record which now exists for every county. This has no statutory force, but it is usually referred to by local authorities on receipt of a planning application. Although some sites will be scheduled as ancient monuments or listed buildings, the record also discloses a great deal of other information such as Roman roads, Saxon burial grounds, medieval parks and similar items which may be of interest, and which may be relevant if the buyer is intending to undertake large scale works.

Under the Hedgerow Regulations 1997, SI 1997/1160, made pursuant to the Environment Act 1995, it is an offence to remove or damage certain stretches of hedge. If a landowner is intending to remove or construct, for example, a gate in a hedge, it is necessary to apply for permission, which will be given if the hedge is not of a type that is to be protected. Protection depends on a number of factors, including historic and landscape importance, and if, for example, a farmer is buying some adjoining fields which he intends to add to his existing land, it may be desirable to check with the local authority whether an application for hedge removal will be granted.

Much land has been designated as sites of special scientific interest (see Chapter 17). This may appear from the local search but, in case of doubt, enquiries of English Nature will disclose whether such sites exist. Areas which are considered to be under threat can be brought under protection quickly, and a buyer may wish to have his own ecological survey carried out to make sure that land which he is proposing to plough up or plant is not the habitat of some rare insect or fungus.

Chapter 26

FINANCE

26.1 INTRODUCTION

The basis of all sale transactions is money, and everything discussed in this book is subsidiary to that principle. A seller is concerned to get the best price for his land, usually in the form of a single payment, although the price may be paid over a period of time, or partly by a single payment and partly by rent. The buyer is concerned to raise the money to acquire the land.

26.2 THE PRICE

Agricultural land is usually sold at a particular price, generally calculated per acre, but sometimes per hectare. Although the transfer document will state a single figure, this can be made up of a number of different elements.

The land will have a market value by reference to the prices being paid for other land of similar quality in the same locality. This is affected by demand (which, in turn, depends on the economy as a whole) and productivity and prices for agricultural products. Agricultural land values can therefore vary greatly, and this has a significance for security (see below). Price calculated by reference to area is also relevant if, for example, the seller is unable to show title to part of the land and damages have to be calculated for breach of contract.

Special factors can, of course, affect the price. These can include temporary features such as the Common Agricultural Policy (CAP) and the availability of set-aside or milk quotas, or, more particularly, the interest of special purchasers. A farmer's expenses are normally divided between fixed costs and variable costs. Variable costs depend on the amount of land, and include things such as the cost of seed and sprays. Fixed costs relate to matters which are not directly affected by the land, such as the cost of buying machinery or employees' wages. Clearly, a large farm will have more equipment and workers than a small farm, but, where a farmer has to take on extra equipment or labour to meet his needs, he may find he then has surplus capacity which can be used on extra land without extra expense. A farmer who has surplus machinery or workforce capacity may wish to spread his fixed costs over a larger area. It may therefore be worth his while to pay more than the normal market price for land adjoining his own, in order to be able to do this, particularly if the new land can be conveniently worked from his existing farm. However, the farmer must check such matters as means of access, particularly since under the Hedgerow Regulations 1997, SI 1997/1160, it may not now be possible simply to open a new gate.

Other factors that can affect the land include the quality of the buildings. A farm with an attractive farmhouse that enjoys good views, particularly if it is in relatively easy commuting distance of a large town or, for example, close to a motorway which can be reached easily but which is not audible, can materially affect the value. Other matters already discussed, such as the prospects of diversification (see Chapter 23), or the availability of environmental grants (see Chapter 21) can also affect the price, and, will be material in the calculation of any damages.

26.3   MORTGAGES

A buyer may not have sufficient cash available to finance the whole purchase, and will need to borrow from a bank or other lender. Other methods of raising finance are, for example, to invite other people to invest in a share in the farm, to spread the purchase around the family with different members owning different areas, or to negotiate for a transaction which comprises a part purchase and a part lease.

Most farming finance is provided by a small number of specialist lenders. Although a large number of lenders, both domestic and overseas, are prepared to lend money on the security of farm land, it is not advisable to borrow from an inexperienced lender (which may not fully understand the nature of farm land as security) as this may lead to problems. The value of farm land can fluctuate, the timing of any sale is important and the rights which affect farm land can be very different to those which lenders normally encounter in other situations. As the farming market is volatile, and particularly having regard to the uncertainties of farming income, it is usually easier to agree a suitable loan and security package with a specialist lender familiar with agricultural matters when, for example, the grain price may be temporarily low but could be expected to rise again in six months.

For many years, the leading agricultural lender was the Agricultural Mortgage Corporation, which was established under the Agricultural Credits Act 1928, and was originally owned jointly by a number of banks. The Corporation is now a subsidiary of one of the major clearing banks, and a number of other specialist lenders now exist in the market. The large clearing banks also have their own specialist agricultural lending sections. As such, even though a farmer usually deals with his local bank manager, it is sensible to arrange borrowing from one of the specialist offices, which may, of course, be part of the same bank.

Specialist lenders will have their own standard requirements of solicitors instructed to handle the mortgage, and will be familiar with problems such as boundaries, tenancies and environmental issues which arise on the solicitor's report on title.

The normal form of agricultural mortgage document of farm land will differ in some respects from the standard printed forms used by lenders as a matter of course. Particular issues include the normal provision in a mortgage that the borrower must not sub-let or grant occupation of any premises which may not be appropriate, where there are employees occupying tied cottages. It is also very common for small areas of land to be released for boundary adjustments, or additional areas to be brought into the charge where the farmer wishes to acquire extra land. In the case of an estate, a number of different mortgages to different lenders may exist, which are granted out of the same title, although in such cases, HM Land Registry will allocate a separate title number to each area of land subject to a separate charge.

In addition, a farmer can give to a bank (but not to any other type of lender) a separate floating charge under the Agricultural Credits Act 1928, over live and dead stock and other matters (see **25.4.3**).

26.4   OVERAGE AND DEVELOPMENT SALES

In addition to its current value, rural land may have the potential in the short or long term to increase in value, typically as building land. This may have to be taken into account on a sale since sellers increasingly seek a share in any possible future uplift (sometimes called overage), while buyers may be unwilling to pay for prospective future value which may not be realised for many years, if at all. A number of devices have been developed to respond to parties' wishes, but at present these are experimental, very few have been tested in court and even the general policy of the law has not yet been settled.

Short-term arrangements may be made with developers. A farmer who owns land on the edge of a town may be approached by a developer who considers that there is a prospect of obtaining planning consent within, say, five years. The normal arrangement is that the farmer continues in occupation as owner, granting to the developer an arrangement under which, in return for an immediate payment, the developer will have a period of time during which he will have exclusive rights to apply for planning consent. This can be a very expensive process, and to recompense the developer, the final sale price will be a proportion, typically 90 or 95 per cent, of the open market value with the benefit of planning consent. The transaction can either be an option, which gives the developer a unilateral right to call for the land once a satisfactory consent has been issued, or a conditional contract, which obliges the developer to seek planning consent, and, if it is given, both parties are automatically bound. The details and issues under such an arrangement are beyond the scope of this book. It is sufficient here to say that such arrangements must be drafted carefully, with a view to the particular requirements of both sides and any other parties, such as the institution funding the developer. From the seller's point of view, the arrangement must be drafted in a form which will not prevent him selling the land, subject to, and with the benefit of, the development agreement if his financial circumstances change.

One option frequently offered by developers is to buy the land outright from the farmer at agricultural value, with a provision for an additional payment if planning consent is granted, and with the right to the farmer to buy back the land if consent is not granted within a given period. Unless the farmer has an urgent need for cash, this is not usually advisable since under such an agreement he must part with ownership, and there is the risk that it may not be possible to recover it, nor, if the developer becomes insolvent, to recover the additional payment. As such, these arrangements are rare. However, since the introduction of farm business tenancies, it may be possible for a farmer to take a long lease on such a basis if cash is needed immediately but he needs to remain in occupation.

26.4.1   Methods of obtaining development value

A variety of methods may be used for longer-term, potential development value. Where the landowner retains other land not involved in development, he can sell a farm or part of it to an agricultural buyer subject to a restrictive covenant that the land can be used only for agriculture. It may be possible subsequently to release the covenant in return for a cash payment. Although such arrangements are common, cases which have come before the courts indicate that the courts consider that a covenant should not be used for this purpose, and if buildings are erected the former landowner may be awarded damages at a much lower level that he could have expected for a proper share of development value. The law on this is developing rapidly at present.

Other methods include a positive obligation on the buyer that if development value is realised he will make a payment to the seller calculated in an agreed way, usually by reference to development value. This constitutes a positive covenant and is therefore not enforceable against successors in title of the covenantor (Chapter 15), but it can be supported in various ways, for example by including a restriction on the register of title that no transfer is to be registered unless the transferee enters into a direct deed of covenant with the original owner who has the benefit of the right to the extra payment. HM Land

Registry will accept such a restriction, but it has not been tested in court, and it is still open to a court to hold that a restriction cannot be used for this purpose.

The original seller may take a rentcharge and right of re-entry. Rentcharges are generally no longer possible under the Rentcharges Act 1977, but a payment of this nature may operate as an estate rentcharge. However, if the seller takes a right of re-entry that itself is a piece of property capable of supporting a further payment. The provision would state that if planning consent is granted, or if building works commence on the land, the original seller will be entitled to take the land back. A provision may be included that the current owner of the land can have this right removed, in return for a payment calculated in a specified way. The House of Lords decided in *Shiloh Spinners v Harding* [1973] AC 691 that such a right of re-entry can work in theory, although in that case the right was designed to protect an immediate interest of the original seller, and it has not yet been established whether such a right is capable of protecting a long-term interest such as overage.

Where geographical circumstances permit, the original seller may keep back an area of land as a ransom. For example, if he continues to control the only access to the potential building land he may be able to charge a sum (typically one-third of the development value under *Stokes v Cambridge Corporation* (1961) 13 P&CR 77) for giving rights of access. However, the buyer or its successor may be able to obtain access by some other route, and there is also the risk that there may be other ransoms available in relation to the same piece of land, which can reduce the value of the original land.

The original seller may keep a charge in the form of a mortgage (either legal or equitable) which will be triggered if development value is secured. Again this has not been tested in law, and under the rules against irredeemable mortgages, it is possible that the courts might allow the owner for the time being to have the mortgage discharged even before development values have been realised. It is generally considered, however, that where the charge is to secure future development value, these rules would not invalidate the charge.

If the buyer is content with less than a full freehold interest, it may be possible for a long lease to be sold. The seller would retain the freehold, and the lease would contain covenants against development, but there may be an option for the tenant to buy in the freehold for a price calculated by reference to development value if planning consent is granted. As the lease will be for a premium, and will usually not command a rent, the lease should be for no more than 300 years to avoid the risk that the tenant enlarges the lease into a freehold under s 153 of the Law of Property Act 1925, but such a length of term is normally acceptable. However, long leases of agricultural land are not common, and would not normally be acceptable to buyers in the market.

None of the above methods of securing overage or realising development value are straightforward and, if they are used, need to be designed specifically for the particular circumstances of each case. Documents must then be drafted carefully in the light of those circumstances.

26.5   SECURITY

It will be evident that competition may arise between the seller or other person entitled to overage, and the bank or other institution lending money for the original purchase, in the event of the insolvency of the owner of the land. Where value can be attributed to development, competition will exist between the previous owner who expects his share of development value, and the lender, who simply wishes to have a debt repaid. In principle, there should be no conflict since one party will have lent on the current value, and the other party will, as part of the terms of the original sale, be seeking a share of the separate development value; however, in practice this can be difficult to distinguish. The lender will therefore wish to ensure that his charge takes priority over any overage, while the original seller will wish to ensure that his interest in the development value takes priority over that of a bank. This possible conflict can have the result of making the land difficult to mortgage (because the lender feels it will not have adequate security) and, therefore (because land which cannot be mortgaged is not attractive to buyers who, even if they have cash, may want to resell to someone who does not) to sell and therefore can have an effect on the original purchase price. Some original sellers who see a prospect of development value in the medium term may be prepared to accept this, and it is a matter for judgement in each case.

Chapter 27

PROCEEDINGS AND NOTICES

27.1 INTRODUCTION

Where an unexpected event occurs, whether or not it is the fault of one of the parties, the result of third party intervention, or an act beyond anyone's control such as an accidental fire, which results in loss to one of the parties, that party will seek compensation and may seek to reverse the transaction. In practice, the vast majority of sales of rural land proceed without a problem.

27.2 BETWEEN CONTRACT AND COMPLETION

The contract creates a legal arrangement between the parties. Where a previous relationship has existed between the parties, for example where the buyer is a neighbour or tenant of the seller, the contract may create rights over the disposal of the land. That relationship continues until completion, when it is replaced by a new relationship. During the contractual period, relations are governed by the terms of the contract and any provisions of the law which supplement or override those provisions. Most contracts for the sale of land incorporate one of the published sets of conditions which include various provisions dealing with the most common types of dispute. In the past, the National Conditions of Sale and the Law Society's Conditions of Sale were widely used. They have now been replaced by the Standard Conditions of Sale which are designed for domestic sales and are not wholly adapted to farm land. In rare cases, the Statutory Form of Conditions of Sale 1925, SR&O 1925 No 779, made by the Lord Chancellor under s 46 of the Law of Property Act 1925, may apply. In general, published conditions provide that minor errors and defects do not cancel the sale, but they do entitle the buyer to compensation, usually by reference to the diminution in value.

A seller may be unable to complete for a number of reasons. For example, he may have insufficient title to the land – although with the spread of compulsory registration and the growing practice of deducing title before exchange, this is now rare. In the past, however, this was very common, and s 49 of the Law of Property Act 1925 laid down a special procedure for a vendor and purchaser summons, under which matters arising out of contract could be dealt with quickly.

In general, the seller is treated as being in a similar position to a trustee of the property between contract and completion, and is under a duty to take care of the property. If the seller has contracted to sell with vacant possession and trespassers move onto the property after contract and before completion, it is usually the responsibility of the seller to remove them. However, it may be agreed, especially in vulnerable country areas where there is a long interval between contract and completion, that this risk should pass to the buyer or should be shared.

Where a local authority makes a requisition, for example if a structure is found to be dangerous and needs urgent works, it will generally be the responsibility of the buyer to comply with the notice. However, if anything of that nature is known to the parties, they should provide for it in advance.

In general, the risk of damage to buildings, for example by fire, is on the buyer as from the date of contract. In practice, sellers keep their insurance policies in place until completion, but if, for example, the property is burnt down between contract and completion, the buyer is normally bound to complete, pay the full purchase price and look to his own insurance policy for recompense. This may be modified in the contract.

If the seller refuses to complete for no good reason (for example because he has changed his mind, or his spouse refuses to move, or he has a related purchase which has fallen through), the buyer is entitled either to terminate the contract after notice and recover the deposit, or to sue for specific performance. The buyer will also have a claim for damages, for example, if he has had to arrange for alternative accommodation because the seller has not moved on the agreed date. Such claims can be very substantial, for example, where it is necessary to arrange fodder for stock, where land cannot be cultivated or crops sown at the right time, or where the buyer has arranged to resell part of the land to a third party and cannot comply with that contract.

Similarly, if the buyer fails to complete, for example because he cannot raise the money, the seller can serve a notice to complete and, if the buyer fails to do so, can forfeit the deposit. This is the most common remedy. The seller may then seek to market the property again and recover any further costs from the buyer. In such a case, credit must be given for the deposit. Alternatively, if the buyer is worth suing, the seller may seek specific performance and possibly also damages.

Where the seller has nothing to sell, for example because he has no rights over the property which are capable of being sold, or is merely the beneficiary under a trust with a life interest and not the owner, there may be a claim for restitution or for breach of warranty of authority.

Where the contract has been induced by misrepresentation, for example because the seller has not been accurate in replies to enquiries, there is a residual power under the general law for the contract to be rescinded. Alternatively, where the defect is relatively minor, the courts can award damages under the Misrepresentation Act 1967.

In general, the normal rules relating to contracts which apply in commercial law will also apply to property law.

27.3 FOLLOWING COMPLETION

Once completion has taken place and ownership of the land has been transferred, it is generally too late to undo the contract. If the seller has given a covenant for title, and in particular if he has given a full title guarantee, the buyer will be entitled to compensation if one of the implied provisions of that guarantee has been broken, for example if the seller was not in fact owner of part of the land or if the land was subject to a financial charge. Under the covenants for title, if a defect can be put right, for example where title depends on a chain of grants of administration from the court to estates of deceased owners and the chain is incomplete, the seller can be required to pay the costs of perfecting the title. A seller may have title over land which will normally be accepted by a buyer but which is not sufficiently clear to be acceptable to the Land Registry, which may then refuse to grant absolute title to the land being acquired. Furthermore, there may be a good documentary title but an adjoining owner may subsequently prove to be the true owner of the land, even though it is fully described in documents. Such problems generally arise only on first registration. Unless the seller has warranted that the buyer will obtain a good registered title (which would be unusual) then simple failure by the Land Registry to accept the title is not itself necessarily a cause for claim for damages, but much would depend on the circumstances.

27.4 THIRD PARTIES

Many of the problems that lead to litigation arise not as a result of the arrangements between the parties themselves, but because of the acts or failures of a third party.

A typical situation is where a tenant owes outstanding rent at the date of completion. If the rent was due before completion, the seller has the right to collect it. It may be agreed that completion will take place on the figures that would apply if the rent were up to date, and the seller will then pursue the tenant for the arrears. Alernatively, it may be easier for the buyer to sue the tenant since, as the subsequent landlord, he will be entitled to forfeit the lease for non-payment of rent even during a period in which he was not the owner. In such a case, it will have to be agreed how the costs of any proceedings will be shared, and it may be necessary for the seller to allow the buyer to use his name in proceedings.

Similarly, if claims are ongoing by or against, for example, local authorities, trespassers, or people who have a claim in nuisance in respect of an activity on the land, it may be a matter for negotiation as to how any such claims will be met. In general, the party who makes or defends claims will be the party who was the owner at the time a breach of duty or contract occurred, or is said to have occurred. However, the parties can agree different arrangements if they wish.

27.5   NOTICES

Where arrangements exist with third parties, those parties will need to be informed of the sale. It is good practice to serve formal notices on tenants requiring them to pay future rents to the new landlord. Under s 3 of the Landlord and Tenant Act 1985, there is an obligation to give notice of the name and address of the new landlord to a tenant of premises which consist of or include a dwelling. Where premises comprise or include a dwelling (other than a business tenancy) then, under s 48 of the Landlord and Tenant Act 1987, the landlord must give notice to the tenant of an address in England and Wales at which proceedings can be served. In the absence of such notice, rent will not be due. Furthermore, where a demand is made for money that comprises or includes a service charge (eg a contribution to maintenance of common access track), then, under s 47 of the 1987 Act, the demand must include the name and address of the landlord.

Where certain types of environmental agreement are in force, for example relating to woodlands or maintenance of the countryside, the agreement will usually contain an obligation to notify the statutory authority of the change of owner.

An employee who will continue to be employed following the sale must be notified of the current employer.

Clearly, it is prudent to notify suppliers, including the statutory undertakers for water, gas, electricity and other services, and it is wise also to notify customers. Where land is subject to rights of common or has the benefit of such rights, there is no legal duty to notify the Commons Registration Authority, although in practice this is usually done. At present, there is no provision for keeping the register up to date, but this may be introduced in the future.

Chapter 28

TAXATION

28.1   INTRODUCTION

The burden of tax, and the steps taken to mitigate it, play an important part in the sale of rural land. Tax liability can have a major influence on the form and timing of the transaction, and is a fundamental consideration for most landowners. The *decision* to buy or sell will be determined by commercial factors, family requirements, debts and the objectives of the parties, but the *way* in which a transaction is carried out will be influenced, to a considerable extent, by tax.

Taxes affect different legal entities in different ways. Some bodies, such as charities, pension funds and local authorities, are not subject to most forms of taxation, although value added tax (VAT) will be an issue (whether or not they can recover it). Such institutions are important players in the agricultural land market and, for that reason, tax considerations are not dominant.

Individuals will, of course, be fully subject to the normal tax rules. However, tax will impact differently on other legal entities, including companies (where different rules apply to large and small companies), trusts (where different rules apply to a person who has an interest in possession and the right to the income from one where there is no such person) partnerships, joint ownerships and estates in course of administration.

Furthermore, the particular history and current legal structure of the land can materially affect tax liability, for example the nature and timing of past expenditure on the land, the date of purchase and the length of period of ownership, whether or not the land is or has been tenanted and, if so, for how long, whether the seller has used the land for business and, if so, whether he acquired it by selling other land used for business, and a number of other historic factors.

As a result it is not possible to give a general picture of tax liabilities as they impinge on sales of land. Each landowner will have their own unique tax position which needs to be considered in the light of their circumstances.

28.2 CAPITAL GAINS TAX

Capital gains tax (CGT) is usually the most significant tax for a seller. In very broad terms, CGT relates to the increase between the cost of the land and the proceeds of sale. The cost includes any expenditure represented in the value and covers expenses of purchase, the cost of construction of buildings, the cost of perfecting title and other reasonable expenditure. Similarly, the proceeds will be reduced by costs associated with the disposal. The acquisition cost will normally be increased to reflect inflation between 1982 and 1998, and the sum charged to tax on disposals after 1998 is reduced in accordance with a scale by reference to the length of ownership.

Where the proceeds of sale of land used for business are rolled over into the acquisition of other business assets, part or all of the gain may be exempt from tax, but the acquisition value of the new land is reduced accordingly. This 'rollover relief' has acted as an incentive for farmers to sell land, for example for development, in order to put their money into other farm land, and has had a material effect, in the past, on agricultural values. However, changes in the Chapter II of Part III of the Finance Act 1998 have reduced the benefits of rollover relief, at least for short-term owners. Where the farmhouse has been the principal residence of the owner, that residence and the immediately adjoining land may also be exempt from tax.

28.3 INCOME TAX

Income tax is normally relevant to the period of ownership rather than the disposal, but it can impact particularly where tax reliefs have been obtained in the past. Tax reliefs apply particularly to farming assets such as cattle or certain plant and machinery, where reliefs have been made available on acquisition. Furthermore, where farming assets have been depreciated in the farmer's accounts and the value on disposal is different to the written-down value, an adjustment may need to be made for income tax. The effect of capital allowances and other factors can therefore materially affect the proceeds, particularly if the seller is a company forming part of another group where reliefs can be passed between different members of the group and set off against corporation tax on income from different assets.

In certain cases, what would otherwise be a capital gain may be charged to income tax instead. For example, under s 776 of the Income and Corporation Taxes Act 1988, where value is derived by reference to the developed value of land (eg the sale of land for building with the price dependent on the value of the house as built), there may be an income tax charge. Similarly, where land has been acquired with a view to making a profit on resale this may be charged to tax either under s 776, or as trading in land or an adventure in the nature of a trade. Thus, if the farmer adopts a practice of selling off parcels of land over a period of time, and particularly if he acquires other pieces of land in order to resell, he may be treated as trading in land. Similarly, where the buyer of an estate resells the land subsequently on a break-up basis (by buying the land as a whole and reselling parts to different sub-purchasers), any profit is likely to be charged to income tax.

Income tax in relation to farming differs from other trades, and this must be considered carefully if the buyer intends to diversify.

28.4 VALUE ADDED TAX

Value added tax (VAT) is European tax and applies to any supply of services or goods. For the purpose of VAT, land is normally treated as goods. Land is generally exempt from tax; as such, tax is not payable on the disposal of land unless the seller has made a specific option to bring the land within the VAT remit, for example in order to recover costs of repairs to buildings. In such circumstances, the seller must collect VAT on disposal. However, where the land is sold as part of a transfer of a going concern, either as the farm business or, in certain circumstances, where the land is tenanted and is sold subject to a continuing tenancy, and where the buyer has also elected, this will be treated as outside the scope of VAT. Special rules relate to specific occupiers where reliefs have been obtained, or the liability has been minimised because of the exempt status of an owner or occupier or the use (eg a charitable use) to which the asset has been put or where buildings have recently been erected.

28.5 STAMP DUTY

Stamp duty is a tax on documents, not on transactions, but in most cases it will be necessary to have a document giving effect to a transfer. In a few cases, such as the surrender of a tenancy, it may be possible to complete the transaction without documents. It is not a criminal offence to fail to pay stamp duty, but any document which should have been stamped and has not been, is not acknowledged for legal purposes. Thus, the buyer of land under a transfer will not be able to register the transfer with the Land Registry unless it has been properly stamped.

28.6 INHERITANCE TAX

Inheritance tax is not usually relevant to sales and purchases. The need to raise money to pay death duties has historically been a major reason for the sale of estates by traditional landed families. The value of agricultural land is now normally exempt from inheritance tax where either the deceased taxpayer has owned and occupied the farm for two years, or has owned it for seven years. The exemption does not, in general, apply to land subject to the Agricultural Holdings Act 1986 where the tenancy was granted before 1 September 1995, although in such cases tax is payable at a reduced rate. Even where agricultural relief is not available, a separate business property relief may apply in much the same way. The relief applies also to equipment used in the agricultural business.

Land of scenic, landscape or historic importance may be exempt from inheritance tax at the discretion of the Treasury, and subject to certain conditions, including public access. Where exempted land is sold sub-sequently, the deferred inheritance tax will become payable.

For the above reasons, rural land may be an attractive investment for prospective owners wishing to protect their assets from death duties for the benefit of their heirs, although the minimum periods of ownership mean that planning should take place at an early stage.

28.7   LANDFILL TAX

Landfill tax is payable by operators of sites used for landfill. It is a factor which must be taken into account on a mineral lease, which will normally include provisions for infilling.

28.8   RATES

In general, agricultural land and property is not subject to rates, but other properties, for example converted barns used for commercial purposes, will be subject to rates. Paddocks let for ponies may also be rated depending on the nature of the equine activities; in general, any non-agricultural activity is potentially subject to rates. Again, this is more significant during the period of ownership than on change, but where rates have not been paid in the past by a former owner, in certain circumstances the local authority can charge rates on the land and recover them from the current owner.

28.9   GENERALLY

The tax treatment of agricultural land, and transactions relating to it, is made up of a mass of detailed rules, and a proper discussion is outside the remit of this book. It is a highly complex and specialised field, and both buyers and sellers should consider taking the advice of a specialist on the subject. Indeed, the knowledge of most specialists tends to be limited to one or another type of tax, so that several advisers may be needed. If the tax position is misunderstood the consequences can be serious, since correct action might make a difference of 40 per cent of final receipts.

Part 2

CHECKLISTS

Checklist (Seller)

(1) Names and addresses of parties.

(2) Capacity of seller to sell: eg board resolution, additional trustee, consent of beneficiary, consent of husband/wife (if matrimonial home), order of Charity Commission or Ministry of Agriculture Fisheries and Food – Settled Land Act.

(3) Names and addresses of surveyors, solicitors to other parties and other professionals.

(4) Large-scale plan to be agreed by surveyors to both parties and checked against title deeds

(5) Check title against sale plan – registered or unregistered. Obtain office copies of title registered or prepare epitome.

(6) Check all occupiers (family, tenants).

(7) Chattels and fixtures to be included in price or paid for in addition.

(8) Sporting and mineral rights, already vested in third parties or to be reserved.

(9) Terms of reservation of sporting, minerals, rights of way and services, including rights needed for adjoining retained properties.

(10) Easements – way, water, drainage, light – existing or to be granted or reserved.

(11) Terms of covenants to be imposed and land to be benefitted. Also, existing covenants and need for indemnity.

(12) If family or company tenants, check all formalities ready for termination. If farming partnership or share farming, check other party fully aware.

(13) If existing tenancy to be terminated, check notices to grant or surrender arrangements and payments to/from tenant, especially timing of notices.

(14) Consider existing public restrictions – inheritance tax undertakings and action to be taken, s 106 (or s 52) agreements and continuing liability.

(15) Details of management agreements (woodland, ancient monument, countryside).

(16) Check tax consequences – is there a desired contract date for CGT? Does sale trigger IHT liability? Corporation tax consequences.

(17) VAT, transfer of going concern, elections.

(18) Agricultural buildings, allowances and other transferable tax reliefs.

(19) IACS forms, milk quota and other set-aside land.

(20) Quota year; IACS; consequences for various subsidies on timing of sale. Consider whether to apportion current year grants and subsidies or provide for them to belong to one or other party. Method of disposal of milk quota: tax implications, IACS form.

(21) Apportionment of grants and subsidies.

(22) Holdover and early entry conditions.

(23) Notify mortgagees and obtain provisional redemption figures. Check if period of notice needed. Check that proceeds of sale sufficient to discharge all charges (including registered local land charges) and consider terms of undertaking to be given on completion.

Checklist (Buyer)

(1) Names and addresses of parties. Available finance: sale of existing property, mortgage, cash in hand.

(2) Names and addresses of surveyors, solicitors to other parties and other professionals.

(3) Large-scale plan to be agreed by surveyors to both parties and checked against title deeds.

(4) Responsibility for boundaries, and any boundary covenants.

(5) Access. Check on width, purposes for which it can be used, any Highway Authority consent for widening. If agricultural, is it for animals or farm machinery?

(6) Available services. Restrictions on use. Title to easements (both existing and new ones to be given by seller).

(7) Meters for mains or estate supply (do they work, is the supply or meter shared?). Route of pipes on plan. Position of springs, collecting chambers and boreholes. Water abstraction licence. Does supply on property also serve other residences not included in purchase.

(8) Chattels and fixtures to be included in price or paid for in addition. Valuation clause; basis of valuation of live and dead stock (market value or value to incomer or written down value). Agree full schedule.

(9) Sporting and mineral rights, already vested in third parties or to be reserved.

(10) Easements – way, water, drainage, light – existing or to be granted or reserved.

(11) If title unregistered, do index map search.

(12) Local authority search, including footpaths and bridleways. Is there a risk of new bridle-ways or footpaths being claimed?

(13) Commons search.

(14) Coal mining search and other mining, if applicable.

(15) Environmental search and enquiries as to past use, especially infilled quarries and farm tips.

(16) Arrange survey. Consider if specialist survey needed, eg suitability for specialist crops, whether there is mining subsidence, business potential for diversification.

(17) Preliminary enquiries, standard and additional.

(18) Check if notifiable diseases have affected crops or livestock.

(19) Does slurry or other disposal comply with Environmental Authority standards?

(20) Planning: check alterations, especially last four years' changes of use – 10 years. Environmental and management agreements. Sites of special scientific interest. Access agreements and other public access including de facto enjoyment. AONB, Heritage Coast, National Park and other constraints. Planning agreements (s 52 and s 106).

(21) Chancel repairs and other ecclesiastical liabilities.

(22) Tax reliefs: buildings allowances, plant and machinery.

(23) Agricultural buildings, allowances and other transferable tax reliefs.

(24) VAT, transfer of going concern, elections.

(25) IACS forms, milk quota and other set-aside land. Quotas, set-aside and arable area payments. Obtain copies of records and registration details. Apportionment of current year.

(26) Holdover and early entry conditions.

(27) Apportionment of grants and subsidies.

(28) Total cost – VAT, stamp duty, fixtures, valuations, survey fee, Land Registry fees, post-completion work, such as renewing management agreements.

(29) Requisitions.

(30) Conveyance/transfer.

(31) Insurance.

(32) Land Charges Search (if unregistered).

(33) Agricultural Credits Search.

(34) Bankruptcy Search (if extra payment, eg for chattels, or if indemnity taken from seller for future liabilities).

(35) Mortgagee requirements.

(36) Assignment of sugar quota – British Sugar Consent.

(37) Land Registry application.

TENANCIES

(1) Agricultural tenancies – succession rights (pre-1985), milk quota rights (pre-1985), lifetime rights (pre-1996).

(2) Residential tenancies; security; Rent Act or assured or assured shorthold. Timing of next review.

(3) Business tenancy; contracted out; length of occupation.

(4) Mining leases.

(5) Compensation rights.

(6) Rent payable in advance or in arrears. Rent review pattern and date of next review. Are there tenants' improvements to be disregarded?

(7) Past conduct of tenant: rent, repairs, use.

(8)   Is identity of land in tenancy defined? Are terms reduced to writing?

(9)   Existing licences: – grazing, occupation, sports such as motor bike scrambling or hang-gliding, use of metal detectors, bird watching, local hunt, local cricket club, climbing in disused quarries, caravans, horse riders.

Part 3

PRELIMINARY ENQUIRIES

Enquiries before Contract

1 THE PROPERTY

1.1 Residential buildings
Are there any residential buildings on the property? If so, when were they first constructed?

1.2 Building works
Please provide approximate dates and brief details of all major building works on the property in the last 20 years.

1.3 Architectural plans
If and in so far as they are still available, please supply copies of the architect's plans, sections and elevations of any buildings on the property as built and of any major alterations, addition or refurbishment.

1.4 Other building documents
Please supply copies of all other design documents including drawings, specifications, bills of quantities and site surveys in the possession or control of the seller.

1.5 Building advisers
In so far as not revealed by any copies supplied in answers 1.3 and 1.4 above and so far as known to or ascertainable by the seller, please provide the names and addresses of all architects, quantity surveyors, structural and service engineers and other professional advisers and all contractors responsible for the design, supervision or construction of the property or of any major alteration, addition or refurbishment.

PART 3 ENQUIRIES

1.6   Prospective alterations

Has the seller, or to the knowledge
of the seller, any predecessor in title,
considered any further development,
alteration, addition or refurbishment,
which has not been carried out but in
respect of which any survey or
design work was carried out? If so,
please supply such documents and
information as are referred to in 1.3
to 1.5 above, as may be in the
possession of, or available to, or
ascertainable by the seller.

1.7   Building materials

Please confirm that the following
materials have not been used in the
construction of any buildings on the
property, or any subsequent
alterations thereto:

(a)   high alumina cement;
(b)   asbestos or asbestos-based
        products (if any such has been
        used please specify type);
(c)   wood wool slabs used as a
        permanent framework for
        concrete;
(d)   calcium chloride concrete
        additives;
(e)   sea-dredged aggregates which
        do not comply with the
        appropriate British Standard;
(f)   polychlorinated biphenyls
        (PCBs);
(g)   materials which may release
        formaldehyde;
(h)   lead, whether pure or as a
        compound in pipework;
(i)   calcium silicate slips or bricks;
(j)   lightweight or air-intrained
        concrete blocks;
(k)   vermiculite plaster;
(m) any other materials currently
        regarded in accordance with
        good construction practice as
        being deleterious, hazardous,
        noxious or otherwise
        dangerous.

1.8 **Adjoining or neighbouring properties**

Does the seller own any adjoining or neighbouring property? If so, please supply a plan indicating the location and extent of it.

1.9 **Boundaries**

1.9.1 Do the physical boundaries of the property differ from those shown on any of the plans supplied on behalf of the seller?

1.9.2 Have there been any disputes concerning, or alterations in the lines or ownership of, any boundaries or any boundary's structures?

1.9.3 To whom do the boundary walls, fences, hedges, ditches, etc belong, or, if the deeds are silent, which has the seller maintained or regarded as his responsibility?

1.9.4 Where the boundaries to the property are formed by ditches, drains or other watercourses, please specify where the boundary lies in each case.

1.10 **Access**

1.10.1 Please supply a plan showing what access routes to the property exist or are, in practice, used by the occupiers of the property.

1.10.2 In relation to each access route:

(a) Is access direct from the public highway?

(b) Is access obtained by way of any unadopted road or footpath or over any adjoining property? If so, please provide details of the owner of the land over which such access is gained, any payments made for such access and anyone else who uses such access. Please also confirm any maintenance responsibilities on the owner of the property towards the upkeep of the access.

1.10.3   If by right, please confirm that the seller's title will be deduced.

1.10.4   If by licence, please supply full details.

1.10.5   Please confirm that there is no liability for any road charges or pavement crosses in respect of those parts of the property that front on to the public highway.

1.10.6   Please confirm that all means of access to the property or benefiting the same are unobstructed and in full use.

1.10.7   Are any services, or is any access, obtained through, over or under the property in favour of any adjoining or neighbouring property? If so, please supply details of all rights granted, whether formal or informal.

1.11   Services
1.11.1   Does the property have surface and foul drainage, water, electricity and gas services?

1.11.2   Which of these are connected to the mains?

1.11.3   Please give details of the routes of all of the services referred to above.

1.11.4   Please supply copies of all relevant easements, grants, exceptions, reservations, wayleaves, licences and consents in respect of all of the services.

1.11.5   In so far as the services are not connected to the mains, please supply the following information:

    (a)   the position of the adopted or public mains connection;
    (b)   the position of the services that remain unadopted and details of where they connect to the public main;
    (c)   the positions of all cesspits and septic tanks on the property.

1.11.6 Please provide a plan showing the position of any land drains on the property.

1.12   Licences
If any of the following facilities are enjoyed exclusively by the property on terms under which any person can control, restrict or terminate or curtail their use, please give particulars:

(a) access for pedestrians and vehicles;
(b) access for light and air;
(c) pipes and wires for services;
(d) rights of entry on to other premises for repairing or maintaining the property.

1.13   Shared facilities
1.13.1 What documents regulate the joint use of any shared roads, paths, drains, wires, pipes, party walls or other facilities or, if undocumented, what evidence is there of the terms of sharing?

1.13.2 Has the seller (or to his knowledge any previous owner or occupier) done any work or been asked to do so or to pay towards the cost, or asked others to do so and is any payment outstanding, disputed or expected?

1.14   Subsisting agreements
Please supply copies of any of the following relating to the property which the purchaser is to have the benefit:

(a) insurance policy, indemnity or guarantee relating to a defective title or breach of any restrictive covenant;
(b) agreement, certificate, guarantee, warranty or insurance policy relating to any repair, replacement, treatment or improvement to the fabric of the property or any buildings on it;

(c) agreement or covenant for the maintenance, by some other person of any road or footpath over which rights of access of the property are enjoyed;

(d) agreement, indemnity, guarantee or bond for payment of the cost of constructing any road on to which the property fronts, or sewers under it, and of road charges on this adoption as maintainable at the public expense.

1.15   Claims under agreements

1.15.1   What defects or other matters have become apparent or adverse claims have been made by third parties which might give rise to a claim under any document mentioned in 1.14.

1.15.2   Has notice of such defect, matter or adverse claim been given? If so, please give particulars.

1.15.3   Please give particulars of all such claims already made, whether or not already settled.

1.16   Fixtures and fittings

1.16.1   In respect of such parts of the property that are being sold with vacant possession, please supply a schedule of all fixtures and fittings forming part of the property, divided into the following categories:

(a) fixtures and fittings included in the sale;

(b) fixtures and fittings which the seller intends to remove.

1.16.2   Is there any fixture, fitting or other thing fixed to the property or included in the property to be sold or intended to be left on the property which does not belong to the seller? If so please state the name and address of the owner of it and particulars of any agreement relating to it.

1.17   Damage to the property
Has any of the following matters
affected the property at any time to
the knowledge of the seller:

(a)   flooding or subsidence;
(b)   structural building or drainage
       defects?

If so, please supply details together
with the relevant plan.

1.18   Reclaimed land
Please confirm that no buildings on
the property have been erected on
reclaimed land by the filling of a
gravel pit, quarry or other
excavation. If any have, please give
details together with the name and
address of the firm responsible for
supervising the infilling work.

1.19   Amenity
Is the seller aware of any matter,
current or proposed, which affects,
or might if implemented affect, the
enjoyment of the property, by noise,
smell, smoke or other emission,
vibration or other nuisance or
otherwise any offensive use current
or proposed of any adjoining or
neighbouring property? If so, please
supply details.

**1.20   Development of neighbouring
         properties**
Is the seller aware of any current or
proposed development or change of
use of any adjoining or neighbouring
property? If so, please supply
details.

1.21   Complaints
Has the seller had cause to complain
against the owner or occupiers of
any adjoining or neighbouring
property in respect of any matter
affecting the property? If so, please
supply details.

1.22   Farming restrictions
Is the property subject to any
scheme, designation or agreement

which imposes, or may in the future
impose, any limitation on the way in
which the property is farmed (eg
sensitive area, nitrate vulnerable
zone, etc)?

1.23   Hedge restrictions
Are there any hedges on the property
which might be the subject of
protection?

1.24   Inclosure awards etc
Are there any inclosure awards or
documents which affect the property
in any way?

2   TITLE

2.1   Covenants etc
2.1.1   In so far as not already provided,
please supply a copy of all
covenants, stipulations, restrictions
and agreements affecting the
property.

2.1.2   In whom is the benefit of such
covenants, stipulations and
restrictions now vested?

2.1.3   Please identify the land for which
the benefit of the restrictive
covenants inures.

2.2   Complaints of breaches
2.2.1   Has any complaint ever been made
alleging any breach of covenant or
restriction relating to the user of the
property or any part of it?

2.2.2   Is the seller aware of any matter or
thing which may give rise to any
such notice or complaint?

2.3   Complaints in respect of buildings
2.3.1   Is the seller aware of there ever
having been any complaints or
objections on the grounds that the
erection of any buildings on any part
of the property is in breach of any
covenants or otherwise?

2.3.2   Is the seller aware of any matter or
         thing which may give rise to such
         notice or complaint?

2.4   Actual breaches
         Please give details of any breaches
         of any covenants relating to the
         property.

2.5   Consents
         Where the consent or approval of
         any person has been required in
         respect of any restrictions affecting
         the property, please supply copies of
         such consent or approval.

2.6   Modification of covenants
         Has any attempt been made, either
         by the seller or by any other person,
         to remove or modify such covenants
         etc pursuant to the provisions of the
         Law of Property Act 1925 (as
         amended) or is any such action
         contemplated?

2.7   Rights over other land
         Please give details of any rights of
         entry, right to inspect, repair or
         replace any facility, any right to
         overhang or eavesdrop or any other
         like rights, facility or services
         enjoyed by the property over other
         property.

2.8   Adverse rights
         Are any of the boundary walls or is
         any open space forming part of the
         property affected by rights of
         support or of access or user which
         are subsisting in favour of
         neighbouring owners?

2.9   Party walls
         Please supply copies of all party
         wall awards or agreements affecting
         the property.

2.10   Benefit of rights
         Is the property sold with the benefit
         of any covenants or easements or
         any other rights? If so, please:

(a) provide copies of all relevant
     deeds and other documents;
(b) identify by plan the servient
     tenement;
(c) state whether the seller, or to
     the knowledge of the seller any
     predecessor, has had cause to
     complain of any breach of any
     such covenant or interference
     with any such easement or
     rights, supplying full details.

2.11   Other adverse rights
Is the seller aware of any rights or
formal arrangements specifically
affecting the property, other than
any disclosed in the draft contract,
which are exercisable by virtue of an
easement, grant, wayleave, licence,
consent, agreement relating to an
ancient monument or land near it or
otherwise, or which are claimed by
any third party or are in the nature of
public or common rights?

2.12   Transactions at an undervalue
Is the seller aware of any transfer,
assignment or other disposal of the
property at an undervalue during the
past five years? If so, please provide
details.

2.13   Treasure finds
2.13.1   Is the seller aware of any
         archaeological or treasure finds on
         the property during their own or any
         previous ownership?
2.13.2   Has the seller drafted any licences to
         treasure hunters or 'metal detectors'?
         If so, please provide details.

3   SPECIFIC TITLE ENQUIRIES
[To be drafted to suit the
circumstances of each case]

4   LAND CHARGES

4.1   Local land charges
Is the seller aware of any matter
which, although not registered, is

capable of registration in the local
land charges registry? If so, please
give details.

4.2 Charges for work done

4.2.1 Is the property subject to any charge
for work done by a local or other
competent authority or to any notice
given by any such authority and not
yet complied with which would not
be disclosed by the usual local land
charges searches and enquiries? If
so, please give particulars.

4.2.2 Is a notice of the type mentioned in
4.2.1 (above) contemplated to the
knowledge of the seller or his
solicitors or agents.

5 OUTGOINGS

5.1 Rates and council tax

5.1.1 Please state the name and address of
the rating authority.

5.1.2 Please state the rates payable in
respect of the property and the area
to which they apply.

5.1.3 In so far as the property or parts of it
are subject to the council tax, as
defined by the Local Government
Finance Act 1992, please supply
details of the value band in which
the dwellings on the property have
been allocated.

5.1.4 Does the hereditament in which the
property is to be sold included for
rating purposes also include any
other property and, if so, what?

5.1.5 Has any alteration been made to any
of the buildings on the property
which is not fully taken into account
in the current gross value? If so,
please supply details.

5.2 Water supply

5.2.1 Please state the name and address of
the water company or undertaker.

5.2.2 Where water rates are payable, what
is the current rate in the pound?

5.2.3   Where the water supply is metered, please supply copies of the past two years' accounts.

5.3   Water abstraction

5.3.1   Please supply a copy of any Water Abstraction Licence affecting or for the benefit of the property, together with any correspondence relating to its renewal.

5.3.2   Please supply copies of any expired Water Abstraction Licences affecting or for the benefit of the property, together with any details available (including correspondence) relating to their non-renewal.

5.3.3   Does the Water Abstraction Licence relate exclusively to the land to be sold.

5.4   Rating disputes
Is the seller disputing or appealing against any rating assessment or property valuation pursuant to the Local Government Finance Act 1992 relating to the property?

5.5   Improvement grants
Please confirm that the property is not affected by any repayable improvement grant.

6   HEALTH AND SAFETY

6.1   Compliance with legislation
So far as the provisions are relevant, please confirm that any relevant provisions of the Factories Act 1961, Offices, Shops and Railway Premises Act 1963, Health and Safety at Work etc Act 1974, Food Hygiene (General) Regulations 1970 and the Shops Act 1950 have all been fully observed and performed.

6.2   Pollution
6.2.1   Does the user of the property or any part of it give rise to the discharge of trade effluent into the drains or otherwise? If so:

(a) please confirm that the Environmental Authority (EA) or the local authority have inspected the property and have approved the same.

(b) please supply copies of any approval and a copy of the relevant consent given by the EA permitting the discharge of such effluent into the public sewer or otherwise.

6.2.2 If such permission was given, subject to conditions, please confirm that the conditions have been complied with since the date of the permission.

6.2.3 If any agreement was entered into in respect of any consent, please supply a copy.

6.2.4 Is the relevant authority considering alterations of any of the terms or conditions of the consent or agreement? If so, please supply copies of all correspondence.

6.3 Special restrictions
Are there any specific statutory or by-law restrictions on the use of the property relating to the area? If so, please provide copies of documentation evidencing the same together with confirmation that all such restrictions or obligations contained therein have been complied with.

6.4 Smoke control
Is there a smoke control order affecting the property? If so, does the property comply in every respect?

6.5 Environmentally sensitive area
6.5.1 Is any part of the property registered as an environmentally sensitive area (ESA)? If so please give details.

6.5.2 Are there any agreements relating to ESAs entered into in respect of the property pursuant to s 18(1) of the Agriculture Act 1986?

6.6   Water works
Is the seller aware of any diversion
or other works carried out to any
stream or watercourse on or under
the property?

6.7   Flood works
Have any flood alleviation measures
been undertaken on the property on
behalf of the EA or the IDB or of
any other body having responsibility
for flood prevention?

6.8   Pollution register
Please provide full details of any
entries relating to the property or
anything undertaken on or from the
property contained in the Pollution
Register maintained by the EA
pursuant to s 190 of the Water
Resources Act 1991.

6.9   Section 86 notices
Has any notice been given by the
EA pursuant to s 86 of the Water
Resources Act in respect of a
discharge of effluent from the
property and, if so, what prohibition
was imposed?

7   COMMON RIGHTS

7.1   Common rights
7.1.1   Is the property to the seller's
knowledge subject to rights of
common or included whether
provisionally or finally in the
registers of common land or of town
and village greens?

7.1.2   Does the property have the benefit of
any rights of common over the land?

7.2   Parish rights
Is the property subject to any
customary or any other parish
rights?

8 PLANNING

8.1 Planning permissions
8.1.1 Are any buildings or operations on site the subject of planning permissions? If so, please supply copies.

8.1.2 In relation to any building not covered by a planning permission, please confirm that such building has stood for at least four years without further development.

8.2 Building alterations
8.2.1 Please supply copies of planning permissions for all additions, alterations, and improvements to the existing buildings which have required planning permissions.

8.2.2 In relation to any such addition, alteration or improvement in respect of which no copy planning permission is provided, please confirm that such addition, alteration or improvement was carried out more than four years ago.

8.2.3 Please supply details of all additions, alterations, improvements and other building or engineering operations carried out, for which it is claimed no planning permission was required, and state why.

8.3 Evidence of planning compliance
In relation to all buildings, additions, alterations, and improvements, please supply evidence of compliance with relevant building by-laws or regulations, including copies of all approvals.

8.4 Other documents
Please supply, where applicable, copies of any:

(a) office development permit;
(b) Industrial Development Certificate;

    (c) Building Control Licence issued in relation to the construction of the property.

8.5   Regional development grants

8.5.1   Has any regional development grant been made in respect of the property?

8.5.2   If so, please supply a copy of any relevant agreement with full details of all conditions attached to the grant, and all payments made by the appropriate authority.

8.6   Conservation area

8.6.1   Is any part of the property in a conservation area? If so, please identify it and state whether any directions have been made under Article 4 of the General Development Order 1988.

8.6.2   If the property is not in a conservation area, is there any possibility of its being included in one? If so, please give details.

8.6.3   If the property is in a conservation area, please confirm that all necessary conservation area consents have been obtained in respect of any demolition works.

8.7   Types of property

8.7.1   Please state the current or most recent use of each part of the property when such use is other than agricultural, and the date of commencement and (if appropriate) cessation of each such use.

8.7.2   Is the current or most recent use of any of them the subject of planning permission? If so, please supply copies of the relevant permissions.

8.8   T and CPA agreements etc

Was any agreement or obligation purporting to regulate development whether under s 52 of the Town and Country Planning Act 1971 or s 106 of the Town and Country Planning

Act 1990 or any other statute
empowering local authorities,
entered into in respect of the
property and any planning
permission? If so, please provide
copies.

8.9   **Established use certificates**
Please supply copies of all
established use certificates or
certificates of lawfulness of existing
use or development.

8.10   **Duration of existing use (subject to
planning permission)**
If any existing use is not the subject
of a planning permission, has it been
carried on in its existing form
continuously from a date prior to the
end of 1963?

8.11   **Existing uses not subject to
planning permission**
8.11.1   If the use of the property or any part
of it is not the subject of a planning
permission, and no established use
certificate or certificate of lawfulness
of existing use or development has
been obtained and the answer to
Enquiry 8.9 is 'none'.

8.11.2   Please state all uses to which each
such part has in the past been put,
with the dates of commencement
and cessation of every such use.

8.11.3   Please provide the names and
addresses of the persons who can
provide statutory declarations as to
such uses and dates, and please
confirm that such persons will do so
if required by the purchaser.

8.12   **Outstanding planning applications**
Is there any outstanding application
for planning permission to develop
the property in any way or change
the use of it? If so, please supply a
copy of the application together with
any plans and other documents
lodged therewith and any draft
agreement with any statutory

PART 3
ENQUIRIES

authority purporting to regulate the
development.

8.13   Outstanding planning appeals
Is any appeal against refusal, actual
or deemed, of permission,
outstanding? If so, please supply
details.

8.14   Court proceedings
Is any appeal to the High Court or
any application for judicial review
by any party pending in respect of
any planning matter?

8.15   Unimplemented permissions
Has any planning permission been
granted for the property or any part
of it, or for any change of use of it,
which has not been implemented? If
so, please supply a copy of such
permission and any agreement with
any statutory planning authority
purporting to regulate development
permitted.

8.16   Planning conditions
Please confirm that all conditions
attached to any permission granted
affecting the property or its use of it
have been complied with by the
seller and the seller's predecessor.

8.17   Planning agreements
Please confirm that the terms and
conditions of any agreement
purporting to regulate the
development entered into with any
statutory authority have been
complied with.

8.18   Refusals of permission
Have any applications for planning
permission affecting the property
been refused? If so, please provide
copies of the applications and
refusals.

8.19   Other planning applications
Have any applications for planning
permission been made and neither

granted nor refused? If so, please
supply details.

8.20   Enforcement proceedings
Have any planning contravention,
breach of condition, enforcement or
stop notices, injunctions or any
enforcement proceedings been
issued or threatened by the planning
authority? If so, please provide
copies of any notices or proceedings
and all relevant correspondence and
give full details.

8.21   Pending enforcement proceedings
Are any appeals or proceedings
whatsoever pending in respect of
any enforcement action in respect of
the property?

8.22   Planning proposals
8.22.1   Is the seller aware of:

(a)   any traffic proposals or schemes
which may affect the property
or the enjoyment of it?
(b)   any proposals involving
compulsory acquisition of the
property or any part of it?

If so, please supply full details.

8.22.2   If any representations have been
made in respect of any effect upon
the property, please supply details.

8.23   Temporary erections
If there are any temporary erections
on the property, please specify them
and confirm that all necessary
consents therefore were obtained.

8.24   Listed buildings
8.24.1   Is any building included in any
provisional or statutory list of
buildings of special architectural or
historic interest, or an ancient
monument? If so, please supply
copies of all relevant listings and
other documents; and answer the
preceding enquiries in this section as
though they applied:

(a) to listed building consent and
     enforcement matters; and
(b) to scheduled monument consent
     and enforcement matters,

supplying full details as appropriate,
listed building and scheduled
monument consent (or give details
of any variation).

8.24.2 Does any part of the property form
        part of the curtilage or setting of any
        listed building or ancient monument
        whether or not comprised in the
        property? If so, please supply
        details.

8.24.3 Has any grant been made in respect
        of any listed building or ancient
        monument? If so, please supply
        details.

8.24.4 Has any agreement been entered into
        with any competent authority in
        respect of the future care of any
        listed building or ancient
        monument?

8.25   Tree Preservation Orders
8.25.1 Are any trees standing on the
        property the subject of a Tree
        Preservation Order or Orders? If so,
        please supply copies.

8.25.2 Have any Tree Preservation Orders
        been breached, and if so are any
        proceedings pending or threatened?

8.26   Area of archaeological importance
        Is the property or any part of it
        designated as an area of
        archaeological importance under the
        Ancient Monuments and
        Archaeological Areas Act 1979, or
        are there any known factors in
        relation to the property which might
        lead to such designation? If so,
        please provide full details.

8.27   Enterprise Zone
        Is the property or any part of it in a
        designated Enterprise Zone? If so,

please identify it and the responsible Enterprise Zone Authority.

8.28 Urban Development Area
Is the property or any part of it in an Urban Development Area? If so, please identify it and the responsible Urban Development Corporation.

8.29 Local structure plan etc
Please state the current status of any local structure or unitary development plan. If any representations or objections have been made in respect of any emerging plan, please supply full details.

9 ENVIRONMENTAL MATTERS INCLUDING RECLAIMED AND CONTAMINATED LAND

9.1 Purchaser's right to inspection
The purchaser reserves the right to carry out his own inspection, survey and other investigations and to raise further enquiries in respect of environmental matters including reclaimed and contaminated land, but the seller is asked specifically to disclose any information it has in relation to any of the following matters and to answer the specific enquiries set out below.

9.2 Reclaimed or unfilled land
Is the seller aware of any part of the land comprising the property, or on which the property is situated, or any adjoining land, having been reclaimed or infilled? If it has, please specify the state and nature of the land before reclamation, stating whether the reclamation involved the filling of a gravel pit, quarry or other excavation or natural feature? If it has, also please give details, including the name and address of the persons or companies responsible for carrying out and

supervising the reclamation and/or
infilling works.

9.3   Former uses of property
Please give details of the present or
former use or uses of the property,
including, in particular:

(a)   use(s) for:
    (i)   manufacturing or other
        industrial activities;
    (ii)   waste disposal (whether
        licensed or systematic or
        not);
    (iii) transport;
    (iv)   defence;
    (v)   gas or other energy
        generation or supply;
    (vi)   winning of minerals;
(b)   the existence of:
    (i)   storage tanks (whether
        above or below ground);
    (ii)   ground water
        contamination.

**9.4   Deleterious substances and
conditions**
If any of the following have affected
the property, please provide details:

(a)   cases of legionnaire's disease,
    humidifier fever or other illness
    or indisposition which is
    associated with 'sick building
    syndrome';
(b)   the presence of substances
    deleterious to health, safety or
    the environment;
(c)   the presence of gases
    deleterious to health, safety or
    the environment, whether
    arising by emission from the
    property or by emission or
    migration from property
    adjoining or in the vicinity or
    however arising, including:
    (i)   methane;
    (ii)   landfill gas;
    (iii) radon;
(d)   anything which might render
    the property prejudicial to
    health or give rise to nuisance.

9.5   **Condition of property**
Please give details of the state and
condition of the buildings and land
comprising the property with
particular reference to anything
which might adversely affect the
value of the property or the
purchaser's use and enjoyment of it.

9.6   **Discharge licences etc**
Please provide copies of all licences,
consents or permissions permitting
or regulating in respect of the
property any discharge or emission
to, or contamination of, the
environment or applications for the
same.

9.7   **Environmental assessments**
Please provide copies of all reports
or assessments carried out in order
to establish whether the property at
that time either contained or
constituted a hazard to health or the
environment.

9.8   **Pollution claims by authorities**
Please give full details of all actions,
claims or notices in respect of any
pollution of, or emission or
discharge to, the environment, on or
from the property, received from, or
threatened by, the EA, HM
Inspectors of Pollution, the local
authority or any other competent
authority.

9.9   **Pollution claims by neighbours etc**
Please give full details of any action
or claim or matter which might give
rise to such action or claim made by
any tenant of the property or owner
or occupier of any neighbouring
property in respect of any nuisance,
discharge or emission from,
contamination of, or defect in the
property. Please also give full details
of any such claim made by any
owner or tenant of the property
against any tenant or owner of the

property, insurance policy in respect
of the property or owner or occupier
of any neighbouring property.

9.10   Removal of waste
Please confirm that all waste or
rubbish will be removed from the
property and that the property will
be left clean.

9.11   Notifiable diseases
Is the seller aware of any notifiable
disease occurring on the property? If
so, please supply full details.

10   INSURANCE

Please confirm that the seller intends
to continue the present insurance
policy up to the date of completion,
and provide details of the existing
cover.

11   CAPITAL ALLOWANCES

In relation to the property, please
state what capital allowances
(including those for agricultural
buildings, minerals, industrial
buildings, plant and machinery,
scientific research and enterprise
zones) and codes are involved and
also:

(a)   the total claimed to date;
(b)   the total and phasing
      outstanding;
(c)   if separately pooled; and
(d)   whether future adjustments are
      possible under the VAT Capital
      Goods Scheme.

12   VALUE ADDED TAX

12.1   VAT on purchase price
12.1.1   Does the seller intend to charge
         Value Added Tax in addition to the
         purchase price?

12.1.2   If so, please provide a copy of:

(a)   the written permission of HM
      Customs & Excise
      Commissioners to the exercise

of waiver pursuant to para 3(10) of Sch 10 to the Value Added Taxes Act 1994 (VATA);

(b) a copy of the notice of election sent to HM Customs & Excise;

(c) copies of correspondence from HM Customs & Excise in relation to the notice and any permission required pursuant to para 3(10) of Sch 10;

(d) a copy of the most recent Value Added Tax invoices rendered by the seller in relation to the property; and

(e) details of any claim made under para 2(9) of Sch 10 to the VAT Act.

12.1.3 Please provide details of any refusal of permission by HM Customs & Excise to the exercise of the waiver on an application under para 3(10) of Sch 10 to the VAT Act, together with copies of all correspondence relating to the same.

12.1.4 If the answer to **12.1.1** is negative, please confirm that no VAT invoice has been issued by the seller or the seller's agents in respect of any sums collected by or payable to the seller in respect of the property.

12.1.5 Please confirm, if no election has been made, that no election will be made in relation to the seller's interests in the property following submission of these enquiries and prior to the completion of the sale without the approval of the purchaser.

13   GRANTS AND QUOTAS

13.1   Grants

13.1.1 Has the land been the subject of a farm amalgamation grant?

13.1.2 Has a grant been received for the repair of, or provision of basic amenities in any farm cottages on the property?

13.1.3   Has a grant been received, save as already disclosed, for planting woodland in connection with its management?

13.2   Quotas

13.2.1   Please supply details of any milk quota and the extent of the registered holding, if different from the property being sold.

13.2.2   Where the land is tenanted, is the tenant entitled to compensation in respect of milk quota on quitting the tenancy?

13.2.3   Has there been any agreement between the landlord and tenant under the Agriculture Act 1986, Sch 1, para 11(6)?

13.2.4   Does the land being sold form the whole of the producer's holding for the purposes of milk quota?

13.2.5   Please supply details of any potato and/or sugar beet quota on the property.

13.2.6   Please supply details of any other quotas in relation to the land.

13.2.7   Please provide copies of Integrated Administration and Control System (IACS) form submitted in respect of the property in the last three years.

13.2.8   Please confirm that all statements in the IACS were correct and complete.

13.2.9   Have there been any breaches of the rules relating to IACS and/or set-aside? If so, please specify.

13.2.10 Please supply copies of any supplementary forms and correspondence with MAFF in relation to registration of the property as eligible or otherwise in relation to the claiming of AAPS or otherwise.

13.2.11 Please confirm that the seller will on completion hand over the originals of all documents relating to the

IACS scheme relating to the
property.

13.2.12 Please supply field plans showing
the crops grown on the property in
the last three years.

14   TENANCIES

14.1   Present tenant's details
Please state the full name and
address and age of the present
tenant.

14.2   Rent revision
When was the rent last revised?
Please supply a copy of the
agreement or award.

14.3   Variations of tenancy
Has there been any adjustment of the
boundaries of the holding subject to
the tenancy, or variation of any
terms of the tenancy since the rent
was last revised? If so, please supply
a copy of the agreement.

14.4   Tenant's improvements
Please supply full details of all
tenant's improvements.

14.5   Statutory succession
14.5.1 Did the present tenant succeed the
preceding tenant by statutory
succession?

14.5.2 If so, did the preceding tenant also
succeed by statutory succession?

14.6   Tenant's relatives
Have the tenants any close relatives
working on the farm?

14.7   AHA 1986 approval
If the approval of the Minister was
obtained under either s 2 or s 3 of the
Agricultural Holdings Act 1986
before the grant of the tenancy,
please supply a copy.

PART 3
ENQUIRIES

14.8   Tenant's compensation
Please supply particulars of any
agreements as between the landlord
and the tenant relating to
compensation payable in respect of
the holding.

15   SUB-LETTING

If the seller is aware of any sub-
letting of all or part of the demised
premises, what are:

(a)   the full names and addresses of
      the sub-tenants?
(b)   the terms of the subletting?

**16   ORDERS, AWARDS OR
          NOTICES**

16.1   Matters affecting letting
Please supply copies of any of the
following which relate to, or affect,
the terms of the letting, or which
affect the use of the property when
let:

(a)   orders or directions of any
      court, tribunal or local
      authority, or arbitration awards;
(b)   notices served on or by the
      local authority and any
      acknowledgement received
      from the local authority;
(c)   undertakings given by the
      landlord or the tenant.

16.2   Compensation awards
Please supply details of any
compensation awarded either to the
tenant or to the landlord under either
the Agricultural Holdings Act 1986
or the Agriculture (Miscellaneous
Provisions) Act 1976 and confirm
whether or not such compensation
has been paid.

**17   GENERAL TENANCY
       ENQUIRIES**

17.1   AHA 1986, s 22 record
Has either the landlord or the tenant
required the making of a record in
respect of the condition of the
holding under the Agricultural
Holdings Act 1986, s 22? If so,
please supply a copy.

17.2   Certificate of bad husbandry
Has application been made for a
certificate of bad husbandry, and, if
so, when and with what result?

18   DISPUTES

18.1   Tenancy dispute proceedings
Have the terms of the tenancy or any
dispute between landlord and tenant
been the subject of proceedings
before any court, tribunal or
arbitrator, or are any such
proceedings pending? If so, please
give details.

18.2   Rent arrears
Is the tenant now, or has he
previously been, in arrears in paying
the rent?

18.3   Tenant's breaches of covenant
Of what other breaches of covenant
by the tenant, continuing or past, is
the seller aware?

18.4   Landlord's breaches of covenant
Has the tenant complained of any
breach of the landlord's obligations?

**19   GENERAL
       MISCELLANEOUS
       ENQUIRIES**

19.1   Changes of circumstances
Please confirm that if there is any
variation in the information given in
the replies to any of these enquiries,
details will be supplied prior to the
exchange of contracts, if the

variation is known by the seller
before exchange or forthwith if the
variation is not known until after
exchange.

19.2   Seller's replies to enquiries

Please confirm that the replies to all
of these enquiries and to any other
enquiries raised in connection with
this transaction are not merely the
replies of the seller's solicitors, but
are the replies of the seller after due
consideration and (as appropriate)
consultation with the seller's
surveyors and managing agents, if
any.

....

Buyer's Solicitors

....

Seller's Solicitors

The foregoing enquiries before contract are based in part upon those produced by the
Solicitors' Law Stationery Society plc.

Part 4

PRECEDENTS

PART 4
PRECEDENTS

1 Restrictive covenant – general form

The buyer covenants with the seller (with the intention of binding each part of the Property) (and for the benefit of each part of the seller's retained land [comprised in title number [   ] *or* shown edged blue on the plan] capable of benefiting as shall not have been transferred on sale or as shall have been transferred with the express benefit of one or more of the following covenants) as follows:

(1) not to use the Property for any purpose except agriculture.
(2) not to erect on the Property any buildings or structures.

---

* material in square brackets [   ] denotes material to be inserted.

2   Right of way

Together with a right of way for the benefit of the Property for agricultural purposes only and with animals and agricultural machinery and vehicles over the track [12] feet wide coloured brown on the plan subject to and conditional on the buyer paying on demand a fair proportion according to use of the cost incurred from time to time by the seller in maintaining, repairing and renewing the track (but without any obligation on the part of the seller to do so) and together also with the right for the buyer (if the seller does not do so) to maintain, repair and renew the track at the expense of the buyer.

3   Drainage

Together with the right to drain foul water and sewage through [the existing line of pipes] [a line of pipes to be laid by the buyer within the perpetuity period of two years from the date of this Transfer] or any replacement in the approximate position shown by a blue line on the plan to the [septic tank/cesspit] in the position shown by the letter 'S' and the right [at all times after the pipe is laid] to drain clarified water from the septic tank/cesspit through the outfall pipes in the position shown on the plan by the word 'outfall' together with the right on giving 48 hours' notice (except in emergency) to enter on the land in which the pipes septic tank/cesspit and outfall ('the drainage system') are situated to inspect, cleanse, maintain, repair and renew them together also with the right to enter on the land in which the septic tank/cesspit is situated with lorries by the route shown by a brown line on the plan to empty it all such rights being subject to and conditional on:

(1) Doing as little damage as possible making good all remediable damage and paying compensation for irremediable damage (including loss of crop).

(2) Adequately fencing all excavations and infilling as soon as possible with a sufficient depth of gravel.

(3) Keeping the drainage system in repair and free from leaks and pollution and forthwith remedying any pollution which occurs.

(4) Indemnifying the owner of the land in which the drainage system is situated against any claim by any neighbouring owner or any statutory body arising out of pollution resulting from the drainage system.

4   Lift and shift

The right to use the [right of way/water pipe/sewer] shall be subject to the right of the seller to divert it so that if at any time during the perpetuity period of 79 years from the date of this Transfer he shall wish to divert the [right of way/water pipe/sewer] or part of it and shall at his expense provide an alternative which shall be reasonably convenient and shall serve on the buyer not less than one month's notice specifying the alternative then on the expiry of the notice the rights of the buyer over the [right of way/water pipe/sewer] (or the part specified in the notice) shall determine and be substituted by rights over the alternative specified in the notice.

5   Existing agricultural tenancy

(1)   The property is sold subject to a tenancy agreement dated etc. and made between etc. and to all claims of the Tenant and his relatives by statute or under that agreement which also affects other land retained by the seller.

(2)   The rent shall be informally apportioned as to £   to the property and £   to the retained land.

(3)   The buyer and the seller mutually agree that each of them will at the request and cost of the other serve or join in all requisite notices and submissions to arbitration and do or join in all other things reasonably requested in relation to review of rent and other matters arising under the tenancy.

(4)   The [buyer/seller] appoints the [seller/buyer] his agent for the purpose of serving notices to arbitrate rent and agree any revised rent and to arbitrate and agree other matters arising under the tenancy subject to the agent at all times having regard to and protecting the interests of his principal and acting throughout prudently and in good faith and indemnifying the principal against any liability arising by reason of the agency [suitable only where the separate area is small].

(5)   The buyer or his solicitor has a copy of the tenancy agreement [and other documents listed in the schedule] and having had the opportunity to raise any enquiries buys with full knowledge and shall not make any objection or requisition in relation to it.

PART 4
PRECEDENTS

6   Minerals – no surface entry

Except and reserving to the seller all mines minerals stone and substrata within and under the property (other than the mines and minerals vested in the National Coal Board by virtue of the Coal Acts 1938 to 1943 and the Coal Industry Nationalisation Act 1946) but without any right or power to enter upon break or use the surface of the property for the purpose of working winning and getting the said mines minerals stone and substrata.

7 Minerals with surface entry

Except and reserving to the seller all mines minerals stone and substrata within and under the property (other than the mines and minerals vested in the National Coal Board by virtue of the Coal Acts 1938 to 1943 and the Coal Industry Nationalisation Act 1946) with liberty for the seller his lessees and licensees and all persons duly authorised by him or them to enter upon the property and there to prospect for and work the said mines minerals stone and substrata and to erect all such buildings machinery and things and to sink and make all such pits shafts levels adits tram rail and other roads and to take and use and divert all such water and do all such other acts works and things under in and about the property as shall be necessary or convenient for prospecting searching for and working the said minerals stone and substrata and getting washing dressing rendering merchantable depositing carrying away and disposing of the same compensation being made to the buyer for any loss or injury or damage which he/she/they may sustain which may be occasioned by such mining operations provided the claim for such compensation be made in writing and left at the address of the seller within six months after the same shall have been sustained the amount of compensation in the case of difference to be settled by Arbitration under the provisions of the Arbitration Act 1996 or any statutory enactment in that behalf for the time being in force.

8   Adjoining land development rights

Except and reserving to the seller and all persons duly authorised by him the right at any time or from time to time hereafter to erect buildings upon the adjoining and neighbouring lands and to use his adjoining and neighbouring lands and buildings in such manner as he may think fit notwithstanding that the access of light and air to the property may thereby be interfered with.

9   Pipes

Except and reserving to the seller and the owners and occupiers for the time being of the adjoining and neighbouring properties the free right at all times hereafter (in common with the buyer) to use together with the right to enter on the giving of prior notice (except in the case of emergency) for the purpose of inspecting maintaining repairing or renewing any pipes sewers drains drainage poles wires watercourses or channels and other works upon in under or over the property which are now and hitherto have been used by such owners or occupiers as the persons exercising such rights making good all damage caused.

10   Future easements

Except and reserving to the seller the unrestricted right of entry for the seller or his workmen servants or licensees to construct and lay within the perpetuity period of 80 years from the date hereof and thereafter to inspect repair or renew pipes sewers drains drainage poles wires watercourses or channels and other works upon in under or over the property And in particular to grant easements or wayleaves to third parties and to retain any rents or considerations payable thereunder making good all damage thereby caused.

11   Sporting (short form)

Except and reserving to the seller free right of hunting over the property and (subject to the provisions of the Ground Game Acts 1880 and 1906) all game hares rabbits and all fish and wildfowl and nests and eggs of game thereon and (subject as aforesaid) the right of preserving shooting fishing and taking the same and the right of entry at all times upon the property for all persons duly authorised by the seller for the purpose of exercising such rights.

12   Sporting (long form)

Except and reserving to the Seller in fee simple as a profit in gross the full and free right of hunting over the property and of shooting fishing sporting and taking away all fish wild birds game and wild mammals which it shall be lawful to kill and take (subject to the concurrent right of the occupier under the Ground Game Act 1880 and the Ground Game (Amendment) Act 1906) together with the right to enter on the property over the route marked [=] on the plan with [not more than   ] persons authorised by the seller with guns and beaters and others [on not more than   days] [between   date and   date in any year] [to be approved in advance by the buyer such approval not to be unreasonably withheld] for the purpose of shooting and killing and taking away such fauna together with the right to stand on the bank for the purpose of fishing and to cut weeds and clear obstructions together with the right to rear game birds subject to and conditional on the seller making good or paying compensation for damage caused including loss of crop.

13   Sporting (*Pole v Peake*)

The following wording received judicial approval in *Pole and Another v Peake and Another*, Court of Appeal (Civil Division) (1998) *The Times*, 22 July.

'EXCEPTED AND RESERVED
unto the Vendors in fee simple, (a) the exclusive right of hunting with hounds and with or without horses in pursuit of deer foxes and hares over and upon all or any of the lands woods and premises hereby conveyed and of taking such animals therefrom and of entering upon all or any part of the lands hereby conveyed for the purposes aforesaid subject and without prejudice to the right of the Purchasers or other the owners or occupiers for the time being of the said lands and premises or any part or parts thereof to farm cultivate afforest and develop the same as they may think fit and in particular but without prejudice to the generality of the foregoing to erect any building or structures thereon and to open gravel pits and quarries and to dig and mine for clay stone or other minerals and subject to making good or paying compensation for all damage which in the excercise of the said rights hereby excepted and reserved shall be done to the said lands fences hedges plantations or crops thereon and pursuant to the rights herein before reserved the Vendors may from time to time authorise the Committee Master or Masters of any recognised Packs of Staghounds Foxhounds Harriers or Beagles to exercise with their servants and followers of such Hunts the right of hunting over all or any of the lands and premises hereby conveyed and of taking deer foxes and hares therefrom hereinbefore excepted and reserved to the Vendors, (b) the exclusive right with or without friends servants and others to hunt shoot fish and sport over and upon all or any part of the lands woods and premises hereby conveyed and to kill and take and dispose of all game rabbits wild fowl and other wild animals and birds and fish upon the said lands woods and premises and for any of the purposes aforesaid and also for the purpose of preserving and rearing game wild fowl and fish to enter upon the said lands woods and premises or any part thereof.'

14   General right

Except and reserving to the seller and his successors in title to the adjoining and neighbouring land of the seller all easements rights and advantages as would by virtue of section 62 of the Law of Property Act 1925 have passed on the conveyance of such adjoining land if the same had been executed one day prior to the date of this transfer.

15 Environmental agreement

(1) The property is sold subject to an Agreement dated etc and made between etc relating to [Woodlands, Environmentally Sensitive Area, Ancient Monuments etc].

(2) The payment for the current year will [belong to the seller] [be apportioned on a daily basis].

(3) The seller will [in the Transfer] [by separate deed] covenant to indemnify the buyer against claims by [statutory body] for breaches of the Agreement prior to completion.

(4) The buyer will [in the Transfer] [by separate deed] covenant to indemnify the seller against claim by [statutory body] for breaches of the Agreement after completion.

(5) The buyer will seek to negotiate an agreement with [statutory body] releasing the seller from future liability [and until that is completed the property shall stand equitably charged to the seller with any sums due from the seller to the [statutory body] in consequence of any breach by the buyer.

PART 4
PRECEDENTS

16   Holdover

(1)   The seller shall have the right of holdover as licensee for the following purposes for the following periods:

1.1   On fields (described by plan or number) until harvest together with the right to harvest the [describe] crop and do all things incidental to it [state whether straw is to be baled and left or removed or other relevant provisions].

1.2   To store grain in the grain store [describe by plan or words] until [date] or earlier emptying together with the right to use electricity and maintain the building subject to the seller paying for all electricity consumed and insuring the grain store against fire and other usual perils.

17 Early entry

The buyer shall have early entry as licensee on fields [described by plan or number] from harvest for the purpose of cultivation and drilling crop provided that if for any reason the sale shall not be completed then at the time of termination of this contract the buyer's licence shall also determine and the buyer shall pay compensation for damage caused but shall not be entitled to compensation for cultivations or growing crops.

18   Milk quota

(1)   The seller reserves the rights in respect of the milk quota of   litres at present registered in the name of [the seller] ('the quota') and it is agreed that the quota is not included in the sale.

(2)   The seller will be entitled to grant before the completion date one or more tenancies of not more than 11 months each to one or more persons wishing to acquire the quota coupled with a management agreement in the form produced to the buyer's solicitors before the date hereof. [add reference to grass keep or other contract as applicable]

[(3)   If such tenancy has not been granted before completion then the seller will on completion grant to the buyer a tenancy of not more than one year in the form annexed.]

(4)   The land to be comprised in the tenancy shall be [define] and the rent shall be [   ] pounds.

(5)   The buyer will at the request and cost of the seller serve or join in any necessary forms (including any consent or sole interest notices) both on transfer of the land and on termination of the tenancy [and appoints the seller his agent for that purpose] and will at the request and cost of the seller authorise the use of his name in any proceedings to protect the title of any person having an interest in quota derived from the property.

[(6)   The buyer will in the transfer covenant with the seller with intent to bind the property and each part of it for the period of five years from the date of transfer and to benefit [define seller's land to which quota is to be transferred and to be used for dairying] not to use the property or any part of it for the purpose of milk production provided that after the end of that period this covenant shall cease to have effect.]

Index

References are to paragraph numbers of Part 1, and to other Parts of the book.

ISBN 0-85308-552-8

9 780853 085522 >